Anti-Racism
&
Multiculturalism

Anti-Racism & Multiculturalism

Studies in International Communication

Mark D. Alleyne

editor

Transaction Publishers
New Brunswick (U.S.A.) and London (U.K.)

This book is printed on acid-free paper that meets the American National Standard for Permanence of Paper for Printed Library Materials.

Library of Congress Catalog Number: 2010017608
ISBN: 978-1-4128-1321-1 (cloth); 978-1-4128-1322-8 (paper)
Printed in the United States of America

Library of Congress Cataloging-in-Publication Data

Anti-racism and multiculturalism : studies in international communication / Mark D. Alleyne, editor.
     p. cm.
Includes bibliographical references and index.
ISBN 978-1-4128-1321-1
    1. Multiculturalism. 2. Anti-racism. 3. Communication, International.
I. Alleyne, Mark D., 1961-

HM1271.A58 2010
305.8009--dc22

                                             2010017608

Dedication

We dedicate this book to our friend, Mark DaCosta Alleyne, a passionate, inspirational, and brave anti-racism activist. As this book was readied for publication, in May 2009, Mark passed away unexpectedly in Guatemala City, where he was leading a study abroad program on behalf of Georgia State University. The idea for this book—thinking globally, historically, and critically about anti-racism—was Mark's from the very beginning and his vision, enthusiasm, and commitment helped bring a sense of unity and cohesion to the diverse topics that we were researching. All of us in our own ways are determined to carry on anti-racist struggles in memory of our colleague.

Contents

Acknowledgments   ix

Anti-Racism as International Communication: 1
An Introduction
Mark D. Alleyne

Part I—Anti-Racism as Naming

Race, Mass Communication, and Modernization: 21
Intellectual Networks and the Flow of Ideas
Hemant Shah

U.S. Treaty Obligations and the Politics of   55
Racism and Anti-Racism Discourse
Sylvanna M. Falcón

Anti-Racist Communication in Soccer: A Spoilt Vocabulary?   73
Floris Müller, Liesbet van Zoonen, and Laurens de Roode

Part II—Anti-Racism as Campaigning

Media Campaigns and Asylum   95
Seekers in Scotland
Jairo Lugo-Ocando

Anti-Racist Campaigning and Nation-Building in Namibia   129
Ingrid A. Lehmann

Celebrating Multiculturalism: European   153
Multicultural Media Initiatives as Anti-Racist Practices
Karina Horsti

The Myth of Racial Democracy: Music and   169
Performance as Interventions into the Public
Discourse on Race in Brazil
   Nakisha T. Nesmith

British Asians and the Cultural Politics of Anti-Racist   187
Campaigning in English Football
   Daniel Burdsey

Anti-Racism as Identity Politics: A Constructivist   213
Approach to the FARE and Ad Council Campaigns
   Mark D. Alleyne

Conclusion: Anti-Racism as International Communication   239
   Mark D. Alleyne

Contributors   249

Index   251

Acknowledgments

We want to thank Irving Louis Horowitz and Mary Curtis at Transaction Publishers for their commitment to publishing this book in Mark's memory. We also thank Andrew McIntosh who patiently guided us through the process of moving the manuscript toward publication. The Toda Institute for Global Peace and Policy Research not only provided funding for this project, but also was instrumental in bringing the contributors together at a conference in Madrid in 2005, where the idea for this book was born. Deva Temple, of the Toda Institute, worked extensively with Mark Alleyne to copyedit the manuscript and in securing Transaction as publisher.

Anti-Racism as International Communication: An Introduction

Mark D. Alleyne

As the manuscript of this book was in its final stages of preparation, an unlikely event in the United States provided perhaps the best possible reminder of this collection's contemporary intellectual relevance. *The New York Times* described it this way: "the ultimate test of racial equality—whether Americans will elect a black president"(Kantor 2008). The event was, of course, the successful run by Barack Obama to secure the nomination of the Democratic Party to be president of the United States. For many anti-racists it was perhaps the most profound example yet of the defeat of racism and the emergence of a color-blind United States. Indeed, when Obama was born in Hawaii in 1961 to a white woman and an black man, miscegenation laws were still on the books, so his parents would had broken the law if they lived in some states; the 1964 Civil Rights Act (needed to support the citizenship rights of African Americans) was still to be passed; and Martin Luther King, Jr. would have just seven more years to live before being gunned down by an assassin in 1968 with so many of his dreams still decades away from realization.

But Obama's ascendancy was as much a symbol of progress in race relations as it was of predicament. The various controversies that Obama's victories and defeats inspired were reminders that the country was anything but color-blind. For example, former vice-presidential candidate Geraldine Ferraro said Obama's color was an advantage rather than a liability. And when his last opponent left standing in the primaries, Hillary Clinton, suggested that she had the more mainstream appeal or made references to the assassination of Robert F. Kennedy in 1968, the racial allusions were not difficult to see. However, if there is one point of agreement among scholars of anti-racism it is that the United States occupies a privileged position in global anti-racist discourse. So even though other countries had long outdone the United States on the matter of symbolic racial inclusion—such as Canada's having a woman immigrant born in Haiti as it governor-general, and Mexico's having presidents of black and indigenous blood even in the 1800s—it was still from the United States that this historic symbol of the triumph of American anti-racism resonated most.

Alastair Bonnett, the prominent scholar of anti-racism, has described the influence of the United States on anti-racist thought and practice as a "master narrative" against which anti-racism in other places is compared:

> The claim to "tolerance" is selfishly guarded by states and other institutions concerned to legitimate themselves by reference to their social egalitarianism. Ironically, this situation accentuates the impact of the one country whose race equity practices do have a global audience, the USA. In the mid- to late twentieth century American racial categories and the American history of race were adopted and adapted across the world. This dominance has ensured that many "national debates" on anti-racism are structured around the conceit of a dialogue between "our approach" and what goes on in the USA. The rise of "global culture" suggests that this situation is likely to become even more common. It also indicates that those traditions of resistance against racial and ethnic discrimination that are unable or unwilling to situate themselves in relation to this master narrative will find themselves increasingly marginal and overlooked (Bonnett 2000, 170).

The case of Obama was a prime example of how this American authority works. The very naming of Obama as a "black" man reflects the system of racial formation in the United States and even exposed the contradictions of the discourse within the USA itself. For example, the subjective and objective construction of Obama's identity as black is testament to the famous "one drop rule" in the country, where a person has been historically racialized and stigmatized as "black" as long as that person has known "black" ancestry. So Obama's achievements are those of a "black" man, just as Halle Berry's winning the Oscar for Best Actress in 2001 was a victory for a "black" woman, her "mixed" background similar to Obama's notwithstanding. In other parts of the world, racial formation has not been that straightforward, has been much more complicated, and so anti-racist thought and praxis has been problematical when sized up against the American model. For example, in South Africa, Obama and Berry would be called coloreds, and in many parts of the Caribbean and Latin America they would be termed mulattos. However, the popularization of the American master narrative of race relations around the world meant that not only that country's racial system was exported, but also its approach to anti-racism that is rooted in that specific scheme of racial classification.

It has given the United States formidable power in structuring anti-racist activism around the world through the power to dictate the form of anti-racist campaigns that can get funding from American aid agencies or the international bodies largely controlled by the USA, such as the World Bank and the Inter-American Development Bank (IADB). However, Bonnett has sought to give the theorization of global anti-racist discourse more depth by noting that the "Americanization" of global anti-racism cannot be accounted for through a simple imperialism hypothesis but by looking at its intersections with globalization and the meaning of the United States as symbolic of counter-authority. The collection of data about the racial composition of populations and creation of social development indices along racial lines are fostered on the grounds that it is part of the process of understanding the marginalization of particular groups and the concomitant squandering of this "human capital" in free markets. The solutions given are based on American race relations practice—i.e., "diversity" campaigns and affirmative action. Bonnett calls it "neo-liberal anti-racism" (Bonnett, 2006).

What will global anti-racist discourse look like in the wake of the Obama phenomenon? All evidence so far suggests that—instead of providing a challenge to the dynamics outlined above—the Obama phenomenon will serve to stifle critique. Obama himself has drawn on the often-used trope of American racial melting pot triumphalism and exceptionalism to frame his rise and success. In his 2008 "Speech on Race," he castigated his former pastor, Jeremiah Wright, for believing that American racial attitudes were static, and he based his faith that the USA would overcome the problem of racism on his belief in the "decency and generosity" of the American people and his own life story:

> I am the son of a black man from Kenya and a white woman from Kansas. I was raised with the help of a white grandfather who survived a Depression to serve in Patton's army during World War II and a white grandmother who worked on a bomber assembly line at Fort Leavenworth while he was overseas. I've gone to some of the best schools in America and I've lived in one of the world's poorest nations. I am married to a black American who carries within her the blood of slaves and slave owners, an inheritance we pass on to our two precious daughters. I have brothers, sisters, nieces, nephews, uncles and cousins of every race and every hue scattered across three continents. And for as long as I live, I will never forget that in no other country on earth is my story even possible. It's a story that hasn't made me the most conventional of candidates. But it is a story that has seared into my genetic makeup the idea that this nation is more than the sum of its parts—that out of many, we are truly one (Transcript 2008).

In other words, he sees himself as the embodiment of how the American master narrative succeeds. Such orations by Obama and the euphoria that his success has engendered actually serve to define even more sharply why a book like this one is needed so much at this time. The critical analyses of anti-racist discourses around the world presented in this volume should add considerably to the rumination about the future of anti-racism in the wake of Obama. All the authors in this book are uneasy with the tendency to arrive at unsophisticated contentment with the increasingly popular anti-racist, diversity programs that have become a common feature of the contemporary international scene. The studies of the various cases in different countries dig deeper, with the help of cutting edge social theory, to provide a sophisticated understanding of what is going on, make theoretical innovations of their own and improve policy formulation.

Anti-Racism as Discourse

All scholarly books are engagements with the existing literature, often the published scholarly work of one established discipline. This book originated with a simple question and modest objectives. My plan was to produce a work that would be in conversation with the literature of international relations even though not being of limited relevance to that field. International relations has been my primary focus not only because it is the area of my formal academic training, but because of international relations' professed goal of having international peace as its central objective. This ethical lens of pondering the best means to achieve world peace is what I used to filter media content that provoked my interest in anti-racism in the fall of 2001.

The attacks on the United States of September 11, 2001, occurred while I was researching and writing my study on the public information program of the United Nations, *Global Lies? Propaganda, the UN and World Order*. For that reason I was probably more attuned to the purpose and effectiveness of international mass media campaigns than I would have been normally. In a matter of days the New York-based Ad Council had launched its "I am American" media campaign with an ostensibly anti-racist message: the American polity accommodated people of all races. As I note in my chapter in this book, it was a curious media strategy in the build-up to war. More fascinating was its historical context in a country where anti-racism media was a rarity.

The campaign inspired my first basic question: Do anti-racist campaigns work? And from that starting point other questions flowed: Why the need to launch an anti-racist media campaign in the wake of the September 11 attacks? What is the relationship between anti-racism and nationalism? How does anti-racism promote international peace?

My research on UN propaganda had given me the background to be skeptical. So my proposal to the Toda Institute for Global Peace was inspired by the now seemingly very limited goal of seeing whether the ambivalence and contradictions I had seen in UN public information policy and practice were reflected in this apparently growing phenomenon of international anti-racist media campaigns. By the time I submitted the proposal in 2004, I had seen already the clear intersections between the topic I had just completed in the book on the UN and my proposed topic for a new tome. A review of the history of UN advocacy revealed that anti-racism was one of the most common themes of UN propaganda in the post-World War II process of constructing a new international order. Indeed, UN campaigns for nuclear disarmament, women's rights and anti-terrorism paled in comparison to the resources invested in anti-racism, such as conferences, media artifacts (such as posters and broadcast programs), the observance of special days, years and decades, etc.

The UN's special attention to race and racism was particularly striking to me because I would not have been aware of that from the literature of international relations, where have avoided the theme like the plague. In place of a sharp focus on race and racism, there has been a preference to write on themes such as international law, nationalism, and war. They are often treated as though they are not strongly related to race, even though they are.

Indeed, as Hemant Shah argues in this volume, the field of international development is heavily steeped in assumptions and theories of racial difference. Race and racism are everywhere in international relations but nowhere at the same time. It is there that we consider the Eurocentric philosophical bias in the governing ideologies of the UN, or when we consider the absence of majority-black countries from the key power centers of the nuclear club and permanent membership in the UN Security Council. We see it also in the gentlemen's agreement that keeps the leaderships of the World Bank and the International Monetary Fund (IMF) in European and American hands. It is there when we ponder the tendency in international politics to form integration movements based on racial/ethnic identity (e.g., the European Union).

This resilience of race is against the backdrop of the ostensible overcoming of race. Although there has been little work on the impact of racial difference on the contours of contemporary international order, there has been a sizeable body of research to abolish the credibility of the pseudo-scientific racism that provided the ideological foundation and justification for imperialism, colonialism, the holocaust and apartheid. Race has been debunked as a myth. Because of this, racism—the ideology bred of human classification according to racial difference—has been found to be intellectually and morally barren. The famous "Statement by Experts on Problems of Race" summed up what was (according to them) "scientifically established" as early as six years after the Nazi defeat:

(1) In matters of race, the only characteristics which anthropologists can effectively use as a basis for classifications are physical and physiological.
(2) According to present knowledge there is no proof that the groups of mankind differ in their innate mental characteristics, whether in respect of intelligence or temperament. The scientific evidence indicates that the range of mental capacities in all ethnic groups is much the same.
(3) Historical and sociological studies support the view that genetic differences are of importance in determining the social and cultural differences between different groups of Homo sapiens, and that the social and cultural changes in different groups have, the main, been independent of changes in inborn constitution. Vast social changes have occurred which were not in any way connected with changes in racial type.
(4) There is no evidence that race mixture as such produces bad results from the biological point of view. The social results of race mixture whether for good or ill are to be traced to social factors.
(5) All normal human beings are capable of learning to share in a common life, to understand the nature of mutual service and reciprocity, and to respect social obligations and contracts. Such biological differences as exist between members of different ethnic groups have no relevance to problems of social and political organization, moral life and communication between human beings (United Nations Economics and Security Council 1951).

This idea of race as a social construction became the common sense of social theory. Those who cling to the idea of race as biological and justify behavior, intelligence and physical prowess based on racial difference have been relegated to the fringe. But this is not to say that assumptions and theories of human difference have gone away. Indeed, it should have been the task of international relations to show the central importance of the United Nations system, and specifically UNESCO, its ideological branch, in establishing new ways of justifying and talking about dissimilarity. The old pseudo-scientific racism was replaced by new ways of explaining human difference that came cloaked as anti-racism, but which effectively produced the same pernicious consequences.

It is this "culturalism of the UNESCO tradition" that is a key pillar of Alana Lentin's sophisticated theorization of anti-racism. UNESCO had sponsored the experts' statement and later modifications of it, which, according to Lentin,

> sought to replace biological theories of human difference with a culturalist definition of diversity. This tendency, which came to dominate the anti-racist approach promoted in the UNESCO vein and to be widely upheld, was opposed by the geneticists and physical anthropologists who wished to retain "race" as a useful tool for the explanation of certain phenomena... Against these reservations, the UNESCO tradition gave rise to terms such as "ethnicity" and "culture." The preference for such terms as markers of human difference, over the racial descriptors that had served previously, was based on the belief that the former were stripped of any implication of superiority and inferiority upon which the idea of "race" was based (Lentin 2004, 76).

The preference for talking about "culture" and "ethnicity" instead of race, according to the UNESCO tradition for which Claude Levi-Strauss was the leading intellectual advocate, established a new axiological principle for international anti-racism. There is a shift away from efforts to refute pseudo-scientific racism—a battle seen as won due to the academic work of Boas and others in the 1930s and 1940s—to: (a) a reification of notions of identity, whether it be at the individual, societal or national levels; and (b) advocacy of the idea that "racism may be combated by a spread of knowledge of different cultures through the education of a future generation in the importance and richness of global cultural diversity" (Lentin 2004, 78).

Work by many, including myself, has shown the key role of the UN system in establishing and propagating the intellectual foundations for many of the ideas that are now taken for granted as the commonsense of international politics, even though many of these principles would have seemed quite implausible a mere 100 years ago (Alleyne 2003; Emmerij, Jolly, & Weiss 2001; Jolly, Emmerij, Weiss, & United Nations Intellectual History Project 2005; T. G. Weiss 2005). Therefore, Lentin's theory of international anti-racism, although written for sociology, resonates in international relations. Central to this resonance is her argument that the common interpretation of contemporary anti-racism as a product of essentialist identity politics (new social movements) is actually wrong because it is really a product of a statist anti-racism that envisions states comprised of reified cultural (or ethnic) groups in the UNESCO tradition.

Missing from Lentin's critique is an explanation of exactly how a doctrine promoted by UNESCO could have achieved so much power as to have defined state behavior. Lentin identifies the force of the UNESCO tradition, but she does not give the intimate details of how this phenomenon achieved traction. This is a question that would animate international relations, concerned as it is with the state as the key organizing unit of political life. And the most straightforward explanation of the power of the UNESCO tradition of anti-racism is the fact the UN system of specialized agencies was established after World War II to be a functional network of international organizations to maintain world peace by doing the business of the international community efficiently. Each of these organizations is assigned a specific brief. That given to UNESCO was that of being the body for propagating the values of Western liberalism that the Allied powers said would be the foundation of a peaceful world order. It is no coincidence that UNESCO is headquartered in Paris, the capital of the country that gave us the "rights of man."

Moreover, UNESCO, like all other institutions of the UN system was founded on the principle of national sovereignty and supreme privilege for the state. So, although Lentin does not delve into the details of this important dynamic, she is quite convincing when she argues that the central feature defining anti-racism in Western democracies and those countries subject to the hegemony of their ideas (i.e., all states that ascribe to the UN's governing principles) is proximity to "public political culture." Drawing on John Rawls, she defines public political culture as "an aggregate of the dispersed elements of political thought that, even in the daily life of its citizens, are associated with the idea of democracy as a principle ordering the modern, western state" (Lentin 2004, 2).

The focus on public political culture provides an axis from which Lentin can expand her theory of anti-racism by posing and answering a number of other questions about anti-racist organizations. What is their relationship to the state? What is the constituency they seek to transform? She shows that anti-racist organizations cannot take money from the state without ignoring, compromising or abandoning critiques of racist state policy and behavior. Likewise, entities that seek to do their anti-racism without state subsidy must be prepared to suffer the consequences, especially as it relates to the ability of the state to marginalize and intimidate. With regards to the second question, Lentin advances the terms *majoritarian* and *communitarian* to describe (respectively) organizations that seek the broadest social appeal and those with approaches more limited to mobilization of racialized groups.

Lentin, like all writers on anti-racism, cannot avoid a departure into the study of communication sooner or later. For example, in introducing the concept of national political culture, she describes its utility as a rhetorical device:

> The defeat of Nazism, *la Resistance* or anti-slavery are portrayed as national legacies, demonstrative of the democratic principles on which the state is purportedly built. Contemporary anti-racist speech recalls these moments and advocates a return to the principles which gave rise to them, considered to be inscribed in national political culture (Lentin 2004, 3).

Similarly, the geographer Alastair Bonnett uses advertising analysis in his effort to show how one well-known transnational firm tried to associate its preferred version of neo-liberal capitalism with "universal values and rights" by deploying imagery of anti-racism and multiculturalism. In the Coca-Cola advertisement

> the camera swooped over a field of young, good-looking representatives of various "racial types." Each clasps a bottle of the product. Upon each bottle the familiar red logo of Coca-Cola, momentarily caught by the camera, is seen in Arabic, Chinese and other languages. The assembled mass, led by a young blonde white woman, sing "I'd like to teach the world to sing in perfect harmony. I'd like to build the world a home and furnish it with love." Here the commodity—Coca-Cola—coheres and gives meaning to the human variety on display. The message is multiracial, multicultural but also universalist; people can live "in perfect harmony," when brought together within white, American commodity culture (Bonnett 2000, 79).

No other contemporary problem on the agenda of modern international relations needs the field of communication as much to provide a sophisticated analysis of how it works. This is not the case with global warming, poverty, nuclear proliferation, or even terrorism. This is so because racism and anti-racism are intellectual, as opposed to physical, phenomena. They are discourses. It is for this reason that the branch of communication research that has had to most to say about racism has been discourse analysis.

Although at its very basic level discourse can be described as "text and talk" (van Dijk 1993, 28), the concept is used in the study of racism and anti-racism to describe a particular *system* that is both a communicative (linguistic) and sociological phenomenon. According to Howarth and Stavrakakis, discourse or discourses are "systems of meaningful practices that form the identities of subjects and objects." They are *political* because, of necessity, their existence is based on the exclusion of certain possibilities and these excluded ideas are always threatening to the established order (Howarth, Norval, & Stavrakakis 2000, 3-4). The creation of a discourse is not necessarily a deliberate, coordinated act. One dictionary of critical theory goes as far as to define discourse as any "organized body or corpus of statements and utterances governed by rules and conventions of which the user is largely unconscious" (Macey 2001, 100). Discourses are ways of describing social phenomena, organizing knowledge and discussing the social world that provide insight into how identities are constructed and how dimensions of social life are understood. Weiss and Wodak describe discourse as "a way of signifying a particular domain of social practice from a particular perspective" (G. Weiss & Wodak 2003, 22).

The basic project of this book is to not only show a variety of ways the study of anti-racism as discourse contributes to international studies, but to also facilitate the scrutiny of anti-racism discourse via more methods than discourse analysis.

Anti-Racism as Naming / Anti-Racism as Campaigning

Despite having just set out a case for more attention to the study of anti-racist discourse in international relations, I must now point out that my chapter is the only contribution from that field to this volume. This fact reinforces my point about the field's neglect of this area of research. In 2004 when I sent out the call for research proposals for this project, funded by the Toda Institute, there were no replies from scholars writing for the literature of international relations. Instead what we have here is the work of a number of scholars from North America and Europe who responded to my call or were recruited into the project by me. The vast majority of the writers are in communication, but the authors include also an ethnomusicologist (Nesmith) and two sociologists (Burdsey and Falcón).

When the group met for the first time in Madrid, Spain, in the spring of 2005 the central task on the table was to find ways to integrate the seemingly disparate collection of chapters into a coherent whole. Until that point the only thing that connected the projects was the belief by the researchers that their work related to the central theme for the book stated in the Request for Proposals (RFP). In the RFP the project was titled *New Technologies and the Transnational Propagation of Peace—Anti-Racist Campaigns,* and the declared goal was to "provide a sophisticated understanding of the relationship between new mass communication technologies and racist, or anti-racist, propaganda campaigns." The central theme of all the studies was their focus on anti-racism, but the problem was how to organize a book of chapters on anti-racist discourses in such a wide variety of locales. The method of organization would also assist readers in evaluating the contribution to knowledge-building of the individual chapters and the book as a sum of those chapters.

A tempting, straightforward means to solving the problem would be to follow Bonnett's typology of six forms of anti-racism (Bonnett 2000, 84-115). However, that would not work with this book because none of the chapters are simple case studies of anti-racism in different places. One of the book's strengths is the fact that the chapters do not accept anti-racist campaigning at face value, and they interrogate and critique the intellectual pre-history of these campaigns. It is for that reason that we collectively decided on an order that would divide the chapters into the two parts now used here.

What we noted in Madrid was that a key feature of anti-racist campaigns launched in the mass media has been the attempt to depict what is racism. For example, public service announcements broadcast in the United States in 2005 by the Advertising Council dramatized cases of what were the creators' views of common racist social practices: extra scrutiny of young black male shoppers in stores, insults directed at immigrant workers because they are assumed to not speak English, weeding out of non-whites from job applicant pools, etc. In contrast, the *Stand Up, Speak Up* campaign launched by Nike for European football, that is assessed in this book, suggested that racism was the insults shouted by a minority of fans at football matches. One key point made in this book is that media campaigns based on such definitions of racism are actually missing the point. It is for that reason that Part I of the book is organized around the idea that the three chapters there are tied together by their scrutiny of anti-racist assumptions about what constitutes racism.

Hemant Shah's archeology of knowledge-building in communication research is an important start to a volume on anti-racism as discourse because he provides the needed explanation of how ostensibly objective scholarship is deeply implicated in what Paul Gilroy calls "raciology." Shah shows how many of the key American thinkers in the 1950s and 1960s on development and communication actually knew each other, and collaborated, or were linked to each other via intellectual networks. The impressively long list of scholars covered by Shah includes (but is not limited to) Daniel Lerner, Ithiel Pool, Edward Shils, Lucian Pye, and Walt Rostow. Assumptions about racial difference and hierarchy provided the contours for this literature's depiction of international development as a problem.

The reader might be forgiven for wondering what the ecology of development communication research has to do with anti-racism. Indeed, the first person I had to convince on this matter early in the project was Shah himself! But the wars in Afghanistan and Iraq and the nation-building projects the United States and United Kingdom in particular have launched in their wake have provoked a revisiting of old debates that show quite clearly the intersection of racial, anti-racist, and modernization discourses. The question of whether it is even possible to establish democracies in these countries provoke arguments about racial and ethnic difference that have a very long history in modernization discourse. And when the American president says he is exporting "freedom" to countries that would otherwise be terrorist threats if they do not become free democracies, it is as much a commentary on the chauvinism of an American political elite as it is a faith in the idea that all humanity (regardless of difference) is capable of such social transformation.

In other words, modernization and anti-racist discourses are often mutually constitutive. Nowhere is this relationship more clearly set out than in Spengler's *The Decline of the West* (Spengler & Atkinson 1926). Spengler's discomfort in discussing race, given his knowledge of then recent arguments of Boas that he cited, presaged the later preference for replacing "culture" with race. This investigation of development communication research by Shah is also important in setting out a point made by both Lentin and Bonnett about the philosophical nature of anti-racism—a belief in anti-racism does not necessarily mean an abandonment of supremacist ideology.

Falcón's analysis of the conflict between the UN and the United States government follows. It is yet another reminder of how crucial the UN and its affiliated organs have been to transnational anti-racist discourse. The UNESCO tradition identified above only set out the philosophical terms of UN praxis. It has been left to organizations such as CERD (the UN Committee to Eliminate Racial Discrimination) to do the bureaucratic and legal work of operationalizing UN anti-racism. Falcón shows that, the shortcomings of UN culturalism notwithstanding, it has still appeared as a radical project to the UN's most powerful member, which abandoned the 2001 World Conference Against Racism. Here anti-racism discourse is "text and talk" within an international organization. While the US government does not deny the persistence of racism within its borders, the specific point of contention has been the UN's preference to define racism in much broader terms than those proposed by the United States.

In the last chapter of the section, Müller, van Zoonen, and de Roode tackle this problem of definition from the angle of culpability. They note the traditional tendency in Europe to define racism as specific acts perpetrated by minorities of soccer "hooligans." They point out that this view is challenged by the increasingly popular "cultural paradigm" of soccer racism research. This paradigm expands the terrain of research of soccer racism to include "interactions between players, coaches and other employees of the soccer club, the institutional arrangements, networks and processes of decision making in various levels of soccer club culture and the role of media in the reproduction of racist discourses and practices in soccer culture."

It uses a refined definition of racism that includes racialization—a process of structuring relations with and between racialized groups. The chapter reports the findings of quantitative research to test how soccer players and fans in Holland responded to specific anti-racist campaigns. They reveal a shocking disconnection between the apparent objectives of the campaigns and how they were perceived. Most striking is the resilience of the idea that racism in soccer can be reduced to the minority of hard-core racists who would not be reached by anti-racist campaigns.

It is important to read the three chapters in Part I before the six in Part II because the many key theoretical questions raised by the first chapters provide sophisticated lenses through which to understand the critiques of the six case studies.

Jairo Lugo-Ocando begins the section by challenging the traditional definition of "campaigns." His fieldwork in Scotland revealed that it can be very myopic to think of campaigns as planned, organized activities by specific entities. What happens when there is a discursive formation advanced by newspapers with specific agendas related to difference and immigration policy? Lugo-Ocando points out that the key challenge for anti-racist campaigners has been the question of how to counteract the campaign from the other side because it is difficult to identify specific entities that structure xenophobic reporting, and such journalism comes cloaked in the assumed respectability of media ethics. The intersection of discourses on refugee policy, national identity, national security, terrorism, racism and anti-racism has been a key feature of contemporary international relations. For this reason it was essential that this book contain a chapter on the topic.

An indispensable chapter on refugees is followed by an indispensable chapter on the UN. Ingrid Lehmann's examination of the UN's anti-racist campaign associated with Namibia's transition to self-rule is actually an introduction to the second dimension of the UN's role in contemporary international anti-racist discourse. The organization operationalizes the culturalism of the UNESCO tradition by running "public information" campaigns of the type seen in Namibia to reinforce its peacekeeping and peace-building missions. Lehmann's chapter is a primary source because she was the UN official who actually designed the campaign. Her perspectives give an insight into how the UN viewed itself and its work in that peace process. For example, Lehmann believes that a multicultural team of UN staff, working in harmony in a region historically torn by racial inequality and conflict provided a powerful demonstration effect to the local population. In other words, the very multi-national character of UN missions is itself a form of anti-racism.

A form of culturalism and identity politics similar to that of the UN is dissected by Karina Horsti in the third chapter of the section. Horsti's decision to explore anti-racist discourses via a Europe-wide prize for multicultural programming is extremely original and innovative. It focuses attention on a form of anti-racist discourse in the media that has got so commonplace in so many countries that it escapes deep intellectual scrutiny. Horsti does an excellent job of putting her study within the context of scholarship on anti-racism, multiculturalism and multicultural programming in Europe. Her exegeses of jury reports, speeches and promotional documents for the Prix Europa Iris for the period 2000-2003 is another validation of Lentin's contention that anti-racism can be theorized according to proximity-distance in relation to public political culture. According to Horsti, "Multicultural media initiatives in the mainstream media are therefore to be treated not only as development of journalism, but also as manifestations of tokenism which construct a multicultural self-understanding of European identity."

Horsti's identification of tokenism originates with her concern about *representation,* a key concept in communication studies and a source of much intellectual trouble for anti-racists. Does anti-racism lose its authenticity and credibility when the leading anti-racists are not members of the racialized groups? When some members of racialized groups are sought to be "the face" of anti-racist groups is this not a sinister form of banal tokenism? What kind of agency do the racialized have in anti-racist discourse? Should their activism be limited to their in group or have the brief of converting the wider public to anti-racism? These are the kinds of questions tackled by Nesmith in her chapter on Brazil. It is the only chapter in the book that focuses exclusively on the anti-racist dimension of what has been theorized as a new social movement, or, according to Lentin, a group with a communitarian brief.

While Latin America, and Brazil in particular, has attracted a considerable amount of writing on the question of racial identity and even racism, there has been less attention to anti-racism in the region. In this first decade of the new century, anti-racism in Latin America has been rejuvenated not only due to the agency of the racialized, but also thanks to the international modernization and development discourses. Latin America is actually a prime example of how the modernization and anti-racist discourses mutually constitute each other (the point made above in this introduction and in the chapter by Shah).

International development agencies, such as the World Bank and the Inter-American Development Bank (IADB), have sponsored studies on racial disparities and identified these particular inequities as obstacles to development in Latin America. This has put pressure on Latin American governments to at least engage in the rhetoric of anti-racism and even implement specific anti-racist policies (Bonnett 2000, 2006). For example, in Colombia a new law made mandatory the teaching of Afro-Colombian history in schools, and in Brazil a new television channel to serve Afro-Brazilians was launched in 2005.

Instead of exploring official anti-racism *from above* by the government, as a political scientist is wont to do, Nesmith, an ethnomusicologist, examines the history and role of a black women's group that is an example of performance-based activism that has gained much popularity in Brazil. Racialized groups frequently utilize this particular form of anti-racist activism because often music and performance are the only spaces open to them. As Nesmith notes, "music has been the most provocative and effective way of addressing a wide range of contemporary social and political issues, and providing important information to black and non-white poor communities that have little access to media and other print resources."

This theme of representation is continued in Burdsey's critique of official anti-racist campaigns aimed at greater inclusion of British Asians in UK football. Burdsey deploys critical race theory as a method of interpretation and praxis. But the dynamic of race relations in the UK is drastically different from that in Brazil. The rise and fall of "political blackness" in Britain requires Burdsey to delve deeper into the shifting meanings of race and to utilize Clare Jean Kim's idea of "positionality" to better understand Asian versus Afro-British subjectivities in UK football. If there is one lesson left by the case studies in this book, it is that just as there are several *racisms* there are also several anti-racisms. However, like the previous chapters by Müller et al., Lugo-Ocando, and Horsti,

Burdsey's analysis reveals how European positive self-identification as democratic and inclusive is an axiological principle that grounds anti-racist campaigns in the region regardless of national location.

I invest a considerable amount of time in the related theme of nationalism in racist and anti-racist ideology in the final case studies of the book. This chapter puts anti-racism within the terrain of international relations theory. The constructivist turn in international relations has opened up new opportunities for collaborative, interdisciplinary research such as embodied by this book. This chapter, and that by Burdsey before it, provides the background needed to get a richer understanding of the lead-up to FIFA's anti-racist posturing at the 2006 World Cup. More importantly, it seeks to show the relevance of anti-racist discourse to the intellectual interrogation of key problems in contemporary international politics, especially terrorism and anti-terrorism, ethnic conflict, post-war reconstruction, neo-liberalism, and war propaganda.

The chapters are tied together in the conclusion by showing how they contribute to the central problem confronting the international system, i.e., the quest for world peace. We do this by considering the volume's relevance to five questions: (1) How does the literature on anti-racism improve our understanding of conflict resolution? (2) How does the analysis of the media's role in racist and anti-racist discourses improve the process of theorizing, writing, and arbitrating international law on hate and war propaganda? (3) How can research on anti-racist discourse improve UN peacekeeping? (4) What implications does the literature on anti-racist discourse have for theory-building and activism for "cultural diversity" in international communication? (5) How and why should the literature on anti-racism expand research in international relations?

When we consider the book's limitations, the volume is best seen as the start of a conversation. Our consideration of anti-racism in international contexts is incomplete without case studies from Asia. Particularly interesting would be a discussion of India's caste system in relation to anti-racist theory. But this book does not claim to set out comprehensive, grand theory. What it does do is pose a number of questions on the border between social and international theory that could inform studies of other geographic regions not covered in this volume.

References

Alleyne, M. D. 2003. *Global Lies? Propaganda, the UN and World Order.* New York: Palgrave.

Banton, M. 2002. *The international Politics of Race.* Cambridge, UK; Malden, MA: Polity Press; Blackwell.

Bonnett, A. 2000. *Anti-racism.* London: New York.

Bonnett, A. 2006. The Americanisation of Anti-Racism? Global Power and Hegemony in Ethnic Equity. *Journal of Ethnic & Migration Studies,* 32(7), 1083-1103.

Emmerij, L., Jolly, R., & Weiss, T. G. 2001. *Ahead of the curve?* : *UN Ideas and Global Challenges.* Bloomington: Indiana University Press.

Howarth, D. R., Norval, A. J., & Stavrakakis, Y. 2000. *Discourse Theory and Political Analysis: identities, hegemonies, and social change.* New York: St. Martin's Press.

Jolly, R., Emmerij, L., Weiss, T. G., & United Nations Intellectual History Project. 2005. *The power of UN Ideas: lessons from the first 60 years: a summary of the books and findings from the United Nations Intellectual History Project.* New York: United Nations Intellectual History Project.

Kantor, J. 2008. Teaching Law, Testing Ideas, Obama Stood Slightly Apart. *The New York Times,* July 30, p. 1.

Lentin, A. 2004. *Racism and Anti-racism in Europe.* London: Pluto Press.

Macey, D. 2001. *The Penguin Dictionary of Critical Theory.* New York: Penguin Books.

Spengler, O., & Atkinson, C. F. 1926. *The decline of the West.* New York: A. A. Knopf.

Transcript. 2008, March 18. Sen. Barack Obama Delivers Remarks on Race Issues. *CQ Transcriptions.*

United Nations Economic and Security Council. 1951. Statement by Experts on Problems of Race. *American Anthropologist,* 53(1), 142-145.

van Dijk, T. A. 1993. *Elite discourse and racism.* Newbury Park, CA: Sage Publications.

Weiss, G., & Wodak, R. 2003. *Critical Discourse Analysis: Theory and Interdisciplinarity.* New York: Palgrave Macmillan.

Weiss, T. G. 2005. *UN Voices: the struggle for development and social justice.* Bloomington: Indiana University Press.

Part I

Anti-Racism as Naming

Race, Mass Communication, and Modernization: Intellectual Networks and the Flow of Ideas

Hemant Shah

In an overview of the ebbs and flows of the "dynamics of accelerating, uneven, and self-contradictory global change," Majid Tehranian (1994) provided a penetrating analysis of multiple waves of modernization through world history. He defined modernization as "a process of change that puts a primary value on science, technological, social, economic, political, and cultural innovations in order to achieve progressively higher levels of productivity, democratic participation, and cultural pluralism" (1994, 72). Tehranian identified "seven modernizations," each with its own temporal, spatial, political-economic, and cultural patterns. The fifth of these modernizations, which began roughly in 1945 at the end of World War II and was characterized by Cold War struggles for the hearts and minds of postcolonial populations, is the focus of this chapter.

Modernization theory was a set of ideas that heavily influenced U.S. foreign policy during the Cold War. The theory posited a model of societal transformation for poor countries made possible by embracing Western manufacturing technology, political structures, values, and systems of mass communication. As a policy initiative, modernization was the centerpiece of efforts to thwart the spread of Soviet communism in Asia, Africa, and the Middle East. A package of Western industrial organization, patterns of governance, and general "lifeways" and values was conceived and offered up as a supposedly superior path to entering the modern post-war world. Mass communication was assigned the key task of making the package attractive and irresistible to residents of the postcolonial world.

This chapter examines some of the intellectual history of modernization and mass communication theory, focusing mainly on the 1950s and 1960s. Specifically, the chapter examines closely the ways in which the theory and its assumptions about people, social change, and media effects were inflected by changing ideas about race and race relations. Recent research on modernization has begun to show that racial thinking had an important impact on the formulation of modernization theory in the post-war era (Borstelman 2001; Layton 2000; Robin 2001). To date, however, few have systematically examined why, how, and with what consequences ideas race and race relations made their way into academic work about introducing mass communication into countries of Asia, Africa, and the Middle East (the "Third World") as important elements of making them "modern."

The chapter will first review an important dimension of the post-World War II socio-political context. Discussions about race were marked by a discursive shift from "biological racism" to "cultural racism," which had important implications for the ways American academics and policy makers thought about the postcolonial world, especially in the context of modernization theory. After providing examples of cultural racism within modernization theory and its mass communication component, the chapter will show how the shift occurred institutionally through intellectual networks. Finally, the chapter will discuss the contemporary consequences of bringing cultural racism discourses into modernization theory.

Bible, Biology, Culture and Racism

Racism refers to a system of thought that classifies "races" on the basis of what is thought to be some shared inherent qualities among individuals and then arranges the subsequent racial categories into hierarchies of superiority and inferiority based on those qualities. James Blaut (1992), the radical geographer, has written persuasively about the complicated ways that racist practices persist even as racial theory—a structure of ideas that purport to empirically explain differences of "race"—changes from epoch to epoch. In other words, racist practice is, to a large extent, an historical constant. Racist practices are upheld, justified, and sometimes masked by changing racial theories that are consistent with the changing intellectual environment of the age.

Blaut identifies three major structures of Western racial theory. Reli-
ﻪ) gious racism, based on the bible, was dominant in the early 19th century.
ᖯ) The dominant racial theory between about 1850 and 1950 was biological

c)

racism, which was based on natural science. Contemporary racial theory is cultural racism, based on certain views of cultural history.

insert

Religious racism stated that God had created white people at the headwaters of the Tigris River, near the Caucasus Mountains, which were thought to be the home of the Caucasian race. God gave white people agriculture, cities, arts, etc., and all of pre-Christian history took place among whites in a region between Rome and Mesopotamia. As some people migrated south out of this region, they became dark and degenerate and lost the civilized life and nature of their white ancestors. The Christian Europeans believed that they were favored by their God and were superior to non-whites.

Biological racism became the dominant theory in the mid-19th century. It did not completely supplant religious racism, as oppression by one people by another in the name of religious superiority did (and does) occur even after 1850. Nevertheless, biological racism attained its dominant status based on versions of the biological theories of Mendel and Darwin. Gobineau proposed a widely accepted view that whites were genetically and culturally superior to non-whites and that those differences were persistent and permanent (Hannaford 1996, 264ff). *insert* Biological racism began to lose its luster a few years after the end of First World War. Anthropologist Franz Boas and his students advanced theories of historical relativism—the idea that all cultures are changing and evolving—in the early years of the 20th century. They argued against the notion of permanent and persistent biological superiority and inferiority. Their ideas had been marginalized by advocates of the biological view of race, but now found favor as biological racism was increasingly discredited.

Biological racism did not completely fall from dominance, however, until the middle of the 20th century, after World War II. After defeating Nazism, American social theorists were uncomfortable with the "American dilemma," Gunnar Myrdal's phrase for the contradiction between the country's egalitarian ideals and racist practice against African Americans and other minorities. Also, in the area of foreign policy, American leaders were compelled to support struggles for national liberation in the former European colonies. A massive effort was organized in American academic circles, funding centers, government and military agencies, and the foreign policy establishment to develop a framework to explain that non-white peoples of the postcolonial world were only *culturally* backward, not biologically inferior. Gradually, a new racial theory emerged to counteract the idea that Anglo Americans were innately superior to postcolonial peoples and non-whites were incapable of change. The new theory proposed that any and all non-white societies could realize their potential and capacity by learning how to think rationally, behave in appropriate ways, and commit themselves to a Western set of values and orientations. The obstacles to such advancement were cultural, not biological. This logic allowed Western academics to substitute, as Samir Amin (1989) pointed out, the racial category white with the cultural category European and American, and the idea that whites are racially superior with the notion that whites are merely culturally superior. Thus, since the gap between whites and non-whites was not biological (and therefore not permanent), it was possible for non-whites to "catch up" to whites.

For two main reasons, a cultural theory of race could not have matched the needs of the moment more perfectly for America in the Cold War era. First, post-war academics needed a way to legitimately dispense with the idea that race was immutable. When Harry Truman announced Point Four in his Inauguration speech in 1949, he told the world that the United States was ready and willing to help "develop" the postcolonial world. Introducing this transitive meaning of the idea of development carried with it an important implication. Truman was suggesting that people of postcolonial lands, believed by European colonizers to be persistently and permanently inferior, could, in fact, be taught to change their outlooks, behaviors, and attitudes in ways that could move nations toward modernity (Shah & Wilkins 2004). In terms of racial theory, to allow the idea that postcolonial people could change the mental, psychological, and moral traits associated with their race into academic discourse, the biological race paradigm had to be replaced. Thus, Boas was brought in from the cold, so to speak, and his ideas revived. His notions that each "culture-group" could develop and change over time and that no cultural group was naturally superior to another were embraced (Hannaford 1996; Pierpoint 2004). Toward the close of the Second World War, Margaret Mead, a student of Boas and an eminent anthropologist in her own right, argued in a paper about "national character" that "the differences in race or sub-race membership are irrelevant, that there are no known psychological differences which are dependent upon race as such" (Mead 1943, 1).

Second, the cultural racism paradigm was perfect for changing intellectual needs because it allowed intellectual space for the notion of development—the teleological notion that all countries inevitably advance out of "backwardness"—and also for modernization theory, which proposed that even supposedly culturally inferior people and countries of the postcolonial world could be modern. Cultural racism allowed the West to retain its notion of superiority over the non-West without resorting to largely discredited theories of biological racism. One of the key players in making these arguments was sociologist Edward Shils. In the summer of 1959, after roughly a decade of modernization research by scholars in a number of disciplines, Shils delivered a keynote address at a conference in Dobbs Ferry, New York, on political development in the "new states" of Africa, Asia, and the Middle East. In the speech, Shils provided a detailed definition of the "modern state." It entailed democracy, the dethronement of the rich and the traditionally privileged, land reform, steeply progressive income taxation, universal suffrage, universal public education, rational technology, scientific knowledge, industrialization, and a high standard of living. "Modern," said Shils, "means being western without the onus of following the west. It is the model for the West detached in some way from its geographical origins and locus" (quoted in Gilman 2003, 2). With this speech, Shils created "foundational certainty" among scholars that the purpose of modernization was to create modern nations all over the world and the blueprint for modern states was America (Gilman 2003, 142). Shils advocated the use of the term modernization to describe the transition from "backward" to "modern" nations, because it steered away from implications of Western superiority suggested by the terms Christianization or Westernization (Gilman 2003, 141; see also Shah 1996).

The theoretical bottom line, then, became that internal conditions in the postcolonial states can be improved it they followed the Euro-American model of overcoming backwardness. In other words, the culturally inferior postcolonial states ought to accept guidance and tutelage of culturally evolved Europeans and Americans who now wanted to altruistically share their wisdom and good fortune with the less wise and less fortunate. This argument was at the center of the notion of cultural racism. And cultural racism is at the center of the theory of modernization as it was articulated in the 1950s and 1960s.

Modernization and Culture

Modernization theory rose to prominence in the years after World War II, as U.S. foreign policy experts recommended a cold-war strategy of winning the hearts and minds of residents living in strategically important nations in Asia, Africa, and the Middle East. As we will see in subsequent sections of the paper, the theory came together as social scientists, funding agencies, and government officials worked with one another under the rubric of anti-communism to theorize, operationalize, and implement a model of societal change for the postcolonial states that would bring them into the U.S. orbit of influence.

It would be wrong to characterize the modernization scholars as religious racists or even, strictly speaking, biological racists. In the context of the era in which they were working, their world-views, their sense of privilege to make declarations about what non-Western world ought to do, and their liberal attitudes toward race and race relations were consistent with what many Americans thought (though the Southern segregationists were a major exception on racial liberalism). At the same time, however, there is little doubt that most of these academics believed they were culturally superior to residents of the postcolonial world. It is rare to find examples of explicit references to residents and cultures of postcolonial states that use the vocabulary of biological racism. That is, it is difficult to find the language common to European colonialism that causally links the physical attributes of, say, a man's hair, skin, and bone, to his mental capabilities, moral temperament, or intelligence. But we can find many, many examples of references to the *cultural* inferiority of non-whites.

The centrality of cultural racism to modernization theory is demonstrated repeatedly in the writing of the main modernization theorists. The first comprehensive statement of modernization theory is Daniel Lerner's *Passing of Traditional Society: Modernizing the Middle East*. The book was based on a six-country radio listener survey sponsored by the Voice of America in 1950 and 1951. In *Passing of Traditional Society*, Lerner proposed a linear theory of modernization: increasing urbanization leading to growth of media (as people would demand news and information) and literacy (as more and more schools are built), which would, in turn, result in economic growth and political participation. Lerner maintained that mass communication was the key factor in helping traditional societies becoming modern. Lerner theorized that radio, television, magazines, and newspapers were important catalysts of the modernization process. The mass media provided information about the modern West and vicarious experiences of modern lifestyles to audiences in the postcolonial world. Audience members with highly empathic personalities—those who could easily imagine themselves in different circumstances—would begin to think and behave in ways that helped transform their countries from tradition societies to modern ones modeled primarily on the United States. In the post-war era and beyond, theory, research, and foreign policy in the mass communication and modernization area were influenced by Lerner's ideas (see Engerman, et al. 2003; Latham 2000).

Early in *Passing of Traditional Society*, describing the rationale for the study, Lerner says that to understand what might happen in the Middle East under modernization,

> "[W]e remind ourselves of what, historically, happened in the West. For the sequence of current events in the Middle East can be understood as a deviation, in some measure a deliberate deformation, of the Western model. This observational standpoint implies no ethnocentrism. As we shall show, the Western model exhibits certain components and sequences whose relevance is global" (Lerner 1958, 46).

In other comparable passages, Lerner writes that modernization involves "an infusion of a 'rationalist and positivistic spirit' against which, scholars seem agreed, Islam is absolutely defenseless" (1958, 46). And further: "modernizers of the Middle East will do well to study the historical sequence of Westernization" (1958, 46). And finally: "A complication of Middle East modernization is its own ethnocentrism—expressed politically in extreme nationalism, psychologically in passionate xenophobia. The hatred sown by anti-colonialism is harvested in the rejection of every appearance of foreign tutelage" (1958, 47).

Lerner is obviously supremely confident about the superiority of the West as a benchmark to measure the progress of "the rest." But he also is certain that what explains the lack of social and economic progress in the Middle East is not a history of European colonialism or imperialism but the notion that the countries deliberately deviated from the path established by the colonialists. And, in classic "blame the victim" rhetoric, Lerner suggests that the "backward" condition of the Middle East is the result of its own racism towards Europeans. The Middle East would be better off, Lerner seems to say, if it had just let colonialism do its job.

Passages similar to these, reflecting a deep belief in the cultural superiority of the West (and concurrent inferiority of the postcolonial nations and peoples), recur frequently in writings of the leading American modernization scholars. In 1951, two important sociologists, Talcott Parsons and Edward Shils, published *Toward A General Theory of Action*, a book that provided a scholarly justification for viewing the West as culturally superior to the non-West. In a co-written chapter, the sociologists introduced a system of "pattern variables," a set of binary pairings representing "value-orientations" that constitute characteristics of social systems (Parsons & Shils 1951, 77). The pairings boiled down to:

Affectivity	Affective neutrality
Self-orientation	Collective orientation
Particularism	Universalism
Ascription	Achievement
Diffuseness	Specificity

Parsons and Shils were careful to claim that their scheme was a merely a heuristic device for analyzing social systems comparatively. However, Walt Rostow, an economist who figures prominently in the intellectual history of modernization, noted in a review of the book: "the most meaningful aspects of the general theory of action lie in some of the assumptions ... built into it" (quoted in Gilman 2003, 87). These assumptions amounted to the idea that the right side of the dichotomous pairs referred to modern or "advanced social systems," such as the United States and the left side to "traditional" or "backward" regions in the postcolonial world. Though Parsons generally avoided explicitly associating a notion of superiority with the United States, Shils did not. He wrote that the United States and Western European nations—those characterized by the value orientations on the right side of the binary—"need not *aspire* to modernity. They *are* modern. Modernity is part of their very nature" (Shils 1960, 267). Shils said the problem with postcolonial society—characterized by the value orientations on the left side of the dichotomy—was that it was handicapped, in part, by its sense of inferiority. Speaking specifically about Indian intellectuals, Shils claimed, "they are ashamed that their country is not a modern country and their institutions are not abreast of the institutions of Great Britain and the modern world. They feel their literature is on the whole inferior to the foreign literature which they read, that Indian science does not stand at the forefront of world science" (Shils 1959, 402). These words could easily have been spoken by many researchers of modernization in a variety of disciplines who readily accepted the views of cultural superiority and inferiority embedded implicitly in the pattern variable scheme and stated more explicitly by Shils.

For example, economist Walt Rostow (1952) of MIT argued that people in the "backward countries" were characterized by certain "propensities" such as aversion to science and technology, rational economic thinking, deferring gratification, and birth control. He and other economists assumed, as Nils Gilman has pointed out, people in such societies were stuck in a "traditional" mindset that was associated with a "lack of political sophistication and susceptibility to political demagoguery" (Gilman 2003, 164). Elsewhere, Rostow (1960) wrote that postcolonial peoples are "pre-Newtonian in science and technology" and "pervaded by fatalism." Political scientist Lucian Pye, also of MIT, argued in studies of Southeast Asian nations that the appeal of communism there was a manifestation of psychopathology related to immature and incoherent political self-identity (Pye 1956, 1961). Pye, influenced by the political psychology approach of his former professors Harold Lasswell and Gabriel Almond, said that as long as these pathologies existed, postcolonial peoples will always be "depressed" about the fact that "modernization...has always been the monopoly of those who were their former masters" (Pye 1961, 310). While political scientist Pye applied theories of psychology to analyze political questions in the postcolonial states, bona fide psychologists also were interested in the process and politics of modernization. Alex Inkeles (1960, 1969) listed features of being modern that could be learned by "backward" residents of the postcolonial states. These included: openness to new experience, independence from traditional authority, abandonment of passivity, high levels of professional ambition, a preference for being on time, a strong interest in civic affairs, and a desire to keep up with international news (Inkeles 1969).

Modernization and Mass Communication

Scholars of mass communication approached modernization and culture in the same manner as their colleagues in sociology, political science and psychology. In fact, the pattern variable scheme casts a long shadow on Lerner's earliest writing on mass communication and modernization, even before he wrote *Passing of Traditional Society*. In an essay summarizing initial analysis of the Middle East survey data, he wrote that most people in the Middle East were "traditional," suffered from "peasant despair" and experienced a "paucity of abstract images of self and society" (Lerner & Reisman 1955, 68-69). In another essay written at about the same time, Lerner declared that certain Arabs are "simple-minded men without the long view of power and its consequences" (Lerner undated, 17). Lerner's descriptions are consistent with the value-orientations listed on the "traditional" side of the Parsons and Shils pattern variable scheme.

The idea of postcolonial peoples as simple-minded readily transfers into the literature that deals specifically with mass communication and modernization. In *Passing of Traditional Society*, Lerner assumes that media images of modern life and rational values depicted in American serials, news, and movies would powerfully and fundamentally alter the attitudes, behaviors, and lifeways of parochial and superstitious non-white people in the Middle East (Lerner 1958, 52ff). In support of this contention Lerner quotes one of the respondents from the survey in Iran who says: "The movies are like teachers to us, who tells us what to do and what not to do" (p. 54). In Lerner's scheme of things, the postcolonial audience was a passive one and vulnerable to manipulation by mass media messages (p. 54). Lerner is more explicit later when he writes that "the importance of media in our theory is that it enlarges a person's view of the world ('opinion range') and his capacity to imagine himself in new and strange situations ('empathy') in ways that will alter action" (1958, 96). In other words, in the language of the social science tradition, mass media content has powerful affective, behavioral, and cognitive effects on media consumers in the postcolonial world.

At the same time Lerner and his contemporaries were writing about powerful media effects on audiences in the Middle East, mass communication researchers in the United States were operating under the "limited effects model" for American audiences. This difference is consistent with the cultural-superiority-of-the-West theory of cultural racism. The underlying argument was that American audiences had evolved to a position of active, sophisticated media consumption, bringing critical faculties to bear on their media consumption choices (see Katz & Lazarsfeld 1955) while the postcolonial audience was still conceived as passive and easily manipulated by media. Lerner argued that Western audiences had once been passive but as they were increasingly exposed to mass media messages they eventually learned the important skill of empathy: "The mass media ... disciplined Western man in those empathic skills which spell modernity" (1958, 54). He expected the same in the postcolonial world—that people there might also be able to eventually develop empathic skills.

For Lerner, empathy had been the key to modernization in the West and it also would be the key to modernization in the postcolonial world. Empathy refers to the capacity for individuals to imagine themselves in situations and conditions different from their own. The greater the proportion of people in a nation with high levels of this empathic skill, Lerner argued, the more modern it is (Lerner 1958, 50). In a paper published in the year before *Passing of Traditional Society* came out Lerner and a colleague wrote that "Western peoples are more able to assume the projective roles of world travelers ... in contrast to findings from the Middle East [analyzed by Lerner in 1953-54]" where questions requiring skills of active projection into unfamiliar situations were met with anxiety and fear (Keller & Lerner 1957). If Middle East audiences were anxious about active projection, Lerner might have reasoned, perhaps passive projection experienced via mass media would be possible for postcolonial audiences. Whatever the reasoning, Lerner concluded that the passive Middle East audience would react to Western mass media, with their contents representing a "vicarious universe" of modern life in the West, in ways similar to that of Western audiences in an earlier age: Postcolonial audiences might be compelled to imagine themselves in modern lives, to aspire to that lifestyle, and to do something about it (Lerner 1963, 348). But for Lerner and the modernization scholars, the modern lifestyle was synonymous with American lifestyle. The modernization theorists seemed to lack a bit of empathy themselves and could not imagine that postcolonial peoples might want and have the capacity to create a modern world of their own making.

Other modernization researchers interested in the role of mass communication made arguments that echoed various parts of Lerner's thesis. Herbert Hyman (Hyman 1963, 147) wrote that because mass media were relatively new to the postcolonial world, he expected them to have "great vitality with powerful consequences for opinion change." McClelland (1963, 250) believed mass media had the power to raise postcolonial people's motivation to achieve and, therefore, push toward a modern life. Pye mentioned powerful societal-level mass media effects in terms of the "amplifying function [that] magnif[ies] actions of individuals to the point that they can be felt throughout the society, in a sense transforming 'man-sized acts' into 'society-sized acts'" (Pye 1963, 6). Wilbur Schramm suggested a number of media functions that can have powerful effects in postcolonial nations. Media can be a watchman, widen horizons, focus attention, raise aspirations, create climate for development, confer status, contribute to interpersonal channels, enforce social norms, help form tastes, and effect lightly held attitudes and slightly canalize stronger attitudes (Schramm 1964, 127ff).

Intellectual Networks and the Flow of Ideas

Ideas related to cultural racism entered modernization thinking primarily through complex and overlapping sets of intellectual networks anchored at various institutions such as government departments, universities, funding agencies, and the Social Science Research Council (SSRC). Many of the best academic minds in the social sciences and humanities worked in some capacity for the military and the government during World War II, resulting in deep and lasting relationships among scholars in a variety of fields. In some cases, institutional anchors are less important than interpersonal contacts over time. In yet other cases, intellectual influences can be deduced simply through evidence of what scholars are reading or through citation analysis. To trace the flow of intellectual ideas, it is most effective to point to the methodological, theoretical, and some key conceptual underpinnings of modernization theory and trace how ideas moved among intellectual networks related to sociology, psychology, foreign policy, communication studies, and race, and then coalesced around a network of academics working on modernization. First, I will describe how behavioralism, the underlying methodological orientation, and structural functionalism, the favored theoretical approach, entered modernization research. Then I discuss two issues—media effects and propaganda—central to the history of mass communication research. The section ends with a look specifically at race-relations research in America and how it is linked to moderniza-tion research. In each of these examples, the assumptions about race and racial difference made by the researchers will be highlighted.

explain *Behavioralism*

Behavioralism was the ascendant methodological approach in the social sciences after World War II. The approach emphasizes the search for social and psychological bases for behavior and advocates the use of precise measurement and quantification in the search for universal laws of behavior (Gilman 2003, 115). Behavioralism can be traced back to the inter-war years at the University of Chicago. Political scientist Charles Merriam (one of the founder of the SSRC) and his student Har-old Lasswell were the most forceful advocates for adopting what was believed to be a value-free method for the social sciences (Smith 1994). Many of Laswell's students, such as Gabriel Almond, Ithiel Pool, and Lucian Pye, among others, pushed the social sciences in the direction of behavioralism. Almond and Pye were directly involved in guiding the direction of modernization research through their activities as di-rectors of the Committee on Comparative Politics (CCP), established within the SSRC in the mid 1950s. It is fair to say, in fact, that in their positions as decision makers for funding and setting the methodological terms and conceptual vocabulary by which to understand social change in the postcolonial world, Almond and Pye helped to create, under the rubric of comparative politics, the dominant paradigm of modernization theory and research. Pye's academic home was MIT, where he had an appointment with the Center for International Studies (CENIS) along with Lerner, Pool, and Rostow. When the Center received an $875,000 grant from the Ford Foundation in 1952 to establish a research focus on international communication, director Max Millikan created a Planning Committee to decide what to do with the money. Lasswell, Shils, and Columbia University mass media researcher Paul Lazarsfeld were all members of the committee (Blackmer 2002, 51).

Social science departments at the University of Chicago had earned a well-deserved reputation for fruitfully using the city as a laboratory for observing human behavior and relationships. The social, political, cultural, and economic life of the city's residents became the object of analysis for a large number of students and faculty from roughly the 1920s onward. Included in this range of study were theses, dissertations, journal articles, and books about the lives of blacks, Asians, and other minorities (see Persons 1987; Yu 2001). In this context of "ethnic studies," Chicago scholars examined such concepts as marginal man, the rural-urban migration axis, the contact-conflict-assimilation cycle, the hobo mind, and other ideas that helped explain race relations in an urban center. Under the sway of behavioralism (initially more so in political science than in sociology), a central tenet of which was to search for universal laws of behavior, postwar scholars drew upon these concepts to study the postcolonial nations. As Pye (2004) recently noted in a reminiscence about the "behavioral revolution":

> "Now [shortly after the end of the war] other places and times could be used as the evidence for comparative findings about the workings of politics" (p. 2).

There are clear parallels within this emerging scholarship between minorities in urban America and residents of newly independent postcolonial nations. For example, as discussed later in the chapter, Park's "marginal man" is similar to Lerner's "transitional" Turkish peasant and Thomas and Znanieki's "rural-urban migration axis" is close to the urbanization stage in Lerner's modernization model. Thus, within the context of the cultural racism theory that was becoming dominant at the time, scholars may have viewed both American minorities and postcolonial residents (who to a large extent shared the feature of being "non-white") as culturally inferior but capable of self-improvement.

Lerner was influenced by behavioralism even before the organization of the CCP. After World War II, Lerner worked with Lasswell and Pool at Stanford. In 1947, they organized the Revolution and Development of

International Relations (RADIR) project, which used detailed quantitative content analysis of dozens of the world's newspapers to determine attitudes toward ideas such as democracy, communism, international organizations, etc. While at Stanford, Lerner also worked closely with Lasswell to edit a 1951 book called the *Policy Sciences: Recent Developments in Scope and Method*, which contained chapters written by the leaders of and converts to behavioralism. In the Foreword, Charles Easton Rothwell, director of Stanford's Hoover Institute Library on War, Revolution and Peace, where the RADIR project was housed, admirably summed up the underlying behavioralist spirit of the book and of the academic age in which Lerner and the modernization scholars were working. Rothwell wrote:

> "In their investigations of the processes of human relations, the students of society are drawing more and more upon the method and discipline of science. Fully aware that intangibles and variables are more numerous and less controllable in the human laboratory than in those of the physical or biological sciences, social scientists have nevertheless found methods for measuring with reasonable accuracy the regularities of human response. By means of statistics, the handmaiden of quantitative investigation, they have been able to convert their observations of human phenomenon into reasonably reliable formulas. [A]s the regularities of human behavior become more apparent, the possibilities of reliable social planning on a local or global scale become greater" (Rothwell 1951, viii).

The book contained chapters by academic "heavy hitters" such as Robert Merton, Edward Shils, Paul Lazarsfeld, and Margaret Mead. Each of these stalwarts of social science would have direct or indirect influence on Lerner's writing of *Passing of Traditional Society*.

Structural Functionalism

Structural functionalism became the theoretical foundation of essentially all modernization research in the post-war era. Walt Rostow, who had strong ties to the US State Department, had worked with the United Nations Economic Commission for Europe following implementation of the Marshall Plan, and is one of the most frequently cited modernization scholars, crafted his "stages of economic development" (Rostow 1960) to align in large measure to the pattern variables put forward by Parsons and Shils. As described earlier, structural functionalism was based on abstracted social, political, and cultural traits of societies that were then arrayed into binaries called pattern variables. In terms of modernization, the United States and Northern Europe possessed characteristics and postcolonial world represented the opposite. These opposing traits were eventually condensed, following Ferdinand Tonnies's famous Gemein-schaft-Gessellschaft distinction (Trevino 2001, xli), into the two master tropes of modern societies (the West) on the one hand and traditional societies (the non-West) on the other. Thus the idea of "modern" was racialized to mean white in that the modernization process took as its normative endpoint the characteristics of predominantly white United States and Northern European countries. Harvard professor Talcott Parsons developed his structural functionalism theory over a number of years beginning in 1931 when he shifted from the Department of Economics to the Department of Social Relations—DSR—where his colleagues included Shils, McClelland and Inkeles. He was motivated by a desire to embed the role of economics within a more general framework of sociological systems (Parsons 1980; Trevino 2001). One of his goals was to go beyond the economists' emphasis on "rational" factors and consider the role of values—from the perspective of "the unconscious," "covert culture," and "latent function"—within a social analysis of human behavior (Gilman 2003, 81).

Taken up readily by modernization theorists interested in transforming societies from traditional to modern, structural functionalism helped explain the blockages to becoming modern and provided a basis for prescribing policies to stimulate comprehensive societal change. In the most comprehensive statement of the theory, *Toward a General Theory of Action*, Parsons and Shils (1951) explained that healthy societies are well-integrated by the smooth functioning of a variety of social structures. Adherence to a common set of values by all members of society was the key underlying mechanism. Too much individualism was a form of social "malintegration" and a recipe for social unrest that prevented the dual goals of social conformity and political stability (Parsons & Shils 1951, 151-153).

Parsons' student Marion Levy was the first to apply structural functionalism to the problem of modernization. He studied societal transformations in China and Japan in the late 1940s and early 1950s (Levy 1949, 1953). For Levy, the key problem of modernization was maintaining political order and social control during a society's transition from traditional to modern. Because postcolonial people were believed to be unsophisticated and susceptible to influence (as per the theory of cultural racism), the postcolonial state had to be strong. Wrote Levy (1953, 175):

> "The problem of coordination involves a problem of control by force if necessary, in cases in which deviance develops or threatens. Most importantly, it requires that there be patterns in operation that tend to minimize the development of deviance."

Levy later assumed a central role in the Committee for Comparative Politics, which was a crucial point of genesis for modernization theory.

Mass Media Effects

As mentioned earlier, the operative framework in America for understanding the impact of mass media messages was the limited effects model. The idea was rooted in two important studies conducted at the Bureau of Applied Social Research (BASR) at Columbia University. (Paul Lazarsfeld was the director and Robert Merton was a powerful presence. Both men had appointments in the sociology department. Lerner was a visiting professor in sociology with an appointment in BASR in the early 1950s when he was involved in analysis of the Middle East survey.) In the first study, Lazarsfeld, Berelson and Gaudet (1948) demonstrated that the media were only one part of an entire web of influences and that media impact often flowed through opinion leaders who interpreted and passed along information to their communities. Later, Katz and Lazarsfeld (1955) produced evidence, heavily criticized later by Gitlin (1978), showing that media audiences were actively determining what media messages to give their attention and even how these messages would affect them, if at all. Together, these studies (along with some others) were the basis for a model that claimed mass media "do not serve as necessary and sufficient cause of media effects" (Klapper 1960).

The limited effects/active audience thesis also served as a counter-argument to the mass culture thesis made popular by members of the Frankfurt School, some who were living, essentially in exile since the 1930s from their native Germany, in New York and California. Their position, based primarily on observation of the American "culture industry," was that mass culture's crude, repetitive content distracted the passive American audience from the fact of their exploitation by capitalist owners of mass media and of their oppression by the state (Horkheimer & Adorno 1972). It was Shils who stood up for the limited effects/active audience side in an acidy retort to the mass culture thesis. Shils viewed the mass culture arguments as an attack on America and its modern-state status. Shils took the critical analysts to task for assuming, in direct contradiction to U.S. social science research, that media content exerted direct and powerful influence on passive audience members. He agreed that mass culture in America could be awful but, he wrote, the critics "go far beyond the limits set by their observations and assume that reading or seeing is evidence of a close correspondence between the content of what is seen and the mind of the person who comes in contact with it" (Shils 1957, 602). In fact, he wrote, "There is no reason at present to believe that men and women in modern Western society or that Americans in particular have much resemblance to the picture of them presented in the works of contemporary social scientists" of the Frankfurt School and their American adherents (Shils 1957, 603). Effectively, Shils and the structural functionalists gave little or no value to Critical Theory perspectives on the question of media effects on American media audiences.

But when it came to residents of the postcolonial world, U.S. scholars, including Shils, were of the opinion that the masses were passive recipients of wisdom from the West: whatever they were shown, they wanted, whatever they were told, they believed. American scholars asserted that there was indeed in the postcolonial world (and *ought* to be in the initial stages of modernization), a correspondence between, as Shils had put it, "the content of what is seen and the mind of the person who comes in contact with it." In fact, in the context of the postcolonial world, Shils claimed that the alienation and depersonalization spawned by mass culture, as described by Adorno, Horkheimer, Dwight Macdonald, and others, was not necessarily a bad thing. As Gilman (2003, 54) notes, Shils felt that in the postcolonial world it was perfectly appropriate that "by giving the people what they wanted *culturally*, elites could avoid making concessions of a concrete *political* sort." For Shils, mass culture represented for the postcolonial world a "non-coercive way of keeping the masses from interfering with elites and intellectuals" as the latter determined the initial directions for society (Gilman 2003, 54). Picking up on Shils's position, modernization researchers, such as Lerner and McClelland, seemed delighted to report that media content from the West could exert powerful effects and move the passive, unsophisticated postcolonial peoples smoothly through what Levy had identified as the dangerous period in the transition from traditional to modern society. Passivity, in the postcolonial context, seemed to be functional for a smooth modernization process.

World War II Propaganda Research

While this topic does not represent a distinct methodological, theoretical, or conceptual tradition that flows through intellectual networks, it is a key activity around which numerous key figures in modernization research interacted. Examining this activity also reveals the military roots of the mass communication component of modernization theory, which can be traced to propaganda research during World War II. One of several centers of U.S. military propaganda was the Army's Psychological Warfare Division in Paris, known as PWD-Forward. This unit was supported by PWD-Rear in London.

Lerner worked in PWD-Forward from September 1944 to May 1945, when he was transferred to PWD's successor agency, the Information Control Division (ICD) of the Office of the Military Government-U.S. in Berlin. At PWD he served as the chief editor of the Intelligence Branch, where his job was to write daily compilations of intelligence reports to be distributed to a wide range of officers working in U.S. intelligence sections throughout Europe. His colleagues included Morris Janowitz, a leading sociologist with whom Lerner occasionally corresponded after the war, C.D. Jackson, a high-ranking editor of *Time* magazine, who as special adviser to President Eisenhower organized important post-war seminars on the issue of foreign aid to postcolonial states, and Murray Gurfein, a future federal judge who heard the Pentagon Papers case in June 1971. At PWD-Rear was the seemingly omnipresent Edward Shils, who was interrogating German POWs with the British psychiatrist Henry Dicks and developing psychological profiles of German "types" to help ascertain the effectiveness of Allied propaganda campaigns.

After the war, Lerner landed at Stanford to work on the RADIR project with Pool and Lasswell. In his capacity as research director he had extensive correspondence and meetings with a wide range of scholars. These include Reinhard Bendix, Bernard Berelson, W. Philips Davison, Paul Lazarsfeld, C. Wright Mills, Margaret Mead, Nathan Glazer, Paul Baran, William Sarnoff, Alex Inkeles, Robert Merton, Gabriel Almond, Bert Hoselitz, Leo Rosten, Leo Lowenthal, Samuel Stouffer, Talcott Parsons, Clyde Kluckhohn, Edward Shils, and others involved to one extent or another in the modernization project or its antecedents.

While at Stanford, Lerner also wrote a dissertation on psychological warfare based on his experiences in Paris. Using intelligence summaries and other documents as his primary data, the dissertation, submitted to New York University in April 1948, was a comprehensive history and assessment of the Allied propaganda efforts between D-Day (June 6, 1944) and V-E Day (May 8, 1945). To aid in the analysis of the targets of Allied propaganda, Lerner turned to the typology developed by Shils and Dicks. Lerner boiled down their manifold typology to three types of Germans: the hard-core Nazis, the anti-Nazis, and the non-politicals. The hard-core was impervious to Allied propaganda and the anti-Nazis needed no convincing to abandon Hitler (see Lerner 1949, 140). Lerner's analysis also claimed that the Allied propaganda experts used the most effective strategy possible by targeting only the non-politicals, the easiest to convert to anti-Nazism, with propaganda messages even though the "members of this group were less likely than others to be stirred by flaming appeals" (Lerner 1949, 140).

Lerner had arranged with Lazarsfeld to be a visiting professor at Columbia in 1951. While there, Lerner became interested in analyzing the data from the Middle East survey, which the BASR was about to complete for the Voice of America's audience analysis specialist Leo Lowenthal, a colleague and friend of Adorno and Horkheimer and member of the Frankfurt School. When Lerner analyzed data from the Middle East survey, the analysis that was the basis for *Passing of Traditional Society*, the propaganda target categories from his dissertation reappeared in a form revised to fit the new situation (Samarajiwa 1987). In *Passing of Traditional Society*, Lerner's categories were "traditionals" who were difficult to convert to modern life, "moderns," who did not need converting, and the "transitionals," the group whose attitudes were most likely to move in the desired direction—that is, toward a modern life.

In other words, Lerner viewed the mass communication and modernization problem in the same way he viewed the propaganda problem. And he said as much in a 1951 BASR report on Turkey:

"The problem of penetrating with new communications ideas down into certain strata of the population or out to the grass roots is not unique with international radio broadcasting to under-developed countries, the same problem has plagued *other propagandists* under different conditions" (Lerner, Scheuller and Stycos 1951, 9, emphasis added).

The parallel he observed between targets of Allied propaganda during World War II and potential targets of Western mass media messages allowed Lerner to abstract without hesitation from studies of white German POWs to create a model of media effects in the Arab and Persian Middle East. He ignored cultural history and differences between Europe and U.S. on the one hand and the Middle East on the other. What Lerner accomplished in the process was essentially to de-militarize propaganda research. But at the same time he racialized the "modern" as white, implying that becoming modern was becoming "white"—in the sense of a symbol standing for all the traits Shils would outline in his Dobbs Ferry speech in 1959.

Race Relations in Post-War America

Comparing the conditions of racial minorities in the United States to the question of modernization in postcolonial nations was not uncommon among modernization writers. Lerner (1958) cited a classic study of "race psychology" among Polish immigrants by University of Chicago sociologists W.I. Thomas and Florian Znaniecki (1927), which investigated the rural-urban migration pattern in both Poland and the United States and suggested a model of social change brought on by the need for "backward" peasants to become modern. Lerner also cites Park (1950) on the importance of cities and urbanization in stimulating the move towards becoming modern. Though it is not cited explicitly, the theory of assimilation that comes out of the Chicago School research seems important to modernization theorists (Shah 2003) because structural functionalism's pattern variables scheme of modern and traditional provided no explanation of *how* a traditional society becomes a modern one (until Parsons, 1964; see Gilman 2003, 89). Assimilation theory, based on the experience of white immigrants, claimed newcomers inevitably go through a contact-conflict-competition-accommodation-assimilation cycle as they are gradually absorbed into the community's new cultural practices and social relationships. Assimilation theory said that one of the primary forces that aided the move from "old ways" to "new" was through contact between distinct cultures (Park 1914; Park 1922; Park & Burgess 1924). Though assimilation has been criticized for its inapplicability to non-whites (Scott 1973, 295), modernization researchers may have drawn from it to predict and explain the traditional to modern transformation in postcolonial nations (Shah 2003). Modernization also appears to elaborate on the idea of intercultural contact by suggesting that even vicarious contact with distant communities and cultures through exposure to media content could provide the stimulus to move postcolonial people towards assimilating into the modern world.

Another connection between race issues in the United States and modernization theory involves the influential book on American race relations, Gunnar Myrdal's *An American Dilemma: The Negro in American Democracy* (1944). The work on *American Dilemma* began before the start of World War II. In 1937, the Carnegie Corporation contracted Myrdal, a renowned Swedish economist, to conduct a definitive study of blacks in America. Carnegie paid unheard of salaries for his handpicked staff as well as expenses for his family to live with him in New York City. Some of the country's leading social scientists were consulted for the project, including Boas students Ashley Montague and Melville Herskovitz, University of Chicago stalwart Louis Wirth, and (of course) Harvard's Edward Shils. Among his research staff and consultants were several leading black intellectuals of the day, including E. Franklin Frazier and Charles S. Johnson, African Americans who both had studied with Park at the University of Chicago. Myrdal's most important associate, however, was the black political scientist Ralph Bunche (Southern 1987). In 1940, with the study in full swing, Myrdal returned home to take part in Swedish resistance to Nazism. But the work continued under the guidance of University of Chicago sociologist Samuel Stouffer. Myrdal returned in late 1941 to complete the project.

American Dilemma was a vitally important book for creating the basis for a post-war liberal race-relations agenda and it had an impact, also, on modernization thinking. The "dilemma" was the discrepancy between the "American Creed"—egalitarianism, fairness, liberty, compassion, etc.—and oppression of blacks. Reflecting the ascendance of the cultural racism paradigm, the thrust of Myrdal's book was that "the Negro" can change culturally and ought to be given the chance to internalize American values and enter the fabric of American life. Recall the similar argument made by modernization scholars in regard to residents of post-colonial nations, that they ought to be given the chance to adopt Western values and enter the modern world. Myrdal also declared in *American Dilemma* that the "Negro problem" was really a white problem because it was white oppression that had created a reactive black culture that was, Myrdal said in a passage that raised the ire of Ralph Ellison (see Ellison 1973) and many other black intellectuals, "a distorted development, or a pathological condition, of general American culture" (Myrdal 1944, 928). Recall again that in an eerily similar statement about the Middle East, Lerner had written: "current events in the Middle East can be understood as a deviation, in some measure a deliberate deformation, of the Western model" (Lerner 1958, 46). Lerner had assigned *American Dilemma* in a course he taught on international political relations at Stanford in 1949 and must have been familiar with Myrdal's work when he worked on *Passing of Traditional Society* in the early 1950s (Lerner 1949).

After publication of *American Dilemma*, Myrdal returned to Sweden to become Minister of Commerce. In 1947, he left that post to become Executive Secretary of the United Nations Economic Commission for Europe (UNECE), based in Switzerland. One of his top aides in Geneva was Walt Rostow. Rostow remained in Geneva until 1952, when he joined the economics department and CENIS at MIT. Rostow wrote some of the key treatises on economic development and modernization during his years at CENIS but he was also the leader of a major effort at MIT in the spring of 1957—the Carnegie-funded "America Project"—that dealt directly with the question of connections between American race relations and modernization.

One component of the America Project was planning for the United States exhibit at the summer 1958 Brussels World Exposition. The United States Information Agency and the U.S. State Department sponsored a "study group" at MIT in April 1957. Rostow thought that the exposition would be a good opportunity to present an image of the United States that could convince the rest of the world that "Americans have become convinced that their destiny lies with the world" (quoted in Gilman 2003, 210). Rostow proposed that one of the exhibits in the U.S. pavilion focus on the question of racial integration. He reasoned that including an exhibit on America's continuing struggle with race relations would "lend credibility to the exhibits, so long as they were contained within a progress narrative" (quoted in Gilman 2003, 210). Rostow also wanted to show that the American "Melting Pot" was working, that blacks had made progress even though the South still practiced segregation, and that complete desegregation was the ultimate goal and inevitable outcome (Gilman 2003, 211). Gilman (2003) perceptively notes that Rostow's proposals reflected the influence of Myrdal, his boss at UNECE. Myrdal had stated in *An American Dilemma* that U.S. race relations would come under scrutiny after the Second World War and that the United States should be prepared to show the new postcolonial nations that it was committed to equality for African Americans. Rostow's idea for the U.S. exhibit was to connect the problems of the postcolonial world with problems of blacks living in the South, thereby suggesting that the American government was interested in the plight of the underprivileged around the world and committed to raising their standard of living. Rostow was saying that overcoming segregation in the South in order to achieve the ideals of the American Creed was, in practical terms, the same as the postcolonial world overcoming traditional belief systems in order to achieve modernity. However, as word about Rostow's proposal reached Southern conservatives, they protested loudly to their representatives in Washington. Southern members of Congress eventually applied enough pressure on the USIA and State Department to kill the exhibit on American race relations and the problems of the postcolonial world. It was replaced just before the start of the Exhibition with a feature on public health.

The second component of the American Project was a series of seminars in Cambridge that culminated in a May 1957 conference "focused on a fundamental re-examination of American society and institutions" (Millikan 1958, vii). An underlying theme, again, was the understanding that to adequately comprehend the postcolonial world, U.S. scholars had to understand their own country—that "their" future was "our" present. CENIS director Max Millikan initiated the conference by saying that "the characteristics of our own society are as important as developments abroad in determining the shape of our foreign relations" (Millikan 1958, vii). The conference was organized around a long paper delivered by Rostow that first told a rather exceptionalist social and economic history of the United States and then attempted to set out the main elements of the "national style," referring to America's "commitment to strive for good purposes" (Rostow 1958, 252). It was an obvious nod again to Myrdal's American Creed idea, which defined the central common values of Americans. In another part of the paper, Rostow wrote: "All of my study confirms Myrdal as being fundamentally correct when he says 'most Americans have most valuations in common'" (Rostow 1958, 147).

In both the conference and the exhibit planning project, it seems Rostow was trying to elaborate on the idea Myrdal proposed earlier: that there is a set of American values and accomplishments that blacks at home and postcolonial peoples abroad could attain if given the chance. Rostow had read *American Dilemma* and almost certainly talked to Myrdal about it during his appointment to the Economic Commission for Europe. Rostow's working relationship with Myrdal undoubtedly enhanced his credibility as he staked out the liberal position in Cambridge in the spring of 1957 that the civil rights question in the United States was linked to the problems of modernization in the postcolonial nations.

The Modernization Critics

A vast majority of American social scientists interested in modernization issues believed in the cultural superiority of the West and were convinced that a policy to bring the postcolonial nations out of tradition and into the modern world was not only politically expedient in the context of a Cold War with the Soviet Union but also morally correct. The communication scholars were mostly convinced about the important benefits to the postcolonial world brought by media messages from the West, as well as related mass communication principles such as freedom of expression.

However, there were a handful of modernization critics in the United States who were uneasy about various aspects of the modernization enterprise, including its shaky theoretical assumptions and its ethnocentrism. For example, at the Dobbs Ferry conference in 1959, Rowland Eggers, a University of Virginia economist, suggested it was inappropriate to think about modernization in the postcolonial states in reference to U.S. history. Yes, Eggers said, we know a lot about American history but "we have not thought enough about the U.S. as an underdeveloped country. We should be humble about this whole area" [of extrapolating American experience into postcolonial contexts] (quoted in Gilman 2003, 147). At the same conference, William Fox, a Columbia University historian, expressed doubt that the United States was the apex of modernization and had only to teach others how to achieve the same status (Gilman 2003, 147).

Almost a decade after the Dobbs Ferry meeting, voices from the academy had become a small chorus of critics. High profile sociologists such as Joseph Gusfield and Reinhard Bendix, though they did in the final analysis believe in the modernization project, pointed out the historically implausible distinction between the "modern" and the "traditional" society, upon which modernization theory rested. Bendix (1967) attempted to "de-ideologize" the tradition-modern distinction by showing that so-called traditional societies are so diverse in their particular characteristics that proposing a single path toward modernization based on the European experience was untenable. Gusfield (1967) also argued that the dichotomy of "traditional" and "modern" was empirically unsupported and that societal features labeled traditional may, in fact, promote social change rather than thwart it. Jessie Bernard, a sociologist at Pennsylvania State University, made similar claims about the ethnocentrism of functionalist theory and its application to problems of modernization in the postcolonial world (Robin 2001, 214).

Marxist economist Andre Gunder Frank (1964) criticized modernization theory for ignoring the history of postcolonial nations—at times even "denying that the underdeveloped countries and underdevelopment even have history" (1969, 73). Several scholars located in the postcolonial world had foreshadowed Frank's thesis. West Indian intellectuals C. L. R. James and Eric Williams (1944), who argued that European industrial development, upon which the theory of modernization is based, was made possible by slave plantations and forced labor. Likewise, Indian scholar Palme Dutt argued that Britain's textile industry was able to modernize only on the basis of appropriating India's dye technology and forcibly suppressing India's textile production (see Blaut 1993, 203).

Another economist, Mancur Olson, demonstrated the fallacy in the modernization theory assumption—popularized by Rostow and held as sacred by Lerner and others—that economic growth and political stability went hand in hand. Olson's research showed, in fact, that while absolute income levels were correlated to political stability, income growth rates were correlated to political *in*stability (see Gilman 2003, 213).

Especially critical of the modernization paradigm's ethnocentrism were, again, the scholars located in the postcolonial world. These writers challenged (at *least* implicitly) the assumptions of cultural inferiority of non-white people embodied within modernization theory and discourse. As such, these thinkers rooted in the experiences of formerly colonized countries, were the vanguard of anti-racist discourse on colonialism, neocolonialism, and modernization. For example, the Guinean Marxist Amilcar Cabral, criticized the assimilationist bias of modernization theory. Writing in the context of a crumbling Portuguese colonial empire, Cabral addressed the "theory of so-called assimilation" that seemed to animate Western efforts to modernize the postcolonial world. He wrote that the idea "is unacceptable not only in theory but even more in practice. It is based on the racist idea of the 'incompetence or lack of dignity' of African people, and implies that African cultures and civilizations have no value" (Cabral 1979, 19).

In a scathing critique of the assumptions of modernization that echoed Cabral, Pakistani economist Inayatuallah (1967) said at a conference sponsored by Schramm and Lerner:

> "[Modernization] presupposes that because the 'traditional' societies have not risen to the higher level of technological development in comparison to the Western society, they are sterile, unproductive, uncreative, and hence worth liquidating. It measures the creativity of the traditional world with a few limited standards such as urbanization and industrialization, like the person who measures the competence of everybody on terms of his own special competence. … It shows remarkable ethnocentrism by equating modern society with paradise and fails to take into account [its own] crisis, especially in the realm of personality, which Erich Fromm and other psychologists have aptly located" (p. 100).

Striking a similar note, Kenyan political scientist and philosopher Ali Mazrui (1968) criticized modernization for its paternalism, noting that the theory gives postcolonial peoples "a capacity to emulate without permitting [them] a capacity to create" (p. 76). Commenting on the shifting paradigm of racial theories, he traced the move in the West from explicit racism to a broad humanism, but noted, "the form of humanism has often been one animated by the self-confidence of ethnocentric achievement" (Mazrui 1968, 82).

Ashis Nandy's critique of modernization, and Western development theory generally, challenges the assumption that Western science and technology inevitably benefits those who participate in modernization (Nandy 1990, 1-23). Rather than accept the functionalist idea that science is always liberating, Nandy reads the history of modernization science in India as violent and oppressive. He argues that an image of modernization as scientific advance has frequently been used to justify death and exploitation of the poor, minorities, and others with relatively little power. He wrote: "Science, as a *raison d'état*, can inflict violence in the name of national security or development..." (Nandy 1990, 10). For modernization theorists, science represented a value-neutral and practical application of knowledge to increase productivity and efficiency that could help transform tradition societies into modern ones (Adas 1989). Thus, modernization science ignored, manipulated, oppressed, and even eliminated the very people it was intended to benefit. In a most perverse ethnocentric twist, some postcolonial scholars have pointed out, the non-white peoples modernization was intended to benefit often were precisely the ones categorized as expendable.

There were also critics of the role of mass communication in U.S. foreign policy initiatives. For example, in 1939 and 1940, the Rockefeller Foundation sponsored a series of seminars on communication research. Lasswell was the driving intellectual force behind a conception of using mass communication as a way for elites to manipulate public opinion in a way that could preserve democracy from authoritarian threat (Simpson 1994, 23). At the seminars, Donald Schlesinger, dean of social science at University of Chicago, challenged Lasswell's position. He pointed out the contradiction of Lasswell's position: "We have thought in terms of fighting dictatorships-by-force through the establishment of dictatorships-by-manipulation" (quoted in Simpson 1994, 23). Apparently, Schlesinger was never invited back to meetings of mass communication research.

However, Lasswell remained an influential presence in mass communication research well into the 1970s. He was Lerner's close friend and mentor and his view of mass communication in processes of general social change was influential in conceptualizing the role of mass communication in modernization. A somewhat softer version of the position Lasswell stated at the Rockefeller seminar was the rationale for targeting opinion leaders in the postcolonial world with pro-democracy media content (see Pye 1963, passim).

Passing of Traditional Society was the first comprehensive statement of the mass communication and modernization theory. It was generally well received, especially among the stalwarts of the networks that have been described in this paper. For example, writing in late 1958 in *Public Opinion Quarterly*, a journal under the editorial control of the leading behavioral social scientists of the day, Middle East expert Morroe Berger wrote in glowing terms that "Lerner had tackled a difficult problem with more success than anyone has any right to hope for in the present state of American social science's acquaintance with the Middle East" (Berger 1958, 426). However, *Passing of Traditional Society* was not without its critics. Among the contemporaneous critics, one noted that the "frail theory" of modernization only seemed to explain the Turkey case with any accuracy while Lebanon, Egypt, Syria, Jordan, and Iran were not at all well explained (Mahar 1959, 110). Other reviewers faulted the book for "generalizing on the basis of meager particulars" (Salem 1959, 129) and uninformed political judgments (Badeau 1959, 1134). Yet another writer labeled Lerner's generalizing from the empathic personality type to a societal typology (that is, the traditional, transitional, modern scheme) "a startling procedure when one considers that specialists armed with full personality data are hesitant to make such a generalization in cases of cultures less complex than the Middle East" (Gulick 1959, 136). A historian, noting a range of contradictory evidence, criticized the assumption of direct and powerful media effects in the postcolonial world, wrote:

> That a high rate of media participation indicates a weakening of the traditional forms of authority and movement toward what Lerner understands by "participant lifeways" is a doubtful proposition (Dawn 1959, 661).

Finally, a sociologist criticized the assimilationist teleology of modernization that leads Lerner to discount the importance of racial, ethnic, and other reference group ties. After noting that in the Middle East there is a strong "presence of racial, religious, and ethnic minorities" and a history of "cross-cultural contacts through commerce, war, and migration," Dalton Potter hones in on "the most important gap in Dr. Lerner's picture of the Middle East" (1959, 118) and reveals the double standard underlying the assumption of media effects in the postcolonial world—the assumption that postcolonial audiences were susceptible to direct media effects while Western media audiences were not. Potter wrote:

> The fictitious "man on the street" or "the man on the other end of the mass media of communications" exists not *in vacuo* but as part of a social group, and he reacts to mass media in terms of the group membership (Potter 1959, 118).

Potter was pointing out, in other words, that people in the Middle East, just as people in the West, live in communities of social networks and effects of media are filtered, deflected, transformed, and moderated by these connections.

Among the more recent critics of modernization theory are political economists such as Herbert I. Schiller (1969) who asserted that Western mass media exported to the postcolonial world are more likely to promote consumerism than political participation, the key outcome in Lerner's model. Among mass communication scholars, serious critique of the faulty assumptions of modernization theory did not begin until the mid-1970s. Scholars based in Latin America, Africa, and Asia challenged the theoretical and methodological assumptions of modernization research as well as the assumptions of cultural shortcomings some Western scholars held about residents of the postcolonial world. These critiques inspired Everett Rogers, a prominent communication scholar, to declare, in words paraphrasing the title of Lerner's book, "the passing of the dominant paradigm" of mass communication and modernization research (Rogers 1976, 121). However, Rogers' declaration may have been premature, as subsequent reviews of the literature have demonstrated the continued influence of some components of Lerner's model as the basis for a multitude of mass communication and modernization studies (Fair 1989; Fair & Shah 1997; Shah 2007).

Conclusions

In the climate of post-war liberalism, American academics were rethinking the role of the United States in international relations. With the nation clearly in a position to ascend to super-power status, networks of intellectuals who had been brought together a decade or so earlier in service to the government (see Cravens 2004) now were holding conferences, writing books, reviewing research proposals, dispensing research dollars, and generally setting the intellectual tone as well as creating the very categories for comprehending the West and "the rest." The modernization project that emerged from these activities asserted the cultural superiority of the West and promoted the idea that the United States and Europe represented the final destination on the road to modernity. If the postcolonial nations wanted to be modern, the prescriptions said, they would do well to emulate the West.

Modernization was not without its critics, as we have seen. Certain dimensions of modernization—the assumptions about race and culture, the teleological theoretical framework, the controversial policy formulations, etc.—came under fire from several directions. Criticism came not only from postcolonial intellectuals such as Cabral, Mazrui, and Nandy, but also from prominent American intellectuals. Conservatives Robert Nisbet and Samuel Huntington criticized modernization for its unfounded optimism and idealism, while from the left, Andre Gunder Frank and Immanuel Wallerstein criticized modernization for, respectively, creating "underdevelopment" (rather than modernity) in postcolonial nations and for its misguided method of using nation-states as the unit of analysis (among other issues) (see the summary by Gilman 2003, Ch. 6). In the 1970s, "neo-modernization" scholars tried to distance themselves from the ethnocentrism of the original modernization paradigm, but retained the emphasis on economic growth, literacy, and democracy (So 1990, Ch. 4).

Despite the criticisms, modernization was firmly embedded within the mainstream of academic thought, the research budgets of funding agencies, and the policy making apparatus within the government. There was little recrimination about the ethnocentric and culturally racist discourses that animated modernization thinking throughout the 1950s and 1960s.

Having reviewed the discursive shift from biological racism to cultural racism and having demonstrated how American ideas about racial difference entered the academic thinking about mass communication and modernization, it is appropriate now to consider the broader implications of having cultural racism as one of the foundation stones of modernization theory. One implication is that it allowed guilt-free promotion of Western superiority, because cultural racism theory helped legitimize the claim by the West that "everyone can be like us." No person, no country, no culture need be inferior forever, the argument went, just follow the path of your colonial fathers and you can be just like us. A related implication is that cultural geopolitics—specifically, the fight for the hearts and minds of postcolonial people—could be legitimized as assistance to help "backward" countries on a natural path toward progress, economic growth, democracy, and global respect. The contending interpretation, that modernization was actually racist neo-colonialism, could be dispensed with all together. Finally, because modernization theory was framed as altruistic aid to the poor and dispossessed, it has persisted as a foreign policy centerpiece despite a lack of strong evidence that modernization policy actually works. Indeed, majestic failures such as growing gaps between rich and poor despite aggregate growth, the failure to establish democracy in Vietnam, and continuing instability in Iraq and Afghanistan in 2010 seem to be the legacy of modernization theory in practice rather than the deeply democratic, fabulously wealthy, culturally rich societies that were promised by Rostow, Shils, Lerner, Pye, et al.

The intellectual history of modernization leaves us with one other lesson. Those who pointed out the problematic assumptions about the culturally racist foundations of modernization are exemplary role models for how academics can resist the intellectual policing of what counts as knowledge. By not succumbing to the liberal-pluralists politics embedded in the dominant paradigm of modernization, by pointing out the ethnocentrism of modernization theory (at the risk of being ostracized and intellectually marginalized), and by training students to cultivate a critical sense for identifying and challenging the ideological assumptions and prescriptions, the critical scholars contributed to anti-hegemonic intellectual discourse within the U.S. academy.

References

Adas, M. 1989. *Machines as the Measure of Men: Science, Technology, and Ideologies of Western Dominance*. Ithica, NY: Cornell University of Press.

Amin, S. 1989. *Eurocentrism*. New York: Monthly Review Press.

Badeau, J.S. 1959. Review of the book *Passing of Traditional Society: Modernizing the Middle East*. *The American Political Science Review* 53: 1133-1135.

Bendix, R. 1967. Tradition and modernity reconsidered. *Comparative Politics in Society and History* 9: 292-364.

Berger, M. 1958. Review of the book *Passing of Traditional Society: Modernizing the Middle East*. *Public Opinion Quarterly* 22: 425-427. Special Issue on Attitude Research in Modernizing Areas.

Blackmer, D. 2002. *The MIT Center for International Studies: The Founding Year, 1951-1969*. Cambridge, MA: CENIS.

Blaut, J. 1992. The theory of cultural racism. *Antipode: A Radical Journal of Geography* 23: 289-299.

Borstelmann, T. 2001. *The Cold War and the Color Line*. Cambridge, MA: Harvard University Press.

Cabral, A. 1979. *Unity and Struggle: Speeches and Writings*. [Trans. Michael Wolfers] New York and London: Monthly Review Press.

Cravens, H. 2004. *The Social Sciences Go to Washington: The Politics of Knowledge in the Postmodern Age*. New Brunswick, NJ: Rutgers University Press.

Dawn, C.E. 1959. Review of the book *Passing of Traditional Society: Modernizing the Middle East*. *American Historical Review* 64: 660-661.

Ellison, R. 1973. *An American Dilemma*: A review. In *The Death of White Sociology*, ed. J. Ladner, 289-309. New York: Random House.

Engerman, D., Gilman, N., Haefele, M., & Latham, M. eds., 2003. *Staging growth: Modernization, development and the global Cold War*. Amherst and Boston: University of Massachusetts Press.

Fair, J.E. 1989. 29 years of theory and research on media and development: The dominant paradigm impact. *Gazette* 44: 129-150.

Fair, J.E. and Shah, H. 1997. Continuities and discontinuities in communication and development research since 1958. *Journal of International Communication* 4: 3-23.

Frank, A.G. 1969. *Latin America: Underdevelopment or Revolution: Essays on the Development of Underdevelopment and the Immediate Enemy.* Monthly Review Press: New York and London.

Gilman, N. 2003. *Mandarins of the Future: Modernization Theory in Cold War America.* Baltimore, MD: Johns Hopkins University Press.

Gitlin, T. 1978. Media sociology: The dominant paradigm. *Theory and Society* 6: 205-253.

Gulick, J. 1959. Review of the book *Passing of Traditional Society: Modernizing the Middle East. American Anthropologist* 61: 135-138

Gusfield, J. 1967. Tradition and modernity: Misplaced polarities in the study pf social change. *American Journal of Sociology* 72: 351-362.

Hannaford, I. 1996. *Race: The History of an Idea in the West.* Baltimore, MD: Johns Hopkins University Press.

Hedebro, G. 1982. *Communication and Social Change in Developing Areas.* Ames. IA: Iowa State University Press.

Horkheimer, M. and Adorno, T. 1972. *Dialectic of Enlightenment* (trans. John Cumming). New York: Herder and Herder.

Hyman, H. 1963. Mass media and political socialization: The role of patterns of communication. In *Communications and Political Development*, ed. L. Pye, 128-148. Princeton, NJ: Princeton University Press.

Inayatullah 1967. Toward a non-western model of development. In *Communication and Change in the Developing World*, eds., D.Lerner and W. Schramm, 98-102. Honolulu: East-West Center Press.

Inkeles, A. (1960). Social stratification in the modernization of Russia. In *The Transformation of Russian Society*, ed., C.E. Black, 338-350). Cambridge, MA: Harvard University Press.

Inkeles, A. 1969. Making men modern: On the causes and consequences of individual change in six developing countries. *American Journal of Sociology* 75: 208-225.

Katz, E. and Lazarsfeld, P. 1955. *Personal influence: The part played by people in the flow of mass communication.* Glencoe, IL: Free Press.

Keller, S. and Lerner, D. 1957. Empathy in cross-national and occupational perspective. Unpublished manuscript. MC336, Daniel Lerner Papers, Box 11, Folder 42. MIT Archives. Cambridge, MA.

Klapper, J. 1960. *The Effects of Mass Communication.* New York: Free Press.

Latham, M. 2000. *Modernization as ideology: American social science and "nation building" in the Kennedy era.* Chapel Hill and London: University of North Carolina Press.

Layton, A.S. 2000. *International politics and civil rights in the United States.* Cambridge: Cambridge University Press.

Lazarsfeld, P., Berelson, B., and Gaudet, H. 1948. *The people's choice.* New York: Columbia University Press.

Lerner, D. n.d. The Arab Intellectual. Unpublished manuscript. MC336, Daniel Lerner papers, Box 11, Folder 5. MIT Archives. Cambridge, MA.

Lerner, D. 1949. International Politics Seminar, course syllabus. Revolution and Development of International Relations (RADIR) Project Papers, Box 10. Hoover Institution Archives, Stanford University. Palo Alto, CA.

Lerner, D. 1949. *Psychological Warfare Against Nazi Germany: The Sykewar Campaign from D-Day to V-E Day.* Cambridge, MA: MIT Press.

Lerner, D., Schueller, G. and Stycos, M. 1951. Mass communication audiences in Turkey. (Report B-0370-5). New York: Bureau of Applied Social research, Columbia University.

Lerner, D. 1958. *Passing of traditional society*. Glencoe, IL: Free Press.

Lerner, D. 1963. Toward a communication theory of modernization: A set of considerations. In *Communications and Political Development*, ed. L. Pye, 327-350. Princeton, NJ: Princeton University Press.

Lerner, D. and Lasswell, H. 1951. *The Policy Sciences: Recent Developments in Scope and Method*. Stanford, CA: Stanford University Press.

Lerner, D. and Reisman, D. 1955. Self and society: Reflections on some Turks in Transition. *Explorations* 5: 67-80.

Levy, M. 1949. *The Family Revolution in Modern China*. Cambridge, MA: Harvard University Press.

Levy, M. 1953. Contrasting factors in the modernization of China and Japan. *Economic Development Cultural Change* 2: 174-190.

Mahar, P.M. (1959). Review of the book *Passing of Traditional Society: Modernizing the Middle East*. *American Journal of Sociology* 65: 110.

Mazrui, A. 1968. From social Darwinism to current theories of modernization. *World Politics* : 69-83.

McClelland, D. 1963. National character and economic growth in Turkey and Iran. In *Communications and Political Development*, ed. L. Pye, pp. 152-181. Princeton, NJ: Princeton University Press.

Mead, M. 1943. Anthropological techniques in war psychology. Harold Fisher papers, Box 13, RADIR Project, Hoover Institution Archives, Stanford University.

Millikan, M. 1958. Preface. *American Style: Essays in Value and Performance*, ed. E. Morrison, pp. vii-ix. Cambridge, MA: MIT Press.

Morrison, E. 1958. *American Style: Essays in Value and Performance*. Cambridge, MA: MIT Press.

Myrdal, G. 1944. *American dilemma: The Negro problem and modern democracy*. New York: Harper and Brothers.

Nandy, A. 1990. Introduction: Science as a reason of state. *Science, Hegemony, and Violence*, ed. A. Nandy, pp. 1-23. New Delhi: Oxford.

Park, R. 1914. Racial assimilation in secondary groups with particular reference to the Negro. *American Journal of Sociology* XIX: 606-623.

Park, R. 1922. *The Immigrant Press and Its Control*. New York: Harper and Brothers.

Park, R. 1950. *Race and culture*. New York: Free Press.

Park, R. and Burgess, E.W. 1924. *Introduction to the Science of Society*. New York: Harper and Row.

Parsons, T. 1964. *Personality and Social Structure*. New York: Free Press.

Parsons, T. 1980. The circumstances of my encounter with Max Weber. In *Sociological Traditions From Generation to Generation: Glimpses of the American Experience*, ed. R.K. Merton and M.W. Riley, pp. 37-43. Norwood, NJ: Ablex.

Parsons, T. and Shils, E. 1951. *Toward a General Theory of Action*. Cambridge, MA: Harvard University Press.

Persons, S. 1987. *Ethnic Studies at Chicago, 1905-45*. Urbana and Chicago: University of Illinois Press.

Pierpoint, C.R. 2004. The measure of America; annals of cultures. *The New Yorker,* March 8.

Potter, D. 1959. Review of the book *Passing of Traditional Society: Modernizing the Middle East*. *American Sociological Review* 24: 117-119.

Pye, L. 1956. *Guerilla Communism in Malaya: Its Social and Political Meaning*. Princeton, NJ: Princeton University Press.

Pye, L. 1961. Personal identity and political ideology. In *Political Decisionmakers*, ed. Dwaine Marvick, (xxx-xxx) Glencoe, IL: Free Press.

Pye, L. 1963. *Communications and Political Development*. Princeton, NJ: Princeton University Press.

Pye, L. 2004. The behavioral revolution and the remaking of comparative politics. Unpublished manuscript, MIT.

Robin, R. 2001. *Making of the Cold War enemy*. Princeton, NJ: Princeton University Press.

Rogers, E.M. 1976. Communication and development: The passing of the dominant paradigm. In *Communication and Development: Critical Perspectives*, ed. E.M. Rogers, 121-148. Beverley Hills, CA: Sage.

Rostow, W.W. 1960. *The Stages of Economic Growth*. Cambridge, England: Cambridge University Press.

Rostow, W.W. 1958. The national style. In *American Style: Essays in Value and Performance*, ed. E. Morrison, pp. 246-313. Cambridge, MA: MIT Press.

Rostow, W.W. 1952. *The Process of Economic Growth*. New York: W.W. Norton.

Rothwell, C.E. 1951. Foreword. In *The Policy Sciences: Recent Developments in Scope and Method*, ed. D. Lerner and H. Lasswell, vii-xi. Stanford, CA: Stanford University Press.

Salim, E. 1959. Review of the book *Passing of Traditional Society: Modernizing the Middle East. Political Science Quarterly* 74: 127-129.

Samarajiwa, R. 1987. The murky beginnings of the communication development field: Voice of America and the *Passing of Traditional Society*. In *Rethinking Development Communication*, ed. N. Jayaweera and S. Amunugama, 3-19. Singapore: AMIC.

Schiller, H.I. 1969. *Mass Communication and American Empire*. New York: A.M. Kelley.

Schramm, W. 1964. *Mass media and national development*. Stanford, CA: Stanford University Press.

Scott, J. 1972. Black science and nation-building. In *The Death of White Sociology*, ed. J. Ladner, 289-309. New York: Random House.

Shah, H. 1996. Modernization, marginalization, and emancipation: Toward a normative model for journalism and national development. *Communication Theory* 6: 143-166.

Shah, H. 2003. Communication and nation building: Comparing US models of ethnic assimilation and "third world" modernization. *Gazette* 65: 165-181.

Shah, H. 2007. Meta-research of development communication research, 1997-2006: Patterns and trends since 1958. Paper presented at the annual meeting of the International Communication Association, May 24-28, San Francisco, CA.

Shah, H. & Wilkins, K. 2005. Reconsidering geometries of development. *Perspectives on Global Development and Technology* 3: 395-416.

Shils, E. 1957. Daydreams and nightmares: Reflections on the criticism of mass culture. *Sawanee Review* 65: 587-608.

Shils, E. 1960. Political development of the new states (I). *Comparative Studies in History and Society* 2: 265-292.

Simpson, C. 1994. *The Science of Coercion: Communication Research and Psychological Warfare, 1945-1960*. New York: Oxford University Press.

Smith, M. 1994. *Social Science in the Crucible: The American Debate Over Objectivity and Purpose, 1918-1941*. Durham, NC: Duke University Press.

So, A. 1990. *Social Change and Development*. Thousand Oaks, CA: Sage.

Southern, D. 1987. *Gunnar Myrdal and Black-White Relations: The Use and Abuse of An American Dilemma, 1944-1969*. Baton Rouge, LA: Louisiana State University Press.

Tehranian, M. 1994. Where is the New World Order: At the end of history or clash of civilizations? *Journal of International Communication* 1: 71-99.

Thomas, W.I. & Znaniekci, F. 1927. *The Polish peasant in Europe and America*. New York: Alfred A. Knopf.

Trevino, A.J. Ed.) (2001. *Talcott Parsons Today: His Theory and Legacy in Contemporary Sociology*. Lanham, MA: Rowman & Littlefield.

Williams, E. 1944 .*Capitalism and Slavery*. Chapel Hill, NC: University of North Carolina Press.

Yu, H. 2001. *Thinking Orientals: Migration, Contact, and Exoticism in Modern America*. New York: Oxford University Press.

U.S. Treaty Obligations and the Politics of Racism and Anti-Racism Discourse

Sylvanna M. Falcón

Introduction

While the scourge of officially sanctioned segregation has been eliminated, de facto segregation and persistent racial discrimination continue to exist. The forms of discriminatory practices have changed and adapted over time, but racial and ethnic discrimination continues to restrict and limit equal opportunity in the United States.
—U.S. government's 2000 CERD report (paragraph 18)

In the midst of the racially turbulent 1960s, U.S. President Johnson signed the International Convention on the Elimination of All Forms of Racial Discrimination (ICERD) in 1966. Nearly thirty years later, U.S. President Clinton ratified ICERD in 1994.[1] ICERD is the premier human rights treaty dealing with racism and racial discrimination and it is one of the few international human rights treaties the United States has both signed and ratified. As required by the treaty, State Parties to the convention submit periodic compliance reports to the treaty monitoring body known as the Committee to Eliminate Racial Discrimination (CERD), which has been in existence since 1970. Having submitted two compliance reports to CERD in 2000 and 2007, the U.S. government must engage in a review hearing with CERD the following year. The purpose of the review hearing, which lasts for six hours over a two-day period, is to evaluate the reporting state's record on ICERD compliance.

In a review hearing, the U.S. government is asked to explain why racial inequality persists and the states' proposed actions to combat it. No other venue exists at either the domestic or international level that *requires* periodic explanations for continued systematic and institutional racism. The exchanges I analyze between CERD members and the U.S. government delegation reveal the U.S. government aims to discursively circumvent its treaty obligations.

In this chapter, I focus on three topics discussed at length during the 2001 U.S.-CERD review—the criminal justice system, freedom of speech, and indigenous rights—to analyze U.S. government discursive strategies. I draw from grounded theory (Bernard and Ryan 2000, 607; Lindlof and Taylor 2002) to analyze several documents[2] pertaining to the 2001 U.S.-CERD review hearing and to identify the discourse deployed by the U.S. government. I make the case that the U.S. government reluctantly complies with their human rights obligations. In addition to the three topics stated above, I also address the legal mechanisms deployed by the government to legally limit the scope and full implementation of human rights treaties.

The U.S. government report focuses almost exclusively on civil and political rights to discuss human rights matters; yet human rights is much broader than this duality as it also includes social, economic, and cultural rights. For this reason, scholars have argued the U.S. government is openly hostile towards international standards because they would empower people of color with additional rights and legitimize their demands for racial justice (Thomas 2000). My chapter supports this argument, especially since racial injustice within the realm of social, economic, and cultural rights are particularly contentious.

ICERD's Definition of Racism and Racial Discrimination

CERD grapples with a wide spectrum of issues, from indigenous sovereignty, land rights, immigration, and labor, to forced sterilization, incarceration, suffrage, the criminal justice system, and poverty to name a few. In its assessment of racial discrimination, CERD is guided by ICERD Article 1's definition of racial discrimination, which states:

> In this Convention, the term 'racial discrimination' shall mean any distinction, exclusion, restriction, or preference based on race, colour, descent, or national or ethnic origin which has the purpose or effect of nullifying or impairing the recognition, enjoyment or exercise, on an equal footing, of human rights and fundamental freedoms in the political, economic, social, cultural, or any other field of public life.

The treaty's definition of racial discrimination is not static. CERD attempts to keep the treaty contemporarily relevant and clarify interpretations of the treaty by issuing General Recommendations, which are official statements adopted by the committee with the purpose of elaborating on treaty obligations. CERD's General Recommendations have dealt with gendered dimensions of racism (see Gallagher 1997) and on the meaning of "non-citizens" and "descent" to name a few.

Since the principles of the treaty apply equally to all reporting governments, the CERD review process can be undertaken systematically, shielding the committee from criticism that it has different standards and basis for evaluation for each reporting government. The committee considers country-specific situations *if* the circumstance, in their view, qualifies under the treaty's definition of racial discrimination.

The ICERD Review Hearings

As directed by Article 9 of the treaty, governments are required to submit their initial compliance report to CERD one year following state ratification and subsequently, two years after that first initial periodic report. After CERD reviews these periodic governmental reports, the committee provides the State Party with documented final observations on its compliance status known as "concluding observations." No penalty mechanism exists for governments that submit reports late, which is unfortunately a common practice. The government periodic reports are based on the first seven articles of ICERD, which includes a series of recommendations for policy and legislative changes for adoption by State Parties. The remaining eighteen articles discuss logistical matters for CERD and State Parties and thus, are not the focus of this chapter.

The U.S. government's discursive strategies aimed at limiting compliance obligations can be seen in two key examples from the 2000 U.S.-CERD review. First, ICERD Article 2 covers a range of policy and legislative requirements, in addition to proposals for new policies and requests for a critical evaluation of existing ones at the government, national, and local levels that may "perpetuate racial discrimination." Article 2 requires states to agree to support multiracial organizations and movements and to not "sponsor or defend racial discrimination by any persons or organizations."

When reporting on their compliance with this Article, the U.S. government cited their federal contracting practices as an example. Paragraph 277 of the U.S. government report maintains, "race-conscious action [is] used only where there is *demonstrable proof* that the effects of racial discrimination continue(s) to hinder minority-owned businesses" (italics added for emphasis) in federal contracting. However, CERD counters the U.S.'s arguments by maintaining that *intent* is harder to legally prove based on U.S. laws. One CERD member, Ms. Britz,[3] states,

[A]ccording to the Supreme Court interpretation, discriminatory intent, as well as disparate impact, [has] to be shown in order to demonstrate a constitutional violation of equal protection. [but] intent [is] much more difficult to prove than impact. Reading between the lines of the [U.S.] report, it [is] clear that its authors [are] aware of the discrepancy.[4]

For the committee, the violation resides in the intent and effects of current public policies, and urges a legal re-assessment of the type of proof needed to assert one's constitutional right of equal protection has been violated. In alignment with this argument, CERD notes that the dismantling of affirmative action policies, after just a mere few decades of existence in light of the hundreds of years of institutional racism, utterly contradicts the purpose and principles of ICERD.

The second example involves the reluctance to enforce economic, social, and cultural rights. ICERD's Article 5 "guarantee(s) the right of everyone … to equality before the law" and cites a broad range of social, cultural, and economic rights that include: the right to security of person and protection by the state against violence or bodily harm (whether by the state or individuals, groups, or institutions); economic and social rights (such as the right to work); the right to form trade unions; the right to education and training; and the right to leave any country, including one's own, and to return to one's country. Paragraph 298 of the U.S. government report states that the rights included in Article 5, which can be characterized as "economic, social, and cultural rights, are not explicitly recognized as legally enforceable 'rights' under U.S. law." Therefore, from the view of the U.S. government, "[A]rticle 5 does not affirmatively require States [P]arties to provide or to ensure observance of each of the listed rights themselves, but rather to prohibit discrimination in the enjoyment of those rights to the extent they are provided by domestic law." The U.S. government attempts to discursively disassociate "prohibit" from "provide" by suggesting that legally prohibiting discrimination does not need to accompany concerted efforts to ensure the meaningful fulfillment of all incarnations of human rights. So for instance, even though no U.S. citizen (unless a convicted felon) is being legally *prohibited* from voting in economically disadvantaged communities, these poor and working-class residents may not be *provided* the equal opportunity to exercise their right to vote due to a lack of sufficient or functioning voting machines. CERD affirms civil, political, social, cultural, and economic rights as interconnected and clarifies that the intent of the treaty is not just to prohibit racial discrimination, but also to ensure all human rights are fully realized.

In reporting on compliance with Articles 2 and 5 of the treaty, the U.S. government representatives in essence argue existing U.S. laws, legislation, and practices adequately fulfill the treaty requirements. However, CERD's mandate is to identify shortcomings and to hold State Parties accountable for their responsibilities to their citizens. CERD pressures the U.S. government to uphold their obligations and not actively try to reduce their responsibilities by highlighting their disagreements with the government delegation. In the next section, I discuss three contentious issues from the 2001 U.S.-CERD review hearing to further expose a level of state complicity and unpack the discourse advanced by the U.S. government to abscond its treaty obligations.

Case One: Racially Disproportionate Incarceration Rates and Death Penalty Sentencing

The section of the U.S. government report discussing Article 5's "right of everyone ... to equality before the law," includes information about the criminal justice system and capital punishment sentencing. The review hearing included a detailed discussion on both topics. Sections of the U.S. compliance report are very forthright about the racial disparities in the criminal justice system; yet other sections of the report simultaneously stress the U.S. criminal justice system is fair. Of grave concern to CERD is the disproportionate representation of people of color in the prison population in general, especially because

> many militant anti-racists and freedom fighters who consider themselves political prisoners [are] being held in American prisons, in particular 100 or so militants opposed to white supremacy and partisans of self-determination for [people of color], [who have been condemned] to excessively severe punishment. Among these detainees [are] 18 Puerto Rican anti-colonialist militants.[5]

The U.S. government report concedes blacks and Latinos/as view the criminal justice system differently than whites and that vastly divergent sentencing exists for crack and powder cocaine arrests, with statistics showing higher numbers of African Americans incarcerated for selling crack compared to whites.

In terms of the death penalty, paragraph 322 of the U.S. government report contains the following startling statistics:

> From 1977 to 1998, a total of 5,709 persons entered prison under a sentence of death. During this period, the U.S. general population was approximately 10-12 per cent Black; however, among those entering prison under a death sentence during that

period, 2,347 (41 per cent) were Black. Of the 500 persons executed during these 22 years, 178 (36 per cent) were Black.

The U.S. government delegation firmly maintains "federal laws [lay] down strict protections to ensure that race [does] not influence decisions to call for or impose the death sentence, whether on the part of judges, prosecutor, or jurors" and that the "Attorney General [makes] the final decision whether to seek a capital sentence."[6] The Department of Justice agrees changes are needed regarding capital punishment, *but not in terms of its practice.* Rather, the changes are about "promot[ing] public confidence in the fairness of the process and to improve its efficiency."[7] A CERD member challenged the U.S. government's position on the death penalty further by arguing "the death penalty [is] incompatible with a high level of civilization."[8]

Even though research indicates capital punishment has been unfairly applied and is ineffective as a deterrent to criminal activity,[9] paragraph 325 of the U.S. government report states that "the U.S. Government remains confident that the death penalty is imposed only in the most egregious cases and only in the context of the heightened procedural safeguards required by our state and federal constitutions and statutes." The report makes no mention of innocent people who have been executed (The Associated Press 2005).

CERD members continued the conversation about death penalty sentences by discussing the inadequate access to legal counsel for poor defendants of color. For CERD,

> [o]ne of the most convincing arguments against capital punishment [is] that 36 per cent of persons condemned to death were blacks who had ended up on death row not because they had committed a particularly odious crime, but because, as socially disadvantaged persons, they had been poorly defended in court. Such rank injustice [is] especially serious when life [is] at stake.[10]

In addition to being one of a small handful of countries around the world that still practices the death penalty, the U.S. is the only democratic, industrialized nation that does so. The U.S. government rejected CERD's calls for imposing a moratorium similar to the one enacted in the state of Illinois in 2000.

During the U.S.-CERD review, the U.S. government delegation expressed the utmost confidence in its justice system, while simultaneously acknowledging racial disparities. In their view, the U.S. justice system works; it is not only fair, but it is never wrong. Despite the research to the contrary, the U.S government ignores its flawed and imperfect justice system when it comes to the disproportionate representation of racial minorities in the prison system, the divergent sentencing between crack and powder cocaine arrests, and the links between poverty and inadequate legal representation in death penalty cases.

Case Two: Racist Hate Speech as "A Consequence of the First Amendment"[11]

> Even if the United States Supreme Court deem[s] cross burning to be a form of expression compatible with the First Amendment, which govern[s] freedom of expression ... such acts [are] not an expression of racial harmony and create[s] a climate of tension within society.
>
> —CERD member Mr. Rechetov[12]

Article 4 denounces propaganda and all organizations based on ideas of racial superiority and that, as a consequence, promote racial hatred. The Article describes ways State Parties can ensure this type of activity is suppressed through legal means. Declaring that "all dissemination of ideas based on racial superiority or hatred, [and] incitement to racial discrimination" should be considered "an offence punishable by law" and prohibited, Article 4 reads, "States Parties [agree to] condemn all propaganda and all organizations which are based on ideas or theories of superiority of one race or group of persons of one colour or ethnic origin, or which attempt to justify or promote racial hatred and discrimination in any form."

This Article raises many issues for the U.S. government. This section of the U.S. report begins with the U.S. government's reasons for inserting a "reservation" for Article 4. A reservation is a unilateral statement by a country upon ratification that modifies or even excludes its legal obligations. The government argues it has constitutional limits to fully implementing Article 4. However, the U.S. government states it complies with this Article in other ways and proceeds to list several hate crimes legislation at the federal, state, and local levels and mentions the work of the "Community Relations Service created by the Civil Rights Act of 1964."[13] The U.S. government ultimately argues that legal restrictions on racist hate speech violates freedom of speech; but CERD questions this rationale, especially because hate speech can result in racially motivated violence.

CERD members argue that by refusing to implement Article 4, the U.S. government is supporting racism, particularly white supremacist groups, by maintaining that their actions are not illegal and that restrictions on their speech violate their First Amendment rights. The U.S. government's main argument for not enforcing Article 4 is that it jeopardizes the integrity of the First Amendment. The U.S. report states in paragraph 286 that the U.S. takes "a reservation to [Article 4]... to make clear that it cannot accept any obligation to restrict those rights (meaning individual freedom of speech, expression, and association), through the adoption of legislation or any other measures, to the extent that they are protected by the Constitution and laws of the United States." But, the U.S. government admits in the review hearing that "certain types of speech intended and likely to cause imminent violence ... could be restricted under the (U.S.) Constitution."[14] Thus, racist speech encouraging violence could be restricted, but racially inflammatory speech in and of itself is protected. According to CERD, oral and written expression of racist ideas warrants as much concern as racist acts themselves because both have "a deleterious effect on peaceful coexistence, racial harmony, and democracy."[15]

Technological advances, such as the Internet, have facilitated the promotion of hate propaganda. A Supreme Court's decision "made it clear that communications on the Internet receive the same constitutional protections under the First Amendment that communications in other media enjoy." According to paragraph 296 of the U.S. government report, restricting racist propaganda on the Internet is complicated. According to the U.S.-based Southern Poverty Law Center, the over 300 U.S.-based "hate sites" are an influential vehicle to advance racist propaganda.[16] CERD's assessment of the situation is as follows:

> [I]n the United States only acts of racial violence and not racist remarks are punishable by law, [making] the chances of successful prosecution for racist propaganda, in particular via the Internet, very limit[ing]. And yet the United States occupie[s] a key position in that area, because in effect it control[s] the Internet.[17]

As indicated in paragraph 150 of the U.S. report, U.S. citizens "applaud the fact that the First Amendment to the U.S. Constitution sharply curtails the government's ability to restrict or prohibit the expression or advocacy of certain ideas, however objectionable." Yet, CERD maintains that Article 4 and the First Amendment of the U.S. Constitution are neither incompatible nor mutually exclusive. "[H]uman rights treaty bodies [have] concluded that there [is] no structural conflict" between "freedom of speech, expression and association" and "equality, respect and non-discrimination" as stated in the Article; all of these elements can co-exist. CERD emphasizes "most of the great democracies [have] taken steps to ensure respect for public order, without having to impinge on freedom of speech for that purpose"[18] based "on the presumption that no human right [is] absolute and no person could claim to have rights without responsibilities."[19] CERD does not accept the argument by the U.S. government about its hands being tied in implementing Article 4 because how [can] "actions of organized racist groups such as the Ku Klux Klan [be tolerated] in the name of freedom of speech, expression, and association?"[20]

ICERD aims to protect "vulnerable communities [who are not] in a position to resist hate speech." If the "reservation concerning freedom of expression relie[s] on the concept of the marketplace of ideas: the good would drive out the bad," according to a CERD member (Mr. Thornberry),[21] then "why not allow the ideas of the Convention to inform the discourse in the United States? Given the force of international obligations, it [is] not clear how Article 4 could be given effect in many cases, but not in others."[22] The representatives of the U.S. government, however, remain unconvinced, arguing the "United States [does] not share the Committee's view that the prohibition of all ideas based on racial superiority or hatred [is] compatible with the right to freedom of opinion and expression." The government delegation defended its reservations to Article 4 by stating they are "deeply rooted in American history and legal and political culture;" therefore, "the right to speak freely [is] virtually an article of faith and the First Amendment, which sharply curtail[s] the Government's ability to restrict or prohibit the expression or advocacy of certain ideas, no matter how distasteful, constitute[s] a cornerstone of American democracy and applie[s] to all media, including the Internet."[23]

The U.S. circumvents its treaty obligations to Article 4 by claiming the U.S.'s constitutional right to freedom of speech prevents the government from denouncing racist propaganda and rendering white supremacist organizations as illegal. In advancing an "as a consequence of the First Amendment" argument, the U.S. government perpetuates a discourse based in an assertion that its hands are essentially tied. However, the Supreme Court case of *Gitlow v. New York* (1925) decided that restrictions in speech are acceptable "if [the speeches] have a tendency to result in action dangerous to public security, even though such utterances create no clear and present danger."[24] CERD is ultimately concerned about how racist hate speech can incite racial violence and contends an "increase in the number of hate crimes in the Untied States" represents a "tolerance towards racists"[25] in the U.S. The government's de facto support of white supremacist groups, under the guise of upholding the First Amendment, represents a lack of political will to proactively and forcefully condemn racist propaganda and prosecute organizations and individuals who advocate white supremacy.

Case Three: Land Abrogation and the Case of the Western Shoshone Peoples

Under existing U.S. laws, Indian tribes are classified as "domestic dependent nations." The U.S. government report mentions it can "abrogate unilaterally" treaties signed between the government and Native Americans "provided [the U.S. Congress] clearly expresse[s] an intention to do so."[26] Therefore, "the land Native Americans possess or use can be taken without compensation by a decision of the Government," which results in continuing the legacy of historical disempowerment of Native communities literally and legally. CERD states that the "domestic dependent nations" classification is racist because Native Americans remain "in a state of helpless inferiority that call[s] for guardianship and protection" by the U.S. government. This legal categorization empowers the government over all aspects of Indian life.[27] The U.S. government conquered Indian lands through the establishment of federal policies and laws to systematically remove land from Indian tribes [as well as engaging in violent wars with Indian tribes]. These policies violate ICERD's Article 2, which urges the evaluation of existing laws that exacerbate racism as well as the adoption of policies and legislation to combat it.

Paragraph 14 of the U.S. government report addresses the adoption of federal policies with the intention of disenfranchising Native communities.

> From 1778 until 1871, the U.S. entered into numerous treaties with Indian tribes, which recognized tribal self-government, reserved tribal lands as 'permanent homes' for Indian tribes, and pledged federal protection for the tribes. Yet, the United States engaged in a series of Indian wars in the nineteenth century, which resulted in significant loss of life and lands among Indian tribes.

This section of the report goes on to state "[The] 'Allotment Policy' resulted in loss of almost 100 million acres of Indian lands from the 1880s until 1934..." The Allotment Policy officially authorized the U.S. president to apportion land to individual Indians on both Indian reservations and on public lands; the land policy completely disrupted the communal ownership tradition of Indians (see Smith 2005).

The struggles over land is directly linked to struggles over environ-mental protection, with CERD members particularly concerned about environmental racism. In the case of the Western Shoshone peoples, U.S. government plans for "expanding mining and nuclear waste storage on Western Shoshone ancestral land, placing their land up for auction for private sale, and other actions affecting the rights of indigenous peoples"[28] violates the Western Shoshone tribe's "right to make use of their ancestral territory." Since [the Bush] administration refused to recognize [that right], the territory in question [has] now been "confis-cated and converted to a zone for nuclear explosions and other military activities."[29]

For CERD, the "domestic dependent nations" classification for Na-tive peoples empowers the U.S. government to act without regard to the citizenship rights of Native Americans and that the "domestic dependent nations" classification is deeply rooted in a U.S. history of racial exclu-sion and disempowerment for indigenous peoples. The U.S. government delegation admits these discriminatory policies exist, but make no indica-tion these policies would be overturned. Because these policies remain, the Western Shoshone peoples have encountered egregious violations of their rights. The struggle over land between the U.S. government and Native groups is far from over and persists to the present day.

Using Treaty Mechanisms to Immobilize the Treaty

As was the case with prior human rights treaties, existing U.S. law provides protections and remedies sufficient to satisfy the requirements of the present Convention.
—U.S. government's 2000 CERD report (paragraph 171)

Reservations, Understandings, and Declarations (RUDs) are available treaty mechanisms for State Parties to ensure compatibility between domestic and international laws. As mentioned earlier, a reservation is a mechanism for State Parties to use to legally absolve themselves from implementing a particular treaty article or section of the article. Understandings and declarations are different than reservations because they do not modify the State Party's legal obligations. They are issued in order to clarify an outstanding issue.

The U.S. government has used RUDs to immobilize the treaty,[30] with an especially excessive number of treaty reservations, according to the committee, that conflict with the spirit of the treaty. The U.S. govern-ment has issued reservations for Articles (or parts of the Article) 2, 3, 4, 5, 7, and 22. The purpose of these reservations can be summarized as follows: resistance to monitoring and curtailing racist hate speech (Articles 4 and 7); exemption for actions engaged in the private sphere (portions of Articles 2, 3, and 5); and restricting the transfer of disputes to the International Court of Justice without U.S. consent (Article 22). CERD considers these reservations as far-reaching and as impeding the full implementation of ICERD.

The issuance of an understanding on federalism (herein "federalism understanding") reinforces the separation between federal and state governments. The U.S. government endorses a federalist approach to governance, reinforcing a separation between federal and state governments and asserting a "states' rights" framework, where states can escape the scrutiny of CERD because the committee evaluates compliance at the federal level. The U.S. government asserts that only individual states can make decisions on what to do (if anything) regarding treaty implementation since the federal government has no enforcement powers over state governments. It ultimately claims that the government implements the treaty to the extent possible, but that states have ultimate control; CERD finds this argument as lacking credibility.

International human rights treaties do not have the force of domestic law because of the issuance of a "non-self-executing declaration," a practice that dates back to the 1950s (Henkin 1995). According to the U.S. Constitution, ratifying a treaty renders it the "Supreme Law of the Land." However, to implement the treaty domestically, a separate legislative process is required as a consequence of the "non-self-executing declaration." If, according to paragraph 170 of the U.S. report, the "declaration does not affect the authority of the Federal Government to enforce the obligations that the United States has assumed under the Convention through administrative or judicial action," then why include it? As CERD member Ms. January-Bardill[31] states, "[h]igh levels of institutional and systemic racial discrimination persist[s], as evidenced for example by a lack of education opportunity, discrimination within the criminal justice system, unequal health care for minorities and disadvantaged women, and continued inequality for the African American population."

When "covert racial discrimination [is] sometimes more dangerous than overt racial discrimination and its effects more devastating"[32] as Ms. January-Bardill argues, then restricting the extent to which ICERD is implemented, demonstrates a disregard with treaty compliance. Maintaining that "[t]he declaration reflects a different choice, one in favour of remaining existing remedies for private parties," paragraph 172 of the U.S. government report acknowledges this choice goes against the committee's and U.S. civil society's preference for "direct inclusion of the Convention into the domestic law." Ultimately though, the government does not want U.S. citizens to have additional rights enforceable by the U.S. judicial process. As stated in paragraph 170 of the U.S. report, "both the Executive Branch and the Senate have considered it prudent to declare that those treaties [referring to U.S.-ratified treaties] do not create new or independently enforceable private rights in U.S. courts."

The U.S. government issues RUDs to effectively and legally limit its legal obligations to ICERD. The misuse of these three treaty mechanisms begs the question of why the U.S. ratified the treaty at all if the goal is to immobilize it in this manner. The answer is not necessarily a simple one. The dismal U.S. record of ratifying human rights treaties does not go unnoticed internationally. Treaty ratification is part political performance, and it is also about a forced, albeit often times reluctant, engagement with human rights. Since the U.N. brokers international agreements and understandings, the U.S. government must remain associated with and not isolated from the work of the U.N. As much as the U.S. government struggles with the U.N., the U.S. government still needs the U.N. Ratifying ICERD gives the perception of U.N. engagement.

The Limitations of CERD and Its Review Process

CERD reviews government reports when they are completed, not necessarily when they are due. CERD possesses little to no power to enforce timely submission of government periodic reports, and State Parties do not experience repercussions for submitting a report late or for merging several reports into one single report. CERD cannot impose sanctions or issue reprimands to convey their disapproval of actions by Member States. To some degree it is remarkable that governments even submit a report. Yet State Parties comply for their own political reasons and because the U.N. treaty monitoring committees use their discretionary powers to the fullest extent to ensure timely report submissions and productive review hearings.

In one instance, the treaty monitoring body for the International Convention on Civil and Political Rights (ICCPR) had not received a report from the U.S. government since 1994. Frustrated by U.S. government's inaction, the committee requested input from U.S. NGOs in compiling a memo stating the ICCPR's concerns about the U.S. government's noncompliance with the treaty. The U.S. government eventually submitted its periodic report to the committee in November 2005 *before* receiving the memo.[33] Once the memo is public, then the U.S. government is obligated to respond to those specific concerns determined by the committee. In this case, the U.S. government may have felt politically pressured to submit their periodic compliance reports, especially once the U.N. committee asked for civil society's involvement.

In addition, CERD does not consider the racial implications of U.S. foreign policy. Its sole focus is on the domestic or national context of racism and ways to combat it. Related to this limited focus is that this treaty does not apply to non-state actors.[34] Therefore, the policies and practices of U.S.-based transnational corporations, which can exacerbate racial and gender inequalities globally, cannot be held accountable to ICERD standards because the U.S. government is not responsible for the actions of U.S.-based transnational corporations.

Despite these limitations, the CERD review hearing requires the U.S. government to publicly discuss racism and be evaluated, just like any other State Party, on its serious deficiencies with ICERD compliance. But why should it matter to NGOs and civil society how governments discuss racism in this particular political space? The outcomes of the CERD review, and any treaty review hearing, expose the government's gaps in compliance and even contradictory positions as well as the deafening silences on issues of importance. And NGOs can use the process of the review hearing in their political organizing (Falcón 2009). In the case of the U.S. government treaty compliance review for the Convention Against Torture (CAT), U.S. activists spotlighted the case of former police commander Jon Burge. Eventually arrested in October 2008 for torturing over one hundred African Americans during the 1970s and 1980s, the NGO press release[35] announcing his arrest acknowledged the CAT committee's support for their demands of an investigation. The CAT committee's attention to the Burge case and referring to these cases of police brutality as acts of torture spotlighted Chicago in an embarrassing manner for local politicians and police investigators (Tars 2009).

Conclusion

> [I]ssues relating to race, ethnicity, and national origin continue to play a negative role in American society. Racial discrimination persists against various groups, despite the progress made through the enactment of major civil rights legislation beginning in the 1860s and 1960s. The path towards true racial equality has been uneven, and substantial barriers must be overcome.
> —U.S. government's 2000 CERD report, paragraph 7

Once a treaty has been ratified, the State Party is required to submit a periodic compliance report. CERD then evaluates the report in a review hearing. The government's periodic compliance reports focus on the first seven articles of ICERD. Disagreements exist on a range of issues between CERD and the U.S. government delegation; in this chapter I analyze three issues of contention: the criminal justice system, freedom of speech, and the rights of indigenous peoples.

RUDs are treaty mechanisms which states can use to modify its treaty obligations to avoid discrepancies between domestic and international laws; but the U.S. utilizes RUDs as a way to severely limit the legal obligations it is subject to as a signatory to this treaty. The high number of ICERD reservations demonstrates the reluctant compliance of the U.S. government and its attempts at discursively evading its obligations. The federalism understanding intends to reify the separation of federal and state governments to the extent in which the federal level has no jurisdiction over states regarding full treaty implementation. And the "non-self-executing declaration" ensures no cause of action under the treaty, no right to sue under the treaty, and prevents the treaty from becoming the "Supreme Law of the Land" without an additional legislative process. CERD strongly urges the U.S. government to remove the RUDs as they are currently enacted.

The U.N. treaty monitoring process offers a unique venue in which to explore the manner in which the U.S. government discursively maneuvers around its stated obligations to the treaty. By highlighting certain topics of disagreement from the 2001 U.S.-CERD review hearing, I analyzed the discrepancies between domestic standards and international ones as a vehicle in which to discuss the politics of racism and antiracism discourse. In this review process, the U.S. government must be prepared to respond to concerns about its lack of compliance; and no other such site exists in the world where the U.S. government must publicly confront its existing racial problems.

Notes

1. According to Louis Henkin, "effective and powerful campaigns to nullify and permanently weaken international human rights treaties represented a move by anti-civil-rights and 'states' rights' forces to seek to prevent—in particular—bringing an end to racial discrimination and segregation by international treaty" (Henkin 1995, 348).
2. I refer to four documents in this chapter: the 2000 U.S. government report to CERD, two sets of summary records which details the 2001 U.S.-CERD review meeting, and CERD's 2001 concluding observations.

3.   Ms. Gabriele Britz (Germany), elected to CERD in August 2001 (term expired on 19 January 2002) is a university professor with research interests in constitutional law, human rights protections, European rights, and the discrimination.

4.   Summary record of the 1475th meeting: United States of America. 22 August 2001. CERD/C/SR.1475, paragraph 13.

5.   Summary Record of the 1474th Meeting: United States of America. 22 May 2003. (First, second and third periodic reports). CERD/C/SR.1474, paragraph 40.

6.   Summary Record of the 1476th Meeting: the United States of America. 22 May 2003 (First, second and third periodic reports). CERD/C/SR.1476, paragraph 11.

7.   Summary Record of the 1476th Meeting: the United States of America. 22 May 2003 (First, second and third periodic reports). CERD/C/SR.1476, paragraph 11.

8.   Summary record of the 1475th meeting: United States of America. 22 August 2001. CERD/C/SR.1475, paragraph 43.

9.   See NGO shadow report submitted by the National Association of Criminal Defense Lawyers for the 2008 CERD review of the U.S. government. The report can be accessed at http://www.ushrnetwork.org/cerd_shadow_2008 by clicking on link to report 11 on the death penalty (last accessed on 22 May 2009).

10. Summary record of the 1475th meeting: United States of America. 22 August 2001. CERD/C/SR.1475, paragraph 43.

11. Summary Record of the 1474th Meeting: United States of America. 22 May 2003. (First, second and third periodic reports). CERD/C/SR.1474, paragraph 5

12. Summary Record of the 1476th Meeting: the United States of America. 22 May 2003 (First, second and third periodic reports). CERD/C/SR.1476, paragraph 54. Mr. Yuri Rechetov's (Russian Federation) term expired on 19 January 2004. He is a long-time diplomat.

13. Committee On The Elimination Of Racial Discrimination Reports Submitted By States Parties Under Article 9 Of The Convention, Third periodic reports of States parties (United States of America) 10 October 2000. CERD/C/351/Add.1, paragraphs 292-295.

14. Summary Record of the 1474th Meeting: United States of America. 22 May 2003. (First, second and third periodic reports). CERD/C/SR.1474, paragraph 5

15. Summary record of the 1475th meeting: United States of America. 22 August 2001. CERD/C/SR.1475, paragraph 24.

16. Southern Poverty Law Center, "Internet Hate and the Law," http://www.splcenter. org/intel/intelreport/article.jsp?aid=288.

17. Summary Record of the 1474th Meeting: United States of America. 22 May 2003. (First, second and third periodic reports). CERD/C/SR.1474, paragraph 55.

18. Summary Record of the 1474th Meeting: United States of America. 22 May 2003. (First, second and third periodic reports). CERD/C/SR.1474, paragraph 64.

19. Summary record of the 1475th meeting: United States of America. 22 August 2001. CERD/C/SR.1475, paragraph 6.

20. Summary Record of the 1474th Meeting: United States of America. 22 May 2003. (First, second and third periodic reports). CERD/C/SR.1474, paragraph 64.

21. Mr. Patrick Thornberry (United Kingdom), elected to CERD on 14 January 2001 (term expires on 19 January 2010), is a professor of international law at Keele University in the United Kingdom. He has written extensively on race, indigenous, and minority issues as it relates to CERD.

22. Summary record of the 1475th meeting: United States of America. 22 August 2001. CERD/C/SR.1475, paragraph 29.

23. Summary Record of the 1476th Meeting: the United States of America. 22 May 2003 (First, second and third periodic reports). CERD/C/SR.1476, paragraph 25.

24. Gitlow v. New York, 268 U.S. 652 (1925), http://www.oyez.org/cases/1901-1939/1922/1922_19/.
25. Summary Record of the 1474th Meeting: United States of America. 22 May 2003. (First, second and third periodic reports). CERD/C/SR.1474 , paragraph 32.
26. Summary Record of the 1476th Meeting: the United States of America. 22 May 2003 (First, second and third periodic reports). CERD/C/SR.1476, paragraph 2.
27. Summary record of the 1475th meeting: United States of America. 22 August 2001. CERD/C/SR.1475, paragraph 3.
28. Concluding Observations of the Committee on the Elimination of Racial Discrimination: United States of America 30 July - 17 August 2001. A/56/18, paragraph 400.
29. Summary Record of the 1474th Meeting: United States of America. 22 May 2003. (First, second and third periodic reports). CERD/C/SR.1474, paragraph 34.
30. Summary record of the 1475th meeting: United States of America. 22 August 2001. CERD/C/SR.1475, paragraph 2.
31. Ms. Patricia Nozipho January-Bardill (South Africa), elected to CERD on 14 January 2002 (term expires on 19 January 2008), is a scholar of race and gender justice who spent 23 years in exile—13 in Lesotho and 10 in the United Kingdom—due to her anti-apartheid activities. She played an advisory role to the new South African parliament in the mid-1990s and was the Director of World University Services in South Africa, which was a non-governmental organization, focused on literacy development in South Africa.
32. Summary record of the 1475th meeting: United States of America. 22 August 2001. CERD/C/SR.1475, paragraph 21.
33. According to the American Civil Liberties Union, the Human Rights Committee sent a letter to the U.S. government on 27 July 2004, which included specific concerns to be addressed in their next report regarding the International Covenant on Civil and Political Rights. The Human Rights committee is the monitoring body for the International Covenant on Civil and Political Rights. Due to lack of U.S. response, the Human Rights Committee wanted to draft its "List of Concerns" about the U.S.'s non-compliance with ICCPR. However, the U.S. submitted their next periodic report regarding ICCPR before the dissemination of this U.N. document. The "List of Concerns" document was eventually released in March 2006.
34. The Convention to Elimination All Forms of Discrimination Against Women (CEDAW) is the only existing human rights treaty that goes beyond state accountability.
35. People's Law Office (Chicago) Press Release, "Former Chicago Police Commander Jon Burge Arrested on Charges Relating to Torture of Over 100 African-Americans," www.ushrnetwork.org/files/ushrn/images/linkfiles/chicago_pressrelease.pdf.

References

Associated Press. "Assembly Democrats announce plans to seek death penalty moratorium" in *The Associated Press State & Local Wire*, June 15, 2005.

Bernard, H. Russell and Gery W. Ryan. 2000. "Text Analysis: Qualitative and Quantitative Methods." in *Handbook of Methods in Cultural Anthropology*, edited by H. Russell Bernard. New York: Altamira Press.

Falcón, Sylvanna. 2009 "Invoking Human Rights and Transnational Activism in Struggles for Racial Justice at Home: Anti-racist Activists and the Committee to Eliminate Racial Discrimination*" Societies Without Borders* 4: 295-316.

Gallagher, A. 1997. "Ending the Marginalization: Strategies for Incorporating Women into the United Nations Human Rights System." *Human Rights Quarterly* 19:283-333.

Henkin, Louis. 1995, "U.S. Ratification of Human Rights Conventions: The Ghost of Senator Bricker," *The American Journal of International Law* 89, 2: 341-50.

Lindlof, Thomas R. and Bryan C. Taylor. 2002. *Qualitative Communication Research Methods*. Thousand Oaks: Sage Publications.

Smith, Andrea. 2005. *Conquest: sexual violence and American Indian genocide*. Cambridge: South End Press.

Tars, Eric. 2009. "Human Rights Shadow Reporting: A Strategic Tool for Domestic Justice." *Clearinghouse Review: Journal of Poverty Law and Policy* 42, 9-10: 475-85.

Thomas, Dorothy Q. 2000. "We Are Not The World: U.S. Activism and Human Rights in the Twenty-First Century." *Signs: A Journal of Women in Culture and Society* 25:1121-1124.

United Nations, Committee on the Elimination of Racial Discrimination Reports Submitted by States Parties under Article 9 of the Convention, Third periodic reports of States parties (United States of America) 10 October 2000. CERD/C/351/Add.1.

———. Concluding Observations of the Committee on the Elimination of Racial Discrimination: United States of America 30 July—17 August 2001. A/56/18, paras. 380-407.

———. Summary Record of the 1474st Meeting: United States of America. 3 August 2001 (First, second and third periodic reports). CERD/C/SR.1474.

———. Summary record of the 1475th meeting: United States of America. 6 August 2001. CERD/C/SR.1475.

———. Summary Record of the 1476st Meeting: the United States of America. 6 August 2001 (First, second and third periodic reports). CERD/C/SR.1476.

Anti-Racist Communication in Soccer: A Spoilt Vocabulary?

Floris Müller, Liesbet van Zoonen, and Laurens de Roode

Introduction

Soccer is a global phenomenon with many local faces, ranging from an impromptu kick-off on a street corner to a symbolic match between rival nations. The response to the equally global problem of soccer racism has, however, been remarkably uniform. Most efforts make the deceptively simple appeal to oppose racism using slogans such as: *"say no to racism," "show racism the red card," "kick racism out of soccer," "love football, hate racism."* At present, little is known about the ways in which soccer fans respond to these messages. Despite their widespread use, it is unclear whether media campaigns that deploy this vocabulary can be considered effective contributions to the struggle against racism in soccer.

In this chapter, we examine these issues by analyzing the content and reception of the two most well-known anti-racist campaigns from Dutch soccer culture of the past decade. These are the campaign *"If Racism Wins, Sports Loses"* by the local Amsterdam municipality and the campaign *"Stand Up, Speak Up"* by Nike. Our investigation is guided by the following three questions: First, how are the anti-racist messages of these two campaigns constructed in visual and textual discourse? Second, how are they received by audiences? Third, what does this tell us about the potentials and limitations of using media campaigns to challenge racism in soccer?

The present study was set up to connect and contribute to ongoing academic as well as societal debates about the nature and extent of racism and anti-racism in soccer. While the vivid images of hooligan racist violence in the 1970s and 1980s have served to put soccer racism on the public agenda, they have also led to the erroneous belief that it is generally found only amongst groups of violent hard core fans (Back, Crabbe & Solomos 2001). This popular misconception ignores the fact that racism also occurs amongst "regular" spectators, players, volunteers and employees at soccer clubs (Back, Crabbe & Solomos 2001; Holland 1997; Jones 2002; King 2004; Müller, van Zoonen, & de Roode 2007). It also does not acknowledge that racism can influence the representations of ethnic players in the media (Carrington 2002; Hermes 2005) and may structure processes of decision making and resource allocation in the board rooms of clubs and football associations (Back, Crabbe & Solomos 2001). Soccer racism should be conceptualized as an aspect of a wider radicalized soccer culture and involves the beliefs, behaviors and interactions of *all* fans, players, volunteers and employees that constitute the practice of soccer in any local context (Back et al. 2001; Garland & Rowe 2001; Holden & Wilde 2004; Horne 1996; Jones 2002; Osler & Starkey 2002).

It is against the backdrop of this understanding of the problem of soccer racism that we approach our study of the reception of the two media campaigns "If Racism Wins, Sports Loses" and "Stand Up, Speak Up." Our empirical interest therefore lies with the ways in which their messages draw audiences into the anti-racist struggle and the domains of soccer racism that are thus addressed by these campaigns. We analyze the impact of both campaigns on their target audiences using in-depth interviews with soccer players and professionals, a survey of local Amsterdam soccer players and a semiotic analysis of campaign materials and discourses.

In the following, we first describe our definition of the problem of racism in soccer, using the work of Back, Crabbe & Solomos (2001) and Garland & Rowe (2001). Next we discuss both campaigns in more detail. This is followed by an explanation of the methodology that we used. Next, we analyze the reception of the two mass media campaigns "If Racism Wins, Sports Loses" and "Stand Up, Speak Up" based on the results of the survey. We contextualize these quantitative findings using material from the in-depth interviews. In so doing, we hope to make clear how certain aspects of the visuals and slogans of the campaigns reverberate with the experiential world of the soccer audiences. The paper ends with a discussion of the implications of these empirical findings for what should be considered an appropriate use of mass media campaigns for anti-racism in soccer.

The Challenge of Anti-Racism in Soccer

Traditional anti-racist practices have focused almost exclusively on the eradication of hooliganism and collective supporter racism such as chanting. This kind of anti-racism has been criticized for ignoring many other areas and aspects in of the problem of soccer racism (Back, Crabbe & Solomos 2001; Garland & Rowe 2001). According to critics a wider definition of the problem of soccer racism should be adopted that implies at least two new challenges for the anti-racist struggle.

First, the domains in which soccer racism may be encountered are much more numerous than previously assumed. Next to spectator behavior, racism may also be found in the interactions between players, coaches and other employees of the soccer club, the institutional arrangements of a club, processes of decision making in various levels of soccer club culture and media that bring soccer to the homes and pubs of its fans (Back, Crabbe & Solomos 2001). Anti-racist practices therefore cannot suffice with attempts to eradicate only soccer hooliganism, no matter how effective those may be. They need to address these other potential domains of racism as well.

Second, anti-racism also needs to take into account the fact that racism comes in many guises in contemporary soccer culture. The reality is that racism is often expressed in contradictory and incoherent ways that are often not immediately recognized as racism. For instance, some soccer fans may cheer on black players on their own team while simultaneously shouting racist abuse at blacks on the opponent's team (Müller et al. 2007). Other examples are (speech) acts that are not intentionally harmful or insulting but nonetheless set black or Asian players apart as different from the group (such racialized remarks or jokes, see Müller, van Zoonen & de Roode 2007). A club culture that alienates players with from an ethnic minority background in subtle ways may also form part of the wider problem of racism (cf. Duyvendak, Krouwel, Kraaijkamp en Boonstra 2001). In more academic terms, this means that anti-racism should not only be concerned with social exclusions and violence but processes of "racialization" as well. Racialization can be defined as the *process* through which social relations between people become structured by the "signification of human biological characteristics in such a way as to define and construct differentiated social collectivities" (Miles 1993, 75). The notion of racialization implicates the wider culture of soccer in which *all* of the people at the clubs and pitches participate in one way or another. Each participant therefore carries both a part of the problem of racism as well as part of the key its eradication.

When these issues are translated to the specific area of anti-racist media campaigns, these theoretical starting points offer a number of avenues for analysis. First, they draw attention to the ways in which the mass media continue to represent soccer players through racialized (visual) discourses (Carrington 2002; Back et al. 1999, Burdsey 2004a; King 2004). Such discourse may, for example, represent black players as (super)naturally athletic, dangerous or even hypersexual and thus reproduce colonial fantasies and fears and racialized social relations (see Hermes (2005) for a discussion of mass media representations of black soccer players in the Dutch media). If campaign makers are not sensitive to these issues, they may easily fall into the trap of drawing on these popular racialized discourses to get their message across. If they do, their media campaign might actually end up reproducing a part of the problem of racism rather than challenging it. For example, racism may be constructed unthinkingly as an issue faced only by "blacks." As a result, some groups that do not fit into this category, such as Asians or Muslims, are not considered or when they are, the specificity of the abuse and exclusion they are facing is not adequately acknowledged (Burdsey 2004b).

The theoretical starting points outlined here give rise to the following focal points in our present study of mass media campaigns against soccer racism. First of all, how can we classify the (visual) discourses the campaigns "If racism wins, Sports loses" and "Stand Up, Speak Up"? How do both campaigns address their audiences and to what extent do they manage to address the wider problem of soccer racism as was just discussed?

Campaigns

We selected two anti-racist media campaigns for this study based on a number of criteria. We sought out two campaigns that were representative of anti-racist media engagements in Dutch soccer by selecting the two largest and most well known campaigns over the last 15 years. Both are briefly described below.

If Racism Wins, Sports Loses

The campaign "If Racism Wins, Sports Loses" was initiated by the Amsterdam municipality in 1993 with the aim to make people involved in local sports aware of the "growing racism" in sports (Dialoog producties 1995). In particular, it focused on people playing sports, members of the boards of sports clubs and other volunteers. The number one goal of the campaign was to "put the topic of racism on the agenda of the boards of sports clubs" and to affect change in club policies regarding non-white players (Dialoog producties 1995). The campaign roughly followed a dual strategy of raising awareness of racism through its slogan ("If Racism Wins, Sports Loses") and realizing change in policies of Amsterdam sporting clubs regarding ethnic minorities. The different strategies for generating publicity began with an official "campaign opening" ceremony during a match between the Amsterdam club Ajax and Rotterdam club Feyenoord. This was the starting signal for several billboard campaigns, television commercials, advertisements on the local trams and the dissemination of free postcards with the slogan and images of the campaign. Sports clubs were targeted with packages of campaign material (i.e., posters, copies of the fanzine, postcards etc.) sent to all Amsterdam sports clubs, which contained an invitation to pledge a promise to the municipality to take up a specifically devised code of conduct in the official club policy. The campaign was held repeatedly throughout the 1990s and changed its visual representations on its posters significantly and ended in 2001.

Stand Up, Speak Up

In January 2005, sports company Nike launched a publicity campaign against soccer racism called "Stand Up, Speak Up" in a number of European countries (Sterkenburg, Janssens & Rijnen 2005). The campaign consisted of a 45-second television ad in which viewers were admonished by a number of celebrity soccer players to "stand up and speak up" against racism in soccer. Nike also produced, distributed and sold 5 million plastic black and white wristbands that carried the slogan of the campaign and its own logo. The wristbands became so popular that they repeatedly sold out. Imitations have now surfaced that are for sale at local Amsterdam markets and the originals are being offered for sale at inflated prices on the Internet. The proceedings of the official Nike sales were, at the time of writing, yet to be donated to local anti-racist and pro-diversity initiatives in Europe as promised. The television advertisement was broadcasted for 3 months on television screens in the UK, the Netherlands, Germany, Belgium, Luxembourg, France, Spain, and Italy. Nike launched a website about the campaign, where the ad can be viewed and some frequently asked questions about the campaign are answered (Sterkenburg, Janssens & Rijnen 2005). The 45-second ad shows a sequence of 15 static shots in which celebrity soccer players are shown asking the viewer to help them combat racism in soccer. Instead of speaking to the viewer, the players remain silent and show the viewer white cardboards on which their anti-racist message is written (see also Müller, van Zoonen & de Roode 2008b).

(Visual) Campaign Discourses

An analysis of the (visual) discourse of the two campaigns reveals that both campaigns contained a very similar message about racism.

Figure 1a
Campaign Visuals from "If Racism Wins, Sports Loses" and
"Stand Up, Speak Up."

Figure 1b

As can be seen in Figure 1a and 1b, the visual material of both campaigns contains remarkable similarities. Both are executed in black and white and feature frontally photographed athletes. Through the combination of direct eye contact with the viewer and a serious facial expression (and a tense body posture in the case of Stand Up, Speak Up), these visuals imply a confrontation with the viewer, and more in particular, people who engage in racist acts. Moreover, the choice for a black and white picture also adds to a sense of stern realism and sobriety to the message. It suggests that a serious topic is being addressed here that tolerates no frivolities. It also further emphasizes the implied confrontation with racism and literally presents anti-racism as a black-and-white matter, in which the viewer is given a clear-cut choice between two differently valued alternatives. On the one side is the good camp of the anti-racists and the victims of soccer racism, represented by the soccer player, and on the other side are the bad racists that have misbehaved and now need to be put in their place.

Both campaigns also featured accompanying texts that served to further anchor their preferred readings. In the first round of posters for "If Racism Wins, Sports Loses," each picture was accompanied by an additional "quote" from the famous athlete on the picture that translates as "[If Racism Wins, Sports Loses] ... *and I am a very poor loser.*" The expression "being a poor loser" generally means losing one's temper or becoming aggressive and in this case therefore implies a threat by the athlete to anyone who might act in a racist way. The commercial for "Stand Up, Speak Up" similarly contained a text that explicated the confrontational approach of the campaign. During the clip, for example, one on lines of text reads, "We need your voices to drown out the racists. Wherever you hear them, say no," thus again reinforcing the notion that soccer culture can be meaningfully and constructively divided up in those groups that are the problem and those that are innocent.

In later years, the visuals and text of "If Racism Wins, Sports Loses" were altered significantly to avoid stressing this confrontation between racists and non-racists. We will return to the contents of this shift in visuals and its implications after a discussion of the general reception of both campaigns.

Data Collection

In order to assess how these two campaigns were received by Dutch soccer audiences, data were collected using a survey amongst soccer players and in-depth interviews with experts and local Amsterdam soccer players.

Survey

The survey was provided to respondents in digital format and could be filled out on the website of the University of Amsterdam. In order to attract respondents from sufficiently diverse ethnic backgrounds, an invitation was posted on a number of Internet forums that catered to ethnic soccer players, ethnic minorities or a combination of both.

A total of 148 respondents signed in to fill out the survey. Unfortunately, a number of respondents did not finish the entire survey and therefore could not be used in the analysis. For the analysis, 113 respondents could be used. The youngest respondent in our sample was 12 years old and the oldest was 68 with a mean of 26 and a standard deviation of 10.8. White Dutch respondents made up 62 percent of our sample and the remaining 38 percent indicated they had at least one parent from an immigrant background. The two main groups of non-Dutch respondents were of a Surinam ethnicity (10 percent) and of a Moroccan ethnicity (9 percent). The remaining 19 percent of our respondents had an English, Turkish, Colombian, Algerian, Egypt, Hong Kong, Indonesian, or South African background. Of these non-Dutch respondents, 50 percent indicated that they had suffered racist abuse in soccer over the last 2 years. Interestingly, 10 percent of the Dutch respondents also indicated that they had been the victim of racist abuse. In terms of participation in local Amsterdam soccer culture, 65 percent of the respondents were currently playing soccer at a soccer club, while an additional 28 percent indicated that they had done so in the past, but were not at the time of filling out the survey.

The survey contained a number of demographic questions that consisted, apart from the usual questions on age, ethnicity and education, of questions on respondent's soccer history. This included the number of years spent playing soccer, the number of soccer clubs that respondents had been a member of and questions on their current soccer team.

Next to these demographic questions, the survey asked respondents about their exposure, evaluation and self-reported effects of "If Racism Wins, Sports Loses" and "Stand Up, Speak Up." All scales consisted of three to five items that required respondents to agree or disagree with a statement on a 5-point Likert scale. The scale measuring exposure consisted of statements on the frequencies with which people had been exposed to the campaigns. An example question of this scale is "*I have seen the Stand Up, Speak Up advertisement on television many times.*" The reliability of this scale was alpha=.81 and .63 for "If Racism Wins, Sports Loses" and "Stand Up, Speak Up," respectively. The scale measuring the respondents' evaluation of the campaigns was made up of 3 questions. An example of these questions is: "*Stand Up, Speak Up is a good way to challenge racism between soccer players.*" The reliability of this scale was alpha=.61 and .72 for "If Racism Wins, Sports Loses" and "Stand Up, Speak Up," respectively. The scale for self-perceived effects of the three cases focused on respondents' own perceptions of the impact of the campaigns on themselves and their peer group. These questions intended to measure both a behavioral and a cognitive component. An example of the questions measuring the cognitive component is "*The campaign "If Racism Wins, Sports Loses" has made me think about soccer racism at my club.*" An example from the questions measuring behavioral change is "*As a result of the campaign, I have talked to my peers about soccer racism.*" The reliability of this scale was alpha=.77 and .85 for "If Racism Wins, Sports Loses" and "Stand Up, Speak Up," respectively.

In-depth Interviews

Nine interviews were held with soccer players from two local soccer clubs and professionals that had been involved in the design and implementation of the campaigns. Using this initial data, the survey was constructed and an interview topic list was devised to guide the further in-depth interviews. These respondents were aged between 18 and 36 years old and were from Dutch, Pakistani, Burkina Faso, Surinamese, and Turkish backgrounds. All of them were playing at a local football club in Amsterdam and were recruited as respondents after or before their training sessions there. In these interviews, respondents were asked about their impressions of both campaigns under study. They were also asked about their experiences with racism and racialization in local Amsterdam soccer. The data from these interviews was used to get a sense of the dominant discourses on racism in local Amsterdam soccer culture as well as some preliminary insights into the reception of anti-racist projects. These interviews typically lasted about one hour and were held either in a room of the respondent's soccer club or at a quiet café in its vicinity.

Campaign Reception

Of the respondents in our sample, 63 percent indicated that they knew what "If Racism Wins, Sports Loses" was. Of these respondents, 81 percent indicated that they had seen the campaign posters during its running time and 85 percent indicated that they had seen the campaign on television. In contrast, 82 percent indicated that they were familiar with the campaign "Stand up, Speak up." These results are perhaps not surprising given the different time periods in which the campaigns had been held. Whereas "Stand Up, Speak Up" had been held a year earlier, "If Racism Wins, Sports Loses," had terminated a few years earlier. Among respondents, 10 percent indicated that they wore the black and white wristbands that were promoted in the campaign and 17 percent indicated that they wore other kinds of wristbands as well.

Taken as a group, the average response on the scales measuring the extent to which they felt the campaign had promoted them and their peers to discuss issues of racism at their club or to change racist behaviors in local soccer culture respondents indicated that they did not feel this was the case. This can be seen in table two under the heading "self-reported effect," which shows that the average response was on the negative side of the five point semantic differentials used for measurement.

Table 1 also shows that despite this negative appraisal of the effects of both campaigns campaign, most respondents did not evaluate either "If Racism Wins, Sports Loses" or "Stand Up, Speak Up" in a negative way. Instead, they expressed a neutral attitude towards both. Further exploratory data analysis suggests that these attitudes towards the campaign were widely shared amongst our respondents. First of all, we were interested to see whether being part of the group of potential "victims" of racism (i.e., member of an ethnic or religious minority in the Netherlands) affected the ways in which the campaign was perceived. We conducted a series of t-tests in order to determine to what extent white Dutch respondents and people with ethnic backgrounds differed on our measures of exposure, self-reported effect and evaluation of the two campaigns. For "If Racism Wins, Sports Loses," differences were found on the measure for self-reported effect for between these two groups. On average, people with an ethnic background were significantly more positive about the effects of "If Racism Wins, Sports Loses" than the white Dutch ($t(86)=-3.258$; $p<.05$). However, the mean scores of both groups seem to suggest that people with an ethnic minority background (M=2,7) were simply expressing a neutral stance in their answers, whereas white Dutch (M=2,1) were actually denying that the campaign resulted in cognitive or behavioral changes in them or their peers. For "Stand Up, Speak Up," we did not find similar results as there were no differences in exposure, self-reported effect and evaluation between Dutch and people with ethnic backgrounds. Second, we explored whether people who indicated they had been the target of racial abuse scored differently on our measures than those who had not. T-tests revealed

Table 1
Mean Exposure, Evaluation, and Self-Reported Effect for the "If Racism Wins, Sports Loses" and "Stand Up, Speak Up" Campaigns.

	Exposure		Evaluation		Self-reported effect	
	N	M	SD	M	SD	M	SD
If Racism Wins, Sports Loses	92	2.8	1.0	2.3	.8	3.3	.6
Stand up, Speak up	113	3.1	.9	2.1	.8	3.3	.8

Note. Some respondents failed to fill out the entire survey. Mean scores were calculated on the answers of all respondents answering a particular question.
*=significant at p<.05

that people who indicated that they had experienced racial abuse did not score differently than people who had not (with a lowest p-value of $t(92)=-1,752; p=.08$).

In order to explore how strongly exposure to the campaign was related to the evaluation of the campaign and self-reported effect, a regression analysis was carried out. These results are shown in Table 2.

As can be seen in Table 2, all models displayed a significant fit with the data (with the highest p-value occurring for the model with the dependent variable "evaluation of campaign" for "If Racism Wins, Sports Loses" ($F(4,86)=2,612; p=.041$)). However, our regression models explained only modest amounts of variance in the dependent variables.

A closer look at the beta loadings reveals that most were not significant, indicating that the influence of these predictor variables is either non-existent in the population from which the sample was drawn or its effect was too small reach significance given the power of our analysis. Considering the size of our sample and the high reliability of our measurement instruments, these results suggest that effects of age and education on evaluation or self-reported effects are too small to be

Table 2
Regression Analysis of Self-Reported Change and Evaluation of "If Racism Wins, Sports Loses" and "Stand Up, Speak Up."

	If Racism Wins, Sports Loses				Stand Up, Speak Up			
	Self-reported changes		Evaluation of campaign		Self-reported changes		Self-Evaluation of campaign	
	Beta	SE	Beta	SE	Beta	SE	Beta	SE
Exposure to campaign	.102	.078	.087	.059	.233*	.078	.212	.081
Self-reported changes	—	—	.272*	.081	—	—	.253	.096
Age	-.044	.008	.178	.006	.045	.009	-.046	.009
Education	-.407*	.049	-.031	.040	-.228*	.046	.118	.047
N	90		90		112		111	
Adjusted R²	.15*		.07*		.08*		.10*	

Note. Only respondents answering all questions were included in the model.
*=significant at p<.05

interpreted meaningfully. It therefore seems that differences in rates of exposure, self-perceived effects and evaluation of both campaigns can not be explained by difference in ethnicity, age, education or even whether one has experienced racism himself. In other words, the data seem to suggest there is a strong consensus amongst these groups in terms of their evaluations of the campaigns and the effects they thought each of them had had.

The interpretation of the quantitative data as showing evidence of a consensus amongst our respondents was further substantiated by the results from our interviews with soccer players. In the following quote, a local Amsterdam soccer player explains his take on the campaign "Stand Up, Speak Up" in the following way:

> [I think] Stand Up, Speak Up is a very good initiative, although I wonder whether you reach the target group that makes these racist expressions, that is those stupid, foolish people that just say what comes to their mind. (…) I wonder if you reach the people who make these expressions and whether they understand what the campaign is saying.
>
> (Surinamese soccer player from Amsterdam World Cup)

The above quote exemplifies the common position in regards to mass-media anti-racist campaigns. After expressing his appreciation for "Stand Up, Speak Up," he immediately questions whether it will reach its "target group" which consists of people that express themselves in racist ways. From the rest of the quote, it is clear that he does not see himself as belonging to this group as he describes these people as stupid, foolish, impulsive, and unable to comprehend the message of the campaign. By constructing this "target group" as a collection of deranged racist individuals, the speaker also implicitly constructs racism as an act of ignorance and positions himself as a conscientious non-racist person.

This rhetorical move was common amongst the people we interviewed and can offer an explanation for the findings from the survey reported above. Most notably, it concurs with the finding that most people felt that even though the campaign has not had an impact on them, they did not feel that this was sufficient reason to question the effectiveness of the campaign. From the point of view explicated in the excerpt above, we can understand this response as the result of an investment in a particular discourse on soccer racism that makes a clear distinction between a small group of racists on the one hand and an innocent majority on the other. Given the absurd proportions to which "racists" are reduced in accounts like this one, everyone but the most hardcore hooligans can and does therefore identify with this innocent majority. The problem of racism is thus reduced to the presence of a group of retarded racists and mass-media anti-racist campaigns like "Stand Up, Speak Up" and "If Racism Wins, Sports Loses" come to be regarded as an attempt to communicate the views of the innocent majority to these racists. Their preferred reading of the campaign may therefore be paraphrased as: "*we, the innocent majority, are against racism and want the deviant racist minority to be removed from their soccer pitches.*" The campaign is thus evaluated positively by most members of the audience as representing their own opinion on the issue and consequently having no consequence for their own actions.

Changing Visions of Anti-Racism

These findings correspond closely to the confrontational (visual) discourse of both campaigns that was discussed earlier. These campaign messages clearly did not stimulate the audience to consider them selves as partly responsible for the problem of soccer racism. The visuals did not challenge the perception that "racists" are evil "others." Nor did they give their audiences any reason to see their own actions, such as those involving joking remarks about race, emotional curses during marches or an intolerant anti-multicultural soccer club culture as anything more than unfortunate but innocent acts that are essentially harmless. However, it is important to note that the visuals from the campaign "If Racism Wins, Sports Loses" were significantly altered in subsequent years as the goals of the municipality changed. Whereas in its early years, the goal was to "put the problem of racism" on the agenda, this changed in its early years to stimulating a positive alternative to racialized soccer culture in its later phases. As such, the aims of the campaign were gradually brought more or less in line with the cultural paradigm that was emerging in the field of soccer racism research during these years as well. This shift was also evident in the posters as the confrontational representations of the early campaign ads were altered.

Visuals were thus introduced like the one shown in Figure 2, in which two individuals from different ethnic backgrounds were depicted together in a way that suggests the opposite of the confrontations of the earlier period and those of "Stand Up, Speak Up." As can be seen in Figure 2, the men were depicted as intimate friends (suggested by their smiles and the fact that they are in physical contact with each other). Although these players also gaze directly at the viewer, their friendly facial expressions and tilted heads do not signify a confrontation with the viewer. Instead, they constitute an invitation to join them in their friendship and intimacy.

Figure 2
Campaign Visuals from the Later Phase of "If Racism Wins, Sports Loses."

By depicting both a white man and a person from a non-white but dif-
fuse ethnic background, this image furthermore seems to stress that the
invitation concerns not only whites and the traditional black victims of
racism, but also non-black ethnic minorities in the Netherlands, such
as Moroccans and Turks. In contrast with the images discussed earlier,
this particular visualization of the actors of anti-racism thus seems to
allude to the possibility of a particular idealized kind of soccer culture,
in which racists, racism, and racialization have obliterated by genuine
interpersonal friendships and love. As such, an effort was made to suggest
an atmosphere of inter-ethnic friendship and intimacy that was absent
in the "Stand Up, Speak Up" images and earlier visuals of "If Racism
Wins, Sports Loses."

Despite these later shifts in the representations of this campaign, however, no differences were found in the reception of both campaigns in our current study. One possible conclusion that may therefore need to be considered is that mass-media campaigns were so ubiquitous in Amsterdam soccer culture that they were hardly taken serious anymore. One interviewee described this in the following way:

> I have to say we don't spend too much attention to these campaigns. I haven't had a proper conversation with people about them, because its not something that really makes an impression on you and that you then need to discuss with your teammates to, like, compare points of view.
>
> (Black player from white middle class club)

As this quote indicates, even mass-media campaigns with a progressive (visual) discourse do not necessarily receive a better reception and can easily remain peripheral to the day to day practices of soccer culture. Much of the visual and textual discourse of both campaigns reinforced the unhelpful notion of a dichotomous confrontation between racists and innocent people. This clearly makes it unlikely that an awareness would develop from exposure of other the wider cultural problem of racism. Moreover, in their sole focus on communicating a particular normative message to players and fans, such campaigns do little to address racism in other domains of soccer than those stereotypically associated with racism (i.e., supporter behavior during matches).

Conclusion

Generally speaking, our analysis shows that both "If racism wins, sports loses" and "Stand Up, Speak Up" construct anti-racism as a confrontation with a small group of immoral racist deviants. Our results furthermore show that audiences, too, conceptualized anti-racism in this way as the striking images of violent hooligans remain etched into their collective unconscious. As a result of this match between the campaign messages and common sense understandings, both campaigns left the majority of the audience feeling like an innocent bystander with no responsibility or part in the fight against racism.

Given the fact that both campaigns were selected as representative of the general approach to communicating anti-racism in soccer, these findings suggest that a critical re-evaluation of the traditional idiom of anti-racism is in order. The results above indicate that confrontational metaphors and a moralistic language of a clear-cut battle between bad "racists" and good "anti-racists" will do little to challenge the wider problem of soccer racism. It is not likely to make the majority of the audiences aware of their own responsibility in the struggle against racism. In a sense, the traditional idiom of anti-racism may therefore be regarded as a "spoilt" vocabulary. This spoilt vocabulary consists of problematic terms ("real" racists, victims, and innocent people) and problematic metaphors (racism as a dark external enemy, a cancerous growth within an otherwise healthy body, a confrontation between good and evil) that prevent an effective and structural engagement with anti-racism.

If we accept this idiom is, to some degree, "spoilt" for the purposes of anti-racism in soccer, how might it be purged of its contra productive elements? The similarities between the reception of the campaign "If Racism Wins, Sports Loses" (which, in its later phases, showed evidence of such an attempt) and "Stand Up, Speak Up" indicate that this is by no means an easy task. They suggest that common sense discourses through which racism is understood in soccer culture are strongly geared towards assimilating any reference to "racism" into a conceptual grid that neatly separates perpetrators, victims and innocent bystanders. Therefore, it appears that small adaptations of this vocabulary of anti-racism in soccer alone are not likely to result in campaigns that challenge racism on a deeper level and wider scale.

An alternative to this spoilt vocabulary therefore also needs to be considered. Media campaigns might also avoid any explicit reference the traditional idiom of anti-racism in order to avoid activating people's own limited and self-serving understandings of the problem of racism. Many attempts in this direction have already been undertaken, albeit not under the general heading of "anti-racism." For example, much of what is currently undertaken in the name of "diversity" policies in the Netherlands and Britain might be understood as experiments in this direction (Shukra, Back, Keith, Khan & Solomos 2004). Some campaigns in soccer may also be interpreted as moves to tackle the problem of racism from a more oblique angle by framing the problem in terms such as social cohesion, lack of trust and interethnic contact (see Müller, van Zoonen & de Roode 2008a).

However, abandoning the "spoilt" vocabulary of anti-racism in soccer carries risks as well. Despite its limitations, the common sense understanding of racism as morally wrong and a social ill is also a powerful tool to rally support for the anti-racist cause (Shukra et al. 2004). The traditional idiom of anti-racism has been the bedrock foundation for the widespread cooperation with anti-racist measures and to discard or alter it therefore risks losing support (Garland & Rowe 2001). While it is certainly true that for many organizations and clubs, their participation in anti-racism thus amounted to little more than lip service, the potential of the traditional idiom of anti-racism for forging broad co-operations and coalitions remains a valuable asset.

A second reason to stop short of the outright dismissal of the traditional anti-racist idiom is that in some situations, it may actually be crucial to be able to distinguish "racists" from "victims" and "innocent majorities." Through its clear-cut language, it provides victims of certain forms of racism the opportunity to claim redress for abuse or exclusion. Moreover, it enables authorities to discipline individuals that commit racist abuse or discrimination knowingly and willingly. Discarding the idiom of anti-racism entirely therefore risks throwing the baby out with the bathwater. Without a common language to discuss soccer racism, refraining from any reference to the traditional idiom of anti-racism may lead to a loss of both widespread support for anti-racism in soccer culture as well as the ability to claim and organize redress and discipline for individual racist incidents.

In the absence of an appropriate but still widely accepted anti-racist vocabulary, any anti-racist engagement with the media will therefore do good to be very conscious about the kinds of messages they seek to communicate and the language that they choose to employ. The need to rally support or seek redress in individual incidents may in some cases necessitate using the "spoilt" traditional vocabulary of anti-racism out of purely strategic reasons. In certain circumstances, particular goals may outweigh the negative effects of failing to challenge the problem at a more structural level. In the long term, however, we cannot afford to be content with such a kind of "strategic essentialism." Our analysis of the campaigns "If Racism Wins, Sports Loses" and "Stand Up, Speak Up" suggests that the communication of anti-racism in soccer has reached an impasse. The traditional idiom of anti-racist media campaigns clearly does not suffice to challenge racism in a structural way. The search is on for improved ways to formulate and communicate the message of anti-racism in soccer culture—an impossible task without a thorough awareness of the mistakes made in the past.

References

Back, L., Crabbe, T. & Solomos. J. (1999). Beyond the racist/hooligan couplet: race, social theory and football culture. *British Journal of Sociology*, *50*(3), 419-442.

Back, L., Crabbe, T. & Solomos. J. (2001). *The changing face of football: racism, identity and multiculture in the English game.* London: Berg Publishers.

Burdsey, D. (2004a). Obstacle race ? 'Race', racism and the recruitment of British Asian professional footballers. *Patterns of prejudice, 38*(3) 280-299.

Burdsey, D. (2004b). 'One of the lads ?' Dual ethnicity and assimilated ethnicities in the careers of British Asian professional footballers. *Ethnic and racial Studies, 27*(5), 757-779.

Carrington, B. (2002). Fear of a Black Athlete: Masculinity, politics and the body. *New formations*, Vol. 45.

Dialoog producties (1995). *Evaluatie onderzoek naar de campagne 'Als racisme wint verliest de sport'.* Amsterdam: Gemeente Amsterdam.

Duyvendak, J., Krouwel, H., Kraaijkamp, A. & Boonstra, B. (2001). *Integratie door sport.* Rotterdam: Erasumus University Press.

Garland, J. & Rowe, M. (1999a). Field of dreams? An assessment of antiracism in British football. *Journal of Ethnic and Migration Studies, 25*, 35-53.

Garland & Rowe (1999b). Selling the game short: antiracism in British football. *Sociology of sport journal, 16*(1), 335-344.

Garland, J. & Rowe, M. (2001). *Racism and anti-racism in football.* Basingstoke: Palgrave.

Hermes, J. (2005). Burnt Orange. Television, Football, and the representation of ethnicity. *Television and new media, 6*(1), 49-69.

Holden, P. & Wilde, N. (2004). *Defense or Attack? Can soccer clubs help tackle social exclusion? Conference Paper.* ISTR Sixth International Conference July 11th-14th 2004 Toronto Canada.

Holland, B. L. (1997). Surviving leisure time racism: the burden of racial harassment on Britain's black footballers. *Leisure Studies, 16*, 261-277.

Horne, J. (1996). Kicking racism out of soccer in England and Scotland. *Journal of social issues, 20(1)*, 45-68.

Jones, R.L. (2002). The black experience within British professional soccer, *Journal of Sport & Social Issues. 26*(1), 47-65.

King, C. (2004). Race and Cultural Identity: Playing the Race Game Inside Football. *Leisure Studies, 23(1)*, 19-30.

Malik, K. (1996). *The Meaning of Race: Race, History, and Culture in Western Society.* New York: New York University Press.

Miles, R. (1993). *Racism after 'race relations'.* London: Routledge.

Müller, F., van Zoonen, L. & de Roode, L. (2007). Accidental racists : expressions and experiences of racism in local Amsterdam soccer. *Soccer and Society, 8(2/3)*, 335-350.

Müller, F., van Zoonen, L. & de Roode, L. (2008a) The social integrative powers of sport. The real and imagined consequences of sport events for multicultural integration. *Sociology of sport journal, 25(3), 387-401.*

Müller, F., van Zoonen, L. & de Roode, L. (2008b) We can't "Just do it" alone! The case of NIKE's anti-racist campaign in soccer. *Media culture and society*, 30(1), 23-40.

Osler, A. & Starkey, H. (2002). Education for citizenship: mainstreaming the fight against racism ? *European journal of education, 37*(2), 143-159.

Shukra, K., Back, L., Keith, M., Khan, A., & Solomos, J. (2004). Race, social cohesion and the changing politics of citizenship. *London Review of Education, 2*(3), 187-195.

Sterkenburg, J. van, Janssens, J. & Rijnen, B. (2005). *Football and racism,* Nieuwegein: Arko Sports Media / W.J.H. Mulier Institute.

Part II

Anti-Racism as Campaigning

Media Campaigns and Asylum Seekers in Scotland

Jairo Lugo-Ocando

Concern over asylum and immigration is not about racism. It is about fairness.
—Tony Blair, former British prime minister
(Campaign speech on April 22, 2005)

The concept of "media campaigns" has largely been defined by political communication studies (McCombs 1975; Arterton 1987; McNair 1995; Backer, Rogers, & Sopory 1992) and Public Relations literature (Grunig 1992; L'Etang & Pieczka 1996; Parkinson & Ekachai 2005). In both areas, the epistemology on media campaigns has included both normative and critical approaches. Over the years, there has been some agreement on the characteristic defining features of these campaigns, such as orchestration, and emphasis. Where there has been less consensus is in the case of intentionality; since it is in some cases methodologically difficult to *operationalize* it as a variable. This approach also presents the problem that it limits the notion of media campaign to overt media efforts that are explicitly presented to audiences as such.

This chapter therefore reconsiders traditional notions of media campaigns in the light of the role they have played in shaping race relations and immigration policy in Scotland. It contends that the media coverage of asylum seekers by London-based tabloids constitutes a media campaign and that it should be assessed alongside other more traditional PR efforts despite its apparent lack of intentionality. The main thesis here is that, to define a media campaign as such, we should look at those features pertaining to agency rather than intentionality.

Media campaigns, the specific area of Public Relations that concern us here, have often been defined as "public communication campaigns"

95

(Rice and Atkin 1989). These types of campaigns have been conceptualized either as "PR media campaigns," when launched by a group or organization for the purpose of issue-management, or as "media advocacy" when they are based on favorable orchestrated efforts, delivered by the media itself in order to address an issue which concerns the community (Dearing and Rogers 1996: 4). According to this framework, the aim of media advocacy is to create awareness, triggering action and ultimately promoting the public good. This is because the understanding of these campaigns departs from an ethical notion of what PR is all about (Seib and Lloyd 1973; Fitzpatrick 1994; Sallot et al. 1998; Somerville in Theaker 2001).

However, there is some evidence to suggest that the explicitness of intention (that relates to deontological ethics) is not necessarily relevant in defining these actions as media campaigns (Lugo 2007, 26). This is not only because intentionality derives from subjective interpretations, but also because the deontology of this definition needs to be considered within the wider picture of racist discourses and practices; at least, when it refers to the way some media outlets operating in Scotland cover asylum seekers and refugees as "issues." Instead, focus, persistence and emphasis should serve to categorize these actions as media campaigns; not because these actions are somehow objective or neutral but because it is possible to identify them with political agency. Hence, campaigns should be considered as discursive acts and as such, they are constitutive in a variety of ways, being largely used to maintain or restore the status quo (Wodak 1998, 8). In this alternative framework, some variety of media coverage can then be categorized as media campaigns that perform the function of discursive acts in terms of race, even if the main actors deny racist intention. By so doing, we are widening not only the concept of campaign but also incorporating the new dimensions that racism has nowadays; which transcends the rudimentary stereotypes based on body features and incorporate cultural constructions of inferiority and barbarism (for a historical deconstruction of this discourse see Fitzgerald 2008, 109).

In order to elaborate upon this re-conceptualization, this chapter examines the way in which anti-immigration campaigns are implemented in Scotland by the British national press, drawing some comparisons with more traditionally structured and explicit media campaigns on asylum seekers developed by the Scottish Government and NGOs. This comparison is based on research that made use of a variety of research strategies including critical discourse analysis, content analysis and participant observation. This is not to suggest that these campaigns can be systematically analyzed as homogenous pieces of individual discourse. On the contrary, it is very rare for a text to be the work of any one person. Instead, as Wodak suggests, texts discursive differences are negotiated; they are governed by negotiations of power which are themselves in part encoded in and determined by the conventions of particular discourses and genres (2001: 11). As sites of struggles, we can also read into these campaigns the traces of differing discourses and ideologies contending for dominance.

In highlighting orchestration and agency in the representation of asylum seekers by the British national press in Scotland, the approach allows us to see the relation of these discursive acts with the structures of power. The analysis distinguishes —but not solely because of methodological reasons— between British and Scottish national newspapers. This refers to the distinctive analysis between those British newspapers with circulation all over the United Kingdom and whose main news desks and editorial policy is ultimately determined in London, against those whose news desks and editorial policy is mainly set in Scotland. This distinctive analysis is increasingly important in a nation that is starting to deal with issues of independence and national sovereignty.

Indeed, as Bailey and Harindranath suggest, the media's *racialized othering* of asylum seekers (2005: 274) has been under-theorized in academic literature. This is because the "issue" has not received the same degree of attention as ethnicity and race in Britain (Bailey and Harindranath 2005, 279), let alone Scotland. Furthermore, as Alberto Melucci argues, racism and anti-racism should not be taken as unified facts, but as pluri-dimensional phenomena:

> The defensive resistance to the "other" is easily transformed into an aggressive attitude against the threat that the other represents. But also the claims to reciprocal understanding and communication are not entirely free from defensive attitudes (in Bulmer and Solomos 1999, 421).

Therefore, the framework used here also characterizes both anti-asylum and pro-asylum seekers campaigns as respectively racist and anti-racist discursive acts. It suggests that anti-asylum media campaigns carried out by some tabloids (and expressed in the form of coverage) should be considered as public communication campaigns in the context of race because their coverage of asylum seekers, although not necessarily having explicit racist intention, are nevertheless orchestrated discursive acts that allow groups and individual actors to articulate implicit racist narratives without violating the racial normative. Therefore, those carrying out these media campaigns are able to deny specific intention, but nevertheless display agency. They can sustain and promote these narratives, without being accused of violating laws and norms that nowadays restrict racist discursive acts; since statutory limitations to freedom of speech are greater in the United Kingdom than in places such as the united States. In similar terms, it is argued here that pro-asylum and pro-immigration campaigns also articulate discourses in terms of race by making use of anti-racist narratives. These campaigns also play a key role in legitimizing those who set and develop them. The cases used here are those of Oxfam's campaign "Asylum Positive Images Network" and the Scottish Government campaign "One Scotland Many Cultures."

In order to deconstruct and contextualize media campaigns in terms of race, it is also necessary to use critical discourse analysis to look at the relations that these discursive acts have in relation to "the politics of *positionality*" (Awkward 1995, 58) and the campaign agents. This will hopefully show that these problems are not media-specific and instead a reflection of more societal issues that have not been properly addressed. Indeed, the issues of *positionality* and *self-referentiality* have already proven to be fruitful subjects of investigation in critical discourse analysis (Awkward 2007, 104).

In using these analytical frameworks, I have looked not only at the wording and text often chosen by news editors and journalists but also at the frequency, timing, and persistency of representing asylum seekers and refugees as a social and political "issue." That is as the source of conflict between identifiable groups over the distribution of resources (Cobb and Elder 1983, 32), which deserve to receive mass media coverage (Dearing and Rogers 1996, 3). It is important to clarify, that the term asylum seeker in the United Kingdom is mainly used to designate those who are in the process of requesting political asylum but who have still not yet receive the status of refugee. It is a sanctioned legal status that allows the person or group of persons to remain in the UK while their case is processed by the legal authorities, but that limits substantially any rights and benefits. The term asylum seekers have acquired very negative connotations in the UK. But this word is nevertheless widely used in conjunction—or associated—with the words "illegal" or "bogus," therefore presenting it as a legal "loophole" when in reality is just a temporary status. The loophole is then often associated in media discourse with terms such as illegal immigrants, Muslim extremist, and African carrying HIV, tuberculosis, or other diseases (Kundnani 2007,

122). The reality often contrasts with what is reported in the media. While tabloid press in the period 2006/7 gave the sensation that there was a huge influx of asylum seekers into Britain, the country in reality received 22,750 applications for refugee status; a decrease of 10 percent in comparison to the previous period of 2005/6. Over 50 percent of the applicants were from Asia and Africa, mainly from places such as Iraq, Afghanistan, and Zimbabwe; places that are confronting crisis mainly provoked or in which it is heavily involved the UK. According to the charity Oxfam, asylum seekers in the UK "receive less basic rights than prosecuted criminals. They are detained indefinitely without trial and there is no automatic independent review of their detention period" (Oxfam 2006). This does not stop the tabloid press in the UK from presenting stories in which asylum seekers "cheat" to obtain state benefits or al placed in "very expensive houses" in the suburbs.

Besides borrowing some methodological elements from the emerging field of Critical Study of Public Relations (L'Etang and Pieczka 2006; Coombs et al. 2006), I have also incorporated some ethnographic data from my own engagement with some of the pro-asylum campaigns. This because I wholeheartedly endorse Paul Gilroy's suggestion that we should pay less attention to the status of race as a distinctive order of social phenomena *sui generis* and instead concentrate upon the primary problem for analysis of racial antagonism, which must be the manner in which racial meaning, solidarity and identities provide the basis for action (1987: 27). This "action," in the case of those of us who deal with this field, requires the deconstruction and contextualization of anti-asylum seeker media campaigns in terms of inferential racism. That is, campaigns that not only have substituted primitive biological racism, but that have also embraced the *cultural othering* as a narrative to bypass existing legal limitations and deliver racist narratives in a covert manner. Furthermore, Mendelberg points out, it is absolutely necessary to categorize these media campaigns as a racist practice—or discursive acts—in order to undermine their power to mobilize voters:

> The injection of race into campaigns poses a great danger to democratic politics—so long as the injection of race takes place under cover. When a society has repudiated racism, yet racial conflict persists, candidates can win by playing the race card only through implicit appeals (…) When an implicit appeal is rendered explicit—when other elites bring the racial meaning of the appeal to voter's attention—it appears to violate the norm of racial equality. It then loses its ability to prime white voters' racial predispositions. As a consequence, voters not only become more disaffected with the candidate but also prevent their negative racial predisposition from influencing their opinion on race (Mendelberg 2001, 4).

Therefore, broadening the notion of media campaigns—in order to incorporate a new dimension and new possibilities to the concept—is not only justifiable in theoretical terms, but also necessary in an ethical sense. Moreover, when the British electorate in light of the recent financial crisis will be almost certainly—once more—inundated with xenophobic appeals in future elections in the UK.

Redefining Media Campaigns

Media campaigns have often been defined as orchestrated, but temporary, efforts to promote specific political goals by means of a given media outlet (Arterton 1987, 40). William Paisley points out that in academic literature, two quite different but complementary definitions of public communication campaigns can be found. One refers to the intention to influence other groups' beliefs; the other to methods employed, such as the use of promotional messages through mass channels to target audiences (in Dearing and Rogers 1996, 16). However, this last definition tends to oversimplify the way in which agenda-setting and media campaigns are inherently part of the same political process. As such, PR (the theoretical matrix from which media campaigns depart) is a political process that goes beyond affecting audiences and news agendas. These collateral effects are instead means to political power. Therefore the primary aim of a corporation, institution, NGO, or a media outlet when they launch a media campaign is not only to influence directly the public or to set a particular orientation for the news agenda, but also to acquire influential political power that can be capitalized in terms of the worldly objectives of that organization. In the same way that the National Rifle Association (NRA) launches media campaigns in the US to stop small arms controls legislation in the Congress, media outlets in the UK create news agendas that they know will mobilize voters towards those parties and sectors that they support and from which media owners will profit once they get into power through indirect or direct association with them (there are of course also altruistic scenarios).

Media campaigns cannot therefore be seen solely as extensions of marketing communication since they are political in every sense. Hence, they need to be rethought beyond the functionalistic and instrumentalist perspectives that still dominate some PR academic research circles, which have tried to confine media campaigns to the area of marketing communication. Some authors have pointed out the necessity of challenging some of the most classical assumptions in the area of PR and have urged scholars to "engage further with media sociological critiques" (L'Etang 2005, 523). The analysis of these media campaigns from a critical perspective is therefore pivotal for their methodological re-conceptualization.

Although these campaigns are not necessarily designed and implemented in order to create and reinforce negative attitudes towards asylum seekers, they do so in order to undermine government administration (or particular members of the government). This is done by means of publicly questioning selective immigration policy, the administration and implementation of immigration legislation oriented to reduce immigration flows, and the effectiveness of measures such as the deportation and incarceration of illegal immigrants and people who fail to be recognized as refugees. In response, the government (in the case Labour) tends to launch what seems to be a counterintuitive but that in reality is part of the same irrationality. In adopting increasing draconian laws and measures, the government fails to recognize the disparity between reality and created fears.

Furthermore, media campaigns by the tabloid press in the UK that emphasize the risk posed by asylum seekers flows tend to articulate racist representations by means of binary distinctions. In representing asylum seekers as "non-individuals" they follow a historically continuous that racializes them as a homogenous group. In so doing, the image of present asylum seekers is framed by earlier representations of "Blacks," "Jews," "Asians," and "Gypsies." This settles in the constructions made by segments of the public familiar pejorative values which are often attached to such representations and that typically convey a "threat" to the imaginary national identity and unity by drawing simultaneously and differentially upon constructions of the Other and the Self (Lynn and Lea 2003, 446).

Indeed, asylum-seekers in the UK are not only a legal category in the immigration system, but also a social construction with meaning in itself for the public's imagination. As a social construction, it is often utilized to isolate the historical nature and political situation of those requiring refugee statuses. In so doing it allows the political actors, the media and the general public to treat the asylum seeker with ambiguity in terms of historical responsibility, to justify their political disfranchisement and to criminalize the individual within the context of what has been called "imagined communities" (Anderson 1983). Although Britishness was not one of Anderson central cases, we could argue that it is currently being promoted and rethought as an ideal of "fairness" and "cohesion." The British Prime Minister, Gordon Brown, whose own legitimacy to power is often questioned because of his Scottish origin, has argued that "he would make the re-articulation of "Britishness" his guiding idea. Brown has gone further to call for "the state to intervene to positively produce a new sense of nationhood" (cited by Kundnani 2007, 121). This particular framing of the political discourse, precisely by those who are supposed to counteract against extremism and xenophobia, facilitates the articulation of anti-immigration and anti-asylum seekers narratives.

For the contextualization of news in the UK media, this means dealing with official news sources that dismiss any historical responsibility towards the incoming asylum seekers. Therefore there is little empathy with families of asylum seekers (including children) being locked in prisons (now euphemistically termed "removal centres"). It also means that it is easier for media outlets to ignore or dismiss voices questioning the legitimacy—let alone legality—of such acts; even in those cases in which they represent mainstream sectors of the society. It also means that the media are allowed to make false distinctions between "moderate" and "extremist" sectors of the society (in the present times Muslims). This in fact is nothing but a continuous of similar historical distinctions made in the past by explicit overt racist narratives; such as "good" *negros* (with the implicitness of obedient and loyal) and "bad" *negros* (as rebels and criminals) and accepted by some then as a response to the accommodation strategy lead by Booker T. Washington (Fairclough 2001, 59).

For the most part, this is the manner in which some right-wing tabloids newspapers cover asylum seekers corresponds; although it must be said that there is also a similar mode in the coverage from many center-left tabloids in Britain.[1] By identifying asylum seekers as an "issue" pertaining to scarce resources and security concerns in their coverage, increasingly so after 9/11 and the July 7, 2005 bombing in London and the financial crisis of 2008, right-wing narratives are reinforced in ways that are reminiscent of Caribbean migrants' treatment in the 1950s by the National Front and politicians such as Enoch Powell (and explored by Gilroy 1987, 48).

Nevertheless, these representations do not take place in a political vacuum. The identification of asylum seekers as a threat is intrinsically linked to the notion of protecting the welfare state. In Europe (as well as in the US), this is a key element of neo-liberal narratives aimed at undermining center-left governments. The discursive acts against immigrants in general, blaming them for the collapse of public services is a very convenient distraction from the fact that neo-liberalism has privileged overspending in the industrial-military complex rather that social investment in improving and widening the welfare state. As some authors point out, the welfare state was implemented in the post-war Britain despite the lack cultural or ethnic homogeneity (Kundnani 2007, 88), but is being dismantled paradoxically using this same theme as an argument. For example, the introduction of ID cards in the UK for foreigners, alongside other control mechanisms, is often justified in terms of preventing "bogus asylum seekers" of abusing the system or "terrorist elements entering Britain." There is little or no reference to military expenditure or banking bailout in explaining why resources in hospitals, schools and unemployment benefit are not there.

The media outlets then tend to collude with the government in dismissing the de-prioritization of the welfare state, emphasizing on how asylum seekers tend to undermine resources and how they are "threat" to national security; but they will do so in the most convenient order for a pre-established news agenda. For example, three out of every five stories in *The Daily Mail* in 2005 that mentioned the terms "asylum seekers" and "terrorist" in the same article, also used "claiming benefit." One example of this was an article on August 6, about the deportation of Sheik Omar Bakri from the UK, which had the title "Deportation not fair, says extremist (on benefits)" (Wilson 2005). The leading paragraph of this article made emphasis on the benefits he received rather than the reasons for his deportation.

> An extreme Muslim cleric whose family has been living on benefits in Britain for 20 years says it would not be 'fair' to deport him.

This case is particularly interesting, since the government had sufficient reasons to question his presence in the UK on the grounds of national security. Instead of focusing on this, the article goes to highlight that the Syrian-born Bakri settled in Britain and his extended family have "raked" in benefits amounting to at least £300,000. The article does not mention the fact that Bakri had been living in Britain since 1985. In other words, it obviates the fact that this represents less than £13,000 per year for the whole family (a low income according to the own government indicators). Neither does the article mention the fact that the figure represents an estimate by the newspaper itself, which has been calculated by adding together council house rent, school tuition, health, and other services provided as a matter of course by the local authorities. Although the article points out that he is registered as a disabled person, it argues that it is due to a leg injury from his childhood, thereby implying the injury preceded his arrival to the UK. It also mentions that he was supplied with a £31,000 Ford Galaxy under the Mobility scheme, but fails to clarify that the car, which has special features, is a local authority property for the use of other disabled people too. Equally deceptive is the reference to his £200,000 (approx. US $395,000) home in London. This house, too, is the property of the local authority and its value relates to the state of the house market in London not on the conditions of the house itself.

Lynn and Lea, in their study of the British press and the coverage of asylum seekers, have identified three rhetorical strategies often apparent by print titles: a) the differentiation of the Other, b) the differentiation of the Self and c) the enemy in our midst (2003: 446). These rhetorical strategies allow those orchestrating these campaigns to identify themselves along a given spectrum, while framing the way that different audiences perceive themselves in relation to asylum seekers. For the tabloids adopting an anti-asylum seeker stance, it allows the promotion of a political agenda that uses xenophobic and racist narratives in "acceptable" terms. As the editor of a tabloid stated before the Commons Joint Committee on Human Rights when being interviewed in relation to media overage of asylum seekers:

> Political correctness should not be imposed on newspapers which have a right and duty to use robust language (BBC 2007).

In using these discursive strategies, the media, which has "the ability to construct and dispense social knowledge" (Fowler 1991; Van Dijk 1991), is able to embrace racist and xenophobic discourses in what seems acceptable terms. However, these discourses are by no means neutral, as Paul Gilroy has pointed out:

> We increasingly face a racism which avoids being recognised as such because it is able to link "race; with nationhood, patriotism and nationalism. A racism which has taken a necessary distance from crude ideas of biological inferiority and superiority and now seeks to present an imaginary definition of the nation as a unified cultural community (in Bulmer and Solomos 1999, 244).

Media campaigns, then, are carried out using narratives that are sustained "in a non-explicit manner" (Bailey and Harindranath 2005). Deploying notions of nationhood and culture to determine who is and who is not part of the national imaginary, they go to argue in defense of "Britain's embattled culture" (Blacklock 2005). This mechanism of exclusion allows racist narratives to make calls for racial segregation without explicitly mentioning "race." Instead, "Removal Centres," TB and HIV testing, and ID cards for foreigners seem acceptable bureaucratic procedures. However, this is not the objective of the discursive acts used by the media to construct its content, but instead a means of promoting another agendas; which have more to do with dismantling the welfare state and bolstering the industrial-military complex.

Ian Ward has described this phenomenon as "dog whistle journalism." In this case, the media uses what seems reasonable language to deliver a calculated message to the target audience (2002: 28). The audiences that Ward refers to in his article about the *Tampa affair in Australia* in 2001 were the undecided voters in that country. As Ward explains, the explicit intention was not necessarily to attack asylum seekers (refugees) as a group, but represent them as a threat in order to achieve an electoral goal. By so doing, the media helps politicians to create moral panics, facilitating the mobilization of voters towards the right. The electorate then "tend to choose those candidates using a more conservative platform when there is a perceived threat" (Lewis et al. 2005, 129).

In Britain, politicians and right-wing tabloids tend to collude in using similar strategies. They tend to portray asylum seekers in a systematic and orchestrated way as a threat to national security (crime, terrorism, etc.) and as a concerning issue in terms of resources (abusing the welfare state, draining resources from public services, etc.). It has already been pointed out that in the case of the UK, the tabloid press that declares itself a supporter of the Conservative party mobilizes the public towards more conservative views by creating moral panics on immigration and asylum issues in the hope that this translates into votes for the right (Law 2002, 91).

These discursive acts displayed mainly—but not solely—by London-based right-wing tabloids, tend to articulate the fear of the invading hordes as a devil folk, mobilizing voters by means of fear tactics. Racism and xenophobia is therefore not an aim in itself but a means to promote other ideologies that push further rightwing and neo-liberal political agendas. Other researches in Europe have already suggested that depending on the situation and context such as interactional function, setting, participants, and audiences, "racist and xenophobic beliefs and ideologies are expressed and used for different aims" (Reisigl and Wodak 2001, 267). These beliefs, which are inherent to the discursive acts, have of course traditions and roots. There are indeed clear historical precedents to the current state of affairs. Indeed, there are clear points of continuity with the xenophobic/racist colonial legacy, which exploited the fear of difference that recurs today in political discourse

(Gale 2004, 325). This is due to the politics of "race" in Britain, which is fuelled by conceptions of national belonging and homogeneity; not only blurring the distinction between race and nation, but also relying on that very ambiguity:

> It specifies who may legitimately belong to the national community and simultaneously advances reasons for the segregation or banishment of those whose origin, sentiment or citizenship assigns them elsewhere (Gilroy 1987, 45).

Media campaigns tend to ride on these same rhetorical strategies, which stress asylum seekers' difference to "us" (Gale 2004), representing them as a threat to "our civilization" (often argued by using "culture" as a sophism of race). They assign customs and practices to supposedly homogenous groups in ways that imply incompatibility with Western "civilization" and values. This is also present in political discourses that refer to terrorist or crime threats and found in everyday news which refers to "honor killings" or "female genital mutilation" to highlight the "barbaric" nature of "these groups." In so doing, they perform the same exclusionist function as biological race discourse did in Nazi Germany, where propaganda portrayed "races" such as Slavs as "barbaric" or "Non-human" before and during World War II. This practice of using essentialized notions of culture and equating them with barbarism is epitomized in an article that appeared in *The Daily Star* under the headline: "Asylum Seekers Eat Our Donkeys."

This article, published on August 21, 2003, claimed that a group of asylum seekers from Somalia stole nine donkeys from South-East London (Nicks 2003). The *Daily Star*, part of the Express Group (owner of *The Daily Express*) and a close ally of the British Conservative party, presented this story as an exclusive. The only police source in the article is an "insider" who claims to be "totally baffled over what has happened to the donkeys." The journalist, Gary Nicks, wrote the article without citing the police source's name:

> One of our main lines of inquiry is that they may have been taken by immigrants who like eating donkey meat as a delicacy. "It's no secret that we have a large African immigrant community here." [non attributed quote] Donkey meat is a speciality in some East African countries, including Somalia. And two areas near Greenwich—Woolwich and Thamesmead—have large numbers of Somalian asylum seekers.

The article implies that the group of Somali asylum seekers living nearby were responsible of the disappearance of the donkey. The journalist attempts to validate this by referring to previous similar reports:

"The donkey rustling follows reports of swans being stolen from ponds and lakes in London by immigrants to eat." However, these reports on asylum seekers eating swans that were published by *The Sun* on July 4, 2003 (Sullivan 2003) were also baseless. *The Sun* in fact retracted from the story with a 79-word apology to its readers inside the newspaper six months later on December 6, 2003. No disciplinary action was taken against the editors or journalists covering either of these stories.

Despite being completely baseless, the *Daily Star* story on asylum seekers eating donkeys was cited by the broadcast media throughout Britain, including several of the BBC radio networks. The story generated hundreds of complaints at the Press Complaints Commission, the main self-regulatory body of the print media in the UK. Of these complaints, only one was upheld and later resolved. This came from Nuradin Dirie, chair of the Somali Coordinating Committee, who argued that the article was inaccurate and therefore in violation of Clause 1 of the PCC Code of Practice. In the complaint, Dirie explained to the PCC that eating this donkey meat was actually prohibited by Islam (PCC 2003), since it was not *halal* ("permissible" by the religion of the alleged perpetrators). It is curious to note that the PCC did not uphold any complaint due to misrepresentation of a group of people or because no source had actually said what the headline suggested even though there was a stronger case for this in ethical and journalistic terms. Following this, the newspaper published an apology for offence caused by the article, pointing out that Islam forbade the eating of donkey meat. However, similarly to *The Sun*, the apology never made it to the front page and was buried inside the newspaper several months later, without a picture or illustration to draw the eye.

These types of articles not only tend to be systematically orchestrated by right-wing tabloids to coincide with electoral years, but they are also used to undermine center-left governments during key debates; shifting the news agenda from a critical issue and affect party politics. Indeed, the "racialized othering of asylum seekers" (Bailey and Harindranath 2005, 274) tends to happen not only in years preceding general elections, but also when other sensitive debates are taking place. As mentioned before the response from the Labour government has been to present a sort of counterintuitive position. For example, the then Commons leader Jack Straw in 2006 claimed that the fundamental problem with the Home Office "is with the people it deals with, rather than its staff." He blamed the problems of the Home Office on asylum seekers who acted as "dysfunctional customers" (BBC 2006).

Conceptual Redefinitions

At this point it is clear that, in the case of Scotland if not for the rest of the UK, the analysis of media campaigns about asylum seekers require recognizing the intrinsic narrative linkages that they articulate. In other words, they need to be a) identified as media campaigns and not merely as legitimate news coverage, and b) these campaigns need to be analyzed as discursive acts that provide positional reference to the actors that articulate them. Correspondingly, there is a need to consider racism as an ideological category within the political communication framework of these campaigns. This category is there to legitimize distinctive agendas, such as in the use of the so-called "race card" (Mendelberg 2001) and subsequently to position the anti-welfare agenda. It does so by presenting an "acceptable face of racism"; one that uses discursive acts based on inferential references to colonial traditions and cultural differences, but without making explicit links to biological race.

If well anti-racist legislation has failed to tackle the roots of racism (Bhavnani et al. 2005), in reality no mainstream media outlet in Britain runs any campaign that openly declares itself as racist or that deploys overtly racist language. The implementation of anti-racist and anti-hatred legislation in the past few years in the UK and Europe have obliged racist narratives and representations, especially in the media, to be more subtle and deceptive. Pieces of legislation in Britain such as the Racial and Religious Hatred Act 2006, the Broadcasting Act 1990, the Public Order Act 1986, the Football Spectators Act 1989 and other international legislation from the European Union such as the EU Race Directive (2000), have created wide possibilities for explicit racial discursive acts in the mainstream media to be legally challenged. These challenges are not confined to media content on news reporting but can also target the nature of the audience that would consume the media product. For example, the main bookshops chains in Britain (Borders, Waterstone's and WH Smith) agreed in July 2007 to remove the comic book character *Tintin* from the children section after the Commission for Racial Equality claimed the book *Tintin in the Congo* depicted "hideous racial prejudice" against Africans (Beckford 2007). For all of this, media campaigns against asylum seekers are nowadays rarely overtly racist. They instead tend to use euphemisms such as "national security," "culture" and "nationhood" to racialize otherness. In so doing, issues such as immigration control and asylum seekers are used to promote racist narratives, without explicitly using racist language. In this context, asylum seekers are often portrayed as the cause of "public service collapse," "social tension" and, more recently, "terrorism." This is particularly the case with the British media coverage of asylum seekers, which increases by about eight percent in the build up to general elections (Law 2002, 58). The fact is that the concept of race still remains central to political debates in Britain on issues such as immigration, national identity (Law 2002, 63) and in issues of culture and religion (Gilroy in Bulmer and Solomos 1999, 246).

Playing Devil's Advocate

The pro-immigration camps in Scotland have often singled out a group of national tabloid newspapers as providing the most systematic anti-asylum coverage: *The Scottish Sun, The Scottish Daily Mail, and The Scottish Daily Express*, all of which are regional editions of the London titles. By this we mean newspapers that are largely constructed in London but that incorporate local content to make a distinctive local edition. Most of these local editions are printed in Scotland and re-branded as Scottish newspapers in their title. These newspapers are among the ten best-selling titles in Scotland. Their re-branding as Scottish editions in combination with successful marketing and editorial strategies has made them leading products in the market.[2]

Although the local editions of the London-based newspaper claim to be Scottish, they in fact follow the editorial policies of London,

Figure 1
Main Newspapers in Scotland - Average 2005
No. of copies sold in Scotland (Source: ABC and JICREG DATA)

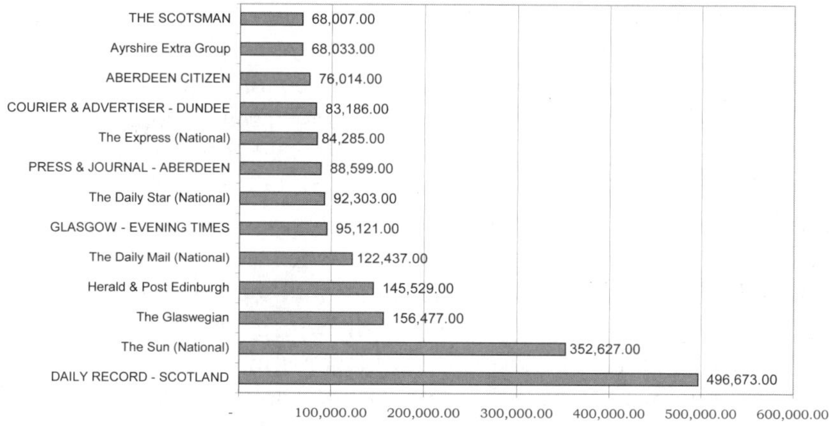
THE SCOTSMAN 68,007.00
Ayrshire Extra Group 68,033.00
ABERDEEN CITIZEN 76,014.00
COURIER & ADVERTISER - DUNDEE 83,186.00
The Express (National) 84,285.00
PRESS & JOURNAL - ABERDEEN 88,599.00
The Daily Star (National) 92,303.00
GLASGOW - EVENING TIMES 95,121.00
The Daily Mail (National) 122,437.00
Herald & Post Edinburgh 145,529.00
The Glaswegian 156,477.00
The Sun (National) 352,627.00
DAILY RECORD - SCOTLAND 496,673.00
-
100,000.00
200,000.00
300,000.00
400,000.00
500,000.00
600,000.00

Figure 2
No. of Articles Published Between Spet. 2003 and Sept. 2004 Using the Term
"Asylum Seekers"

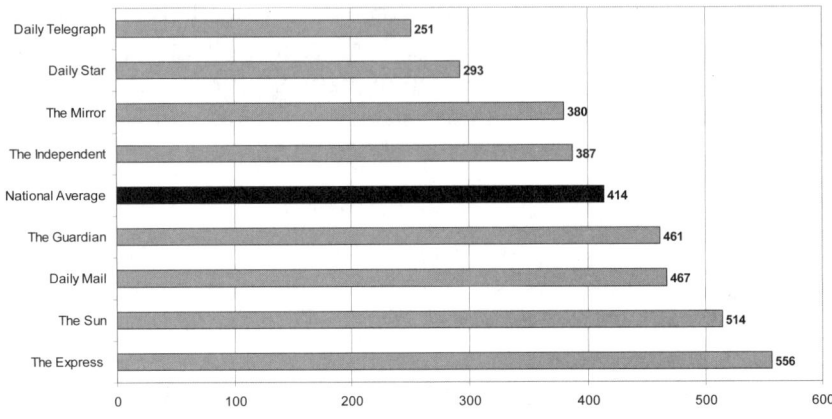

something that has been already highlighted by a number of authors (Schlesinger et al. 2001 and N. Blain and Hutchison 2007; Lugo-Ocando 2007). Because of this, these titles tend to incorporate news items that are not necessarily related to the issues raised by Scottish public opinion, while ignoring others that are much more urgent. Similarly, right-wing tabloids dedicate far more articles to asylum seekers matters than the national average for British newspapers.

This difference between national averages is even more noteworthy when we compare the coverage of asylum seeker issues of these three titles with the number of articles that the Scottish press dedicate to the subject on average. For example, in 2004, London-based tabloids operating in Scotland set aside far more space and headlines to issues such as asylum seekers than to other issues such as Scottish independence, flooding in the Highlands or even pressing economic matters, such as the decline in investment (all of which affected far more people's lives in Scotland than asylum issues). Between September 2003 and September 2004, these three tabloid newspapers published twice as many articles on the issue of asylum seekers than their closest Scottish competitors and three times more than the Scottish average.

This data suggests that the "issue" of asylum seekers is a debate that is brought to Scotland by the coverage of British national papers. Not only have these three newspapers have taken a more proactive role in covering asylum, but they have done so from an anti-asylum perspective.

Figure 3
National vs. Scottish Coverage of "Asylum Seeker"

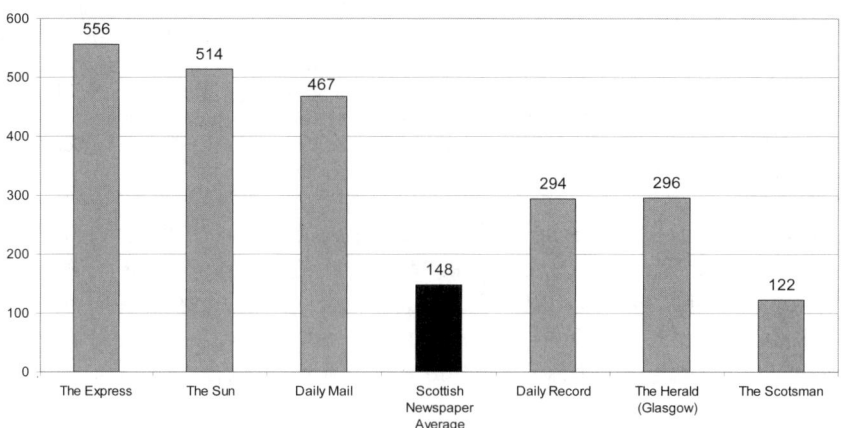

In evidence given to the Joint Committee on Human Rights of the UK parliament, the representative of The United Nations High Commissioner for Refugees (UNHCR), Bemma Donkoh, pointed out:

> Asylum seekers in the UK have been subjected to particularly hostile reporting in recent years by some sections of the UK press. It is the view of the UN High Commissioner for Refugees that the negative effects of this tone of reporting have not been tempered by enough substantive reports on conditions in countries of origin behind the claims of persecution and war, or stories highlighting the individual asylum claimants and their reasons for fleeing abroad.

Donkoh, went to suggest that:

> Guidance from authorities such as the Press Complaints Commission needs to be enhanced and expanded to take into account the shift in the misuse of terminology, in particular, towards a conflation of issues in regard to migration and refugee movements, as well as media reports that equate asylum seeking with terrorism suspects.

These observations from the representative of UNHCR are also highlighted by research done by Anthea Irwin from the University of Glasgow Caledonian. Irwin's work, which was commissioned by Oxfam's Asylum Positive Image Network, suggests that the indigenous Scottish press tends to be far less anti-asylum that their British counterparts:

> It is clear that the Scottish papers (as opposed to the Scottish editions of British papers) have a neutral to pro-asylum stance and the dominant discourse is that many asylum seekers are refugees who have fled from intolerable situations in their home countries and should be welcomed and treated with respect and dignity in Scotland.

Within this, though, there are sometimes nuances of meaning that contradict or confuse this discourse. When we include the Scottish editions of British papers (which
a great many people read) the picture is not so positive and a discourse that says
asylum seekers cause problems to the people of Britain (either individually or as a
result of government policy) is very much in evidence. It is interesting to note that
the British paper with a Scottish edition that is most pro-asylum, the Scottish Daily
Mirror, could be argued to be well contextualised for a Scottish audience whereas
the other three, the Scottish Daily Mail, the Scottish Daily Express and the Scottish
Sun, are much more problematic in this regard (Irwin 2006, 21).

Some additional data supports these claims. For example, the coverage of
asylum seekers has been emphasized by the pro-Conservative tabloid press
during Labour's term in office. For example, since the landslide victory of
the Labour party in 1997, *The Daily Mail's* readers have seen a substantial
increase in column inches dedicated to asylum-seeker issues:

Figure 4
The Daily Mail on Asylum Seekers 1996-2005

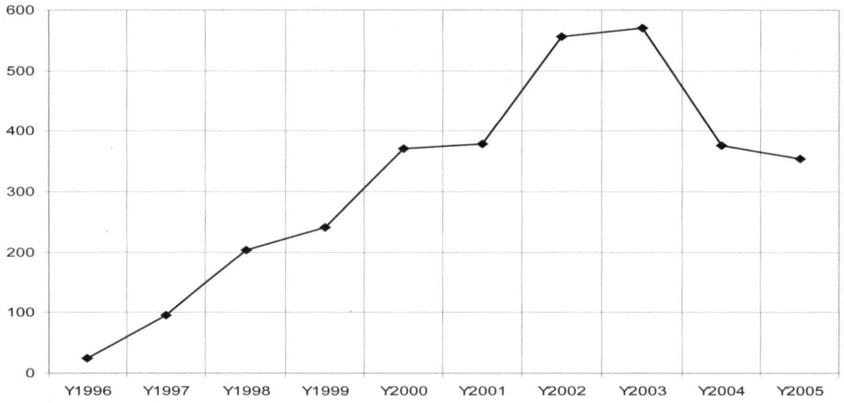

The peaks here correspond with the run-up to general elections in
both Scotland and the UK. Furthermore, a comparative analysis of the
coverage *The Scottish Sun* and the *Express* shows a similar trend. However, there was a slight difference in the Rupert Murdoch-owned paper,
The Scottish Sun, which seems to show a fall in the number of articles
published on the subject on 2001 in the run up to the general elections.
This apparent anomaly to the expected hypothesis of pre-electoral emphasis on asylum and immigration matters could be explained by the fact
that this newspaper supported Tony Blair's New Labour platform since
1995; after a meeting between the then leader of the opposition and the
head of News International, Rupert Murdoch in Australia (Herman &
McChesney 1997, 169).

However, as was discussed previously, the persistent negative cover-age of asylum seekers should not only be seen simply as a strategy to undermine Labour and mobilize a potential Conservative victory, but also as a way of strengthening the most right-wing voices inside all the politi-cal parties (including the Labour party in itself). This practice, which precedes even Enoch Powell's infamous xenophobic and racist "Rivers of Blood" speech[3] (Jones 1999, 9), allows those politicians who adopt a strong stance against asylum seekers and immigrants to increase their media exposure. The practice was rapidly incorporated into the notion of Thatcherism (Hall 1978) and mutated into New Labour, which constantly needed to demonstrate its hawkish attitude towards immigration.

Between 2001 and 2004, the biggest winner of this perverse prac-tice was perhaps David Blunkett, Member of Parliament for Sheffield Brightside, who as Home Office Secretary during these years, promoted some of the most draconian measures against immigrants and asylum seekers in recent times. Although resigning twice from the cabinet due to corruption scandals, he was rewarded with a column in the *Sun*. The biggest losers in this same period, on the other hand, were those politi-cians who have taken a more moderate stand in favor of immigration and asylum, who were sidelined.

Immigration policy has been identified as a key target for the oppo-sition in the past two general elections (2001 and 2005). In the last of these elections, the then Conservative leader, Michael Howard, enlisted the help of Lynton Crosby, the same man who advised Australia's Prime Minister, John Howard, in the last four elections as Liberal Party of Australia's chief electoral strategist. Crosby was responsible for the slo-gan "we decide who comes here" for the 2001 campaign in that country after the *Tampa Affair*. It is reported that he advised the Conservatives in the UK to repeat some of these same tactics in Britain (Watt 2005), including asking pro-Conservative papers to intensify their coverage of asylum seekers. The New Labour government in order to prove its hawkish credentials then responded by also toughening its immigration policy and discourse; something that they have done since then

However, after disappointing electoral results in the 2005 election, this strategy seemed initially exhausted. The new leadership of the Con-servative Party, headed by David Cameron went for a while softening its position on asylum seekers and immigration. He called on his follow-ers to embrace "genuine" asylum seekers fleeing from persecution and Cameron went to criticize former Home Secretary, David Blunkett, for his irresponsible language against asylum seekers:

He [Blunkett] was the person who talked about us being swamped: he used irresponsible language at the same time as having a chaotic immigration policy. I want the Conservative party to do the opposite: use moderate, reasonable, sensible language, and to have a policy that actually delivers (Hinsliff 2005).

This was not, however, a complete departure from the view of asylum seekers as an "issue." In that same interview for the Sunday paper *The Observer*, Cameron praised the cultural and economic benefits of immigration, but added:

We will have a big amount of emigration and immigration, but will also recognise that a responsible government needs to look at the level of net migration in terms of also providing good public services and having good community relations.

Furthermore, in the same piece Cameron promised to review the policy of capping at their numbers for the next manifesto, which technically meant to withdraw from the Geneva Convention of 1951.[4] This apparent new, softer approach was nevertheless short lived. After restraining itself on the topic of asylum seekers for a while, the *Daily Mail* published the headline "Asylum Seekers to get luxury houses" (March 15, 2006). This happened just a day after that the first ICM poll showed David Cameron and the Conservatives losing popular support among voters and slipping back into second place in the polls behind Labour.

Re-Conceptualizing Media Campaigns

One of the most important observations we can make at this stage in light of existing evidence is to suggest that the coverage of asylum seekers issues by tabloid newspapers in Scotland is done in such a way that its orientation and framing suggests agency. This systematic bias contributes in weakening liberal and progressive sectors among both main political parties. However, it is also important to recognize that the orchestration of racist narratives is only a means to push forward other agendas and interests.

Some of the research made into the newsrooms of these tabloids suggests no specific evidence of journalists being explicitly asked to adopt positions against asylum seekers or immigrants.[5] Instead, it can be argued that the organizational culture serves as the framework for the newspaper agenda, defining the way in which stories regarding asylum seekers will be covered. Because of this, there is awareness among staff in these newsrooms of the angle that they are expected to take and the sources that they need to interview. This was made clear to journalists who read the editorials published by these three tabloid newspapers during the year previous to the general election of 2005. For any journalist wanting to make a career inside those organizations, this was an unequivocal sign of what to write and what angle to take.

Between September 2004 and September 2005 the *Express* had 28 editorials and 104 headlines with the term "asylum seekers" which carried overwhelmingly negative connotations. The numbers in the cases of the *Sun* and the *Daily Mail* are similar. In that same period The *Sun* published 45 opinion pieces and editorials criticizing asylum seekers and immigration policy with little or no balance (that is, without a source contradicting the main assertion of the article) while the *Daily Mail* had 53 editorials and opinion pieces on this subject, equally excluding alternative points of view. Journalists of these newspapers follow this editorial line without necessarily having to be asked. Journalists of the *Express* wrote 238 articles that associated the term "asylum seeker" with "problem" and 123 articles associating "immigration policy" with "problem." This same newspaper published 175 articles that associated the word "terrorism" with "asylum seekers" and 145 with "immigrant."

It is important to observe that these newspapers are careful to avoid presenting these associations as an explicit attack coming from the Conservative party. One explanation could be that once explicitly presented as a political message of the Conservative party, the attack loses its power to mobilize the electorate since its render as partisan. During the same September 2004 and September 2005 period, the *Daily Mail,* for example, dedicated 244 articles to asylum seekers that questioned the ability of the Labour government to manage the issue of immigration (an issue in which both parties had a stake). However, of these only 81 made reference to Conservative party sources. In many cases, the practice violates the editorial policies of these same newspapers requiring journalists and sub editors to balance every piece with government sources and interviews with the opposition on matters of public policy. The explanation is simple, if the editor had complied with their own rule then the attack would have been explicitly rendered as a partisan discursive act. Instead, it is presented as a legitimate issue.

Particularly interesting is the way in which certain news pieces are orchestrated with other news subjects to reinforce criticism to government policy in other areas. For example, the *Sunday Express* published a feature article with the headline "Got AIDS? Welcome to Britain." This article, published on April 7, 2002 was about a Tanzanian woman who successfully managed to appeal under article three of the Human Rights Act against the decision of the British government to deny her asylum claim on "medical grounds." The article argued that asylum seekers with AIDS, TB, and other killer diseases were gaining permanent entry to Britain by exploiting what the article called "a dangerous loophole in the law" created by the European Convention of Human Rights. The feature was published at the time Labour's record on investing in and modernizing the National Health System (NHS) was being questioned as well as at the time that the euro was introduced to most of Western Europe. The article suggested that it would cost taxpayers some £15,000 a year to treat this woman and other similar "infected" asylum seekers. The campaign had a very clear objective: having fuelled fears among the general public by attacking the National Health System's growing waiting lists, newspaper articles like these redirected those fears towards new patients who were perceived impostors. This piece was also addressing tangentially at the anti-European position of the newspaper. The article presented the case as a loophole associated to Europe, this despite the fact that the European Convention of Human Rights is not part of the European Union's body of legislation.[6] This was, of course, never explained to the audiences.

Where Are Pro-Asylum Campaigns Failing?

If the right-wing tabloid press have tended to ride on rhetorical strategies that frame asylum seekers in racial terms (Gale 2004), this is not limited to newspaper campaigns alone. Baker and McEnery (2005) have already noted that, not only in British newspapers but also in the websites of institutions such as the Office of the United Nations High Commissioner for Refugees, it is possible to observe patterns that revealed linguistic traces of prior colonial discourses. Pro-asylum campaigns carried out by many non-governmental organizations (NGOs) also tend to frame their pro-asylum seeker campaigns in terms of race. As Melucci has highlighted:

> Racism and antiracism as collective phenomena should be located within the framework outlined above and not taken as unified facts, but as pluri-dimensional phenomena. The defensive resistance to the "other" is easily transformed into an aggressive attitude against the threat that the other represents. But also the claims to reciprocal understanding and communication are not entirely free from defensive attitudes (in Bulmer and Solomos 1999, 421).

This is because anti-racist campaigns in Europe are based on rhetorical constructions that derive from colonial racism. Alana Letin believes that because of this, anti-racism cannot be researched sociologically without a concomitant and interrelated historicization of the political idea of race and the rise of modern racism. This is "fundamental to a full understanding of the political project of anti-racism" (2004: 9).

My own observations of anti-racist campaigns in Scotland indicate that they also tend to respond with similar *racialized* criteria, that is *othering* asylum seekers in their own narratives (Lugo 2007). This is particularly important since by so doing the pro-asylum camp broadly uses and reinforces the same rhetorical strategies and stereotypes when making their own case in defense of asylum seekers. In this sense, Karim Murji has highlighted the lack of awareness about how these images might be read in diverse ways and questions those who launch these campaigns (2006). Examining the campaign launched by the Commission of Racial Equality (CRE) in the UK, Murji concludes that the use of racial stereotypes by anti-racists in the UK is "questionable" (2006: 278). In the case of the two pro-asylum campaigns used here, Oxfam Positive Image Project and One Scotland Many Cultures of the Scottish Parliament, there is a recurrent feature to refer to asylum seekers as an issue; highlighting the problematic discursive structure put in place by the mainstream media. One of the main problems is that these campaigns are designed to counterbalance negative coverage and perceptions, therefore expected to refer to the same categories in similar terms. Hence, the embrace the concept of asylum seeker without questioning its moral and legal validity in terms of international law; they tend to draw from present and past experiences but without questioning the fundamental function of exclusion that derives from nationhood and overall they fall short—because of institutional compromises—from highlighting the use of implicit racial narrative by media partisan interests. The positive aspects however is that they do recognize that the problem goes beyond media practices.

Another important point to highlight is that they present the characteristics of media campaigns in the most classical terms. In fact, NGOs and grassroots movements, which dominate this camp are aware of the need to deploy PR strategies and deal with public opinion in a sophisticated manner (Demetrious 2002, 151). This is nothing new; back in the early 1990s, the Scottish Refugee Council (SRC)[7] launched a media campaign that incorporated the most important elements of media campaigns in terms of creative strategy, media strategy and marketing. The campaign, which stills runs, aimed at changing attitudes towards asylum seekers and refugees. The chief executive of the SRC, Sally Daghlian has highlighted the need to "use every means available to counter negative public attitudes."[8]

In more recent decades, NGOs and grassroots movements in Scotland have come to understand also that they need to embrace practices such as media relations, communication management and marketing, research of target audiences, definition of messages and discourses, media strategy and evaluation of objectives against achievements (Backer et al. 1992, 31). These groups and organizations are well aware that, in some cases, they are an "NGO brand," a brand that sets ethical standards and that is perceived as a legitimate voice of "society" (Beaudoin 2004, 369), therefore able to communicate politically with the rest of the mainstream society.

In this context, Oxfam can also be described as an NGO that raises legitimate concerns and counters prevalent discourses to a certain extent. It is part of the institutionalization of militant demands that can now articulate alternative discourses within the mainstream. Therefore, these types of campaigns require analysis in terms of the *positionality* and *self-referentiality* of the institutions and actors involved. The same can be said in relation to the Scottish Parliament's campaign "One Scotland, Many Cultures," overall in its quest for legitimacy after being established by the Scotland Act in 1998.

Despite having fewer resources than the Scottish Executive's campaign (One Scotland, Many Culture), Oxfam-Scotland has embraced the need to adopt similar practices to those of the government and corporations in terms of marketing their messages and targeting specific audiences. Norma McKinnon, leading officer of the Asylum Positive Images Network (APIN) in Scotland between 2004 and 2005 recalls that this effort began with an assessment of the problem:

> The first objective for the Asylum Positive Images Project was to measure the current situation by studying the language used in news paper reports. It then looked at the effect this has on what the public and politicians think. For this we commissioned two independent MORI polls. Then we surveyed 100 asylum seekers asking them which newspapers they read and what they thought about the coverage of asylum issues.[9]

Oxfam's officers were not only aware of the fact that it was important to conduct research before launching their campaign; they were also very conscientious about the need to understand the parameters and direction of that research. McKinnon points out that before launching the campaign, the project looked at emerging debates in Scotland, which she believed differed from the rest of the UK. From the beginning, "the project aimed at building further bridges with the media in Scotland." In terms of classical PR models, it can be said that this campaign went beyond the press agentry model described by Jim Grunig (Fawkes in Theaker 2001, 11), adopting the "public information model," where "practitioners both sought information from, and gave information to, publics" (Grunig and Grunig in Grunig 1992, 312).

The original concept of APIN was developed in Wales (Threadgold 2005) and later transplanted to Scotland. It was based on the notion of "building bridges," which promoted networking between different actors involved in asylum issues, the media and official bodies. It produced several leaflets and books for journalists in conjunction with organizations such as the National Union of Journalists and Amnesty International. It also organized forums and events with the aim of gathering journalists and asylum seekers in the same room. The most important leaflet of the campaign was a guide for journalists on how to cover issues relating to asylum seekers. "Fair Play: a guide for journalists in Scotland" was produced by a team of experts who summarized the most important aspects of the subject and addressed the most common mistakes made by journalists. The guide was comprehensive, but there is no evidence that it made a difference to London-based tabloids (who did receive the booklet according to the organizers). The explanation is simple; the campaign was premised on the institutionalized assumption that anti-asylum campaigns were founded on a lack of awareness rather than on a structural bias in explaining anti-asylum campaigns. I say that Oxfam "institutionally assumed" this position, because, as a participant in the steering group that oversaw the design and implementation of the campaign, I became increasingly aware of the unwillingness to confront directly the tabloids (even though this was never the intention). The leaflet was nevertheless well received by most of the media people (which it is not the same thing as saying it was adopted in everyday newsroom practices). It tended to preach to the converted (I found that the center-left tabloids made far more use of this leaflet and other resources offered to them). The project was somehow more successful in altering the norm. For example, after intense lobbying from Oxfam and other institutions and political leaders, the Press Complaints Commission asked newspapers to moderate their coverage of asylum seekers and to stop using terms such as "illegal" or "bogus" asylum seekers. Even though some tabloids persist in using these terms, there are now at least some grounds for making formal complaints.

The other case study, "One Scotland, Many Cultures" campaign was launched on September 2002 by the Scottish Executive. It was originally designed to tackle racism and raise awareness of racist attitudes, high-lighting its negative impact on society. The campaign later dealt with issue of sectarianism between Catholics and Protestants in Scotland, although it still places particular emphasis on asylum seekers, both in terms of message and image. It was one of the first media initiatives from the recently created Scottish Executive after devolution[10] and not only included the media campaign but a series of other initiatives such as legislation for the workplace and the monitoring of minorities' rights. In the context of this campaign, the Executive offers practical support and funding for a range of initiatives to tackle racism and provides information on the campaign's web site. The most recent phase of this campaign made used of advertisement efforts, for which a budget in 2005 of almost £800,000 was been assigned (US $1.4 million). This amount was aimed at developing, producing and airing ads for radio and television, placing newspaper ads and banners on buses and on the high street. This budget was up 36 percent in 2007 from the previous year, but down 45 percent from the first year of the campaign, when allocated £1.4 million (US $2.5 million). The reasons for the variable nature of this allocation throughout its three years are unclear, although it could be suggested that had more to do with the political process of budgetary discussions in Parliament than with the actual achievements or needs of the campaign; which received assessment from an independent company hired by the Scottish Government.

Despite the amount of resources and the implementation of a system of evaluation, the "One Scotland, Many Cultures" campaign has not escaped criticism. Positive Action in Housing, a charity that works closely with Scotland's ethnic minorities, has questioned the success of the Scottish Executive's efforts to tackle racism by means of this campaign in its 2005 annual report. This NGO claims that it has had no significant impact on reducing racism:

> Primarily because its message is drowned out and rendered ineffective by the constant scapegoating of asylum seekers and the xenophobic and Islamophobic outpourings from some politicians and the media (BBC 2005a).

The campaign made a series of television adverts that were only broadcast on Scottish Independent Television and some cable channels in Scotland. One of the adverts figured an Eastern European man and his son who appear to be talking about their arrival experience, saying that, despite things being hard at first, they were later welcomed by the native population. At the end, however, the advert makes it clear that this was not this man's words but those of a Scottish man who emigrated in the 1950s from Scotland to Canada. The intention is clear; to draw a parallel between the situations lived by Scottish people in the past and that of asylum seekers now arriving to Scotland. The problem with this ad is that, visually speaking, the agents are all also too similar: a white man talks to other white men.

A second ad presented a group of people from different ethnic backgrounds performing diverse tasks. The main message is that Scotland is a place of diversity. The ad however portrayed in most cases the traditional stereotypical role assigned to the individuals of each ethnic origin. The Indian old man as a shopkeeper, the young Pakistanis as kitchen workers, the Chinese woman as a doctor and so on. The notion of diversity is then sidelined by the underlying narrative that everyone has their place, namely the traditional role that society assigned them. This was, at least, my own reading of the commercial as an immigrant living in Scotland. This also suggests that the reading of this ad needs to be assessed not only in terms of the intended target-audience but also with regard to the subject it refers to.

The third television piece features a man who enters a cybercafé and sends an email with a racist joke. The message immediately starts spreading out to other computers in garages, schools and offices. The email causes the screens to go black and the computers crash one by one until the computers in the cybercafé crash too. The people looking at all the computers happen to be from ethnic minorities and the man who sent originally the message looks around him in shame. The final message is on the screen of a computer in the form of an email saying: "Don't spread racism, it's a virus." The problem with this third ad is that a) the man who sends the original racist joke is a white working-class young man (thereby reinforcing the stereotype that racism is predominantly a working class problem) and b) it assumes that it racism operates underground, when in reality it is in the mainstream media that we find the most obscene racist narratives.

As some authors have already suggested, the reading of these types of television adverts need to be read using a dual perspective: semantic and pragmatic (Molero de Cabezas 2002). The "One Scotland, Many Cultures" campaign shows that, irrespective of the amount of resources deployed, this type of campaign cannot counter the reiterative and orchestrated messages delivered by the media. Not because they are under exposed or under-resourced, but because they have fundamentally they fail to challenge the predominant narratives.

Indeed, it is already widely accepted that anti-racist efforts in many places have had little impact on public attitudes since they fail—in many cases—to address underlying everyday racist attitudes and behaviors, which frequently are allowed to go unchallenged (Essed 1991; Bhavnani et al. 2005). If we add to this the fact that anti-racist campaigns in Scotland have to compete against powerful racist media campaigns that are presented as legitimate media coverage, then we start to understand why the pro-asylum campaigns seem so ineffective. In defense of pro-asylum campaigns we should say that this is not something that other campaigns have had to confront in the past. Campaigns against drink driving, disability awareness and domestic violence developed in Scotland, and often compared to anti-racist campaigns in academic and professional analysis, had no contradictory narrative coming from the mainstream media to neutralize their message. At least not on the scale that anti-racist campaigns have had to deal with. Anti-racist campaigns in general and pro-asylum campaigns in particular, are often overwhelmed by a torrent of messages that undermines each and every argument made. Using a common metaphor, we can say that they are just a drop of water in a very wide ocean; they should be at least as distinctive as a drop of oil.

Indeed, the other problem that these campaigns face is that, as discursive acts, they relate to the discursive subject using similar categories. Therefore their function as counter discursive acts is nullified by the fact that they play the same game in narrative terms. In so doing, they hold to boundaries imposed by the implicit racist appeals rather than expositing them as such. Direct confrontation with the right-wing tabloid press is too much of a risk for some NGOs, as the experience of the Red Cross in the UK demonstrates (vilified and attacked by the tabloid press). There are precedents for this type of behavior in civil rights, for example in the US the anti-lynching campaigns by the NAACP in the 1920s rarely questioned the fundamental premises of those narratives supporting lynching as racist (such as the suppose inferiority or "natural" rape tendencies of African-Americans). In the same way, pro-asylum seekers campaigns in the UK rarely expose their counterparts as racist. Neither have they have gone yet as far as to object the use of terms such as "asylum seekers," "removal centres" or "tolerance." In order to do so, they would have to question some of their own language and premises. This is perhaps too much to expect from institutions that operate and depend on broad normative acceptance. In any case, more than the institution itself, it is the established norm that prevents the bar from being raised in order to deliver more radical discursive acts. In other words, the problem with these campaigns is the complexity of their own *positionality* in reading anti-asylum campaigns. A reading that strategically uses a responsive *self-referentiality* in order to claim the moral high ground but that fails to essentialize and question the disturbing basic terms that frame and define anti-asylum campaigns in Scotland as London-based colonial nostalgia.

Conclusions

Of course, we cannot blame solely campaigns for the riots in Paris or in Birmingham in 2005. These events, which have increasingly become a recurrent and mediated spectacle for Europe, are the manifestation of a deeper and far more complex set of problems linked to racism as an ideology, which is both institutionalized in the State and spread across vast segments of society. In the case of Scotland, the situation is worsened by the fact that pro-refugee campaigns have to compete with powerful and well-resourced media campaigns by London-based right-wing tabloids. These pro-asylum campaigns, even though well intentioned, nevertheless compete by embracing in their own discourses similar categories to that of their counterparts.

Anti-asylum campaigns delivered by the London-based tabloids create an additional problem, neutralizing efforts to change public perceptions of asylum seekers in Scotland. Indeed, everyday racist discursive acts are constantly being reinforced by subtle and overt narratives from media outlets with a political agenda that stirs up moral panic to mobilize opinion towards the political right. In doing so, they further undermine the possibility of success of anti-racist efforts. Therefore, their responsibility is not only in exacerbating existing tensions but also in preventing efforts to reduce those tensions. To make matters worse, since the London bombings of July 7, 2005, the binary distinctions that use nationalism and culture to sustain racist narratives in the media, which retain the imprint of colonial values, have increasingly become legitimatized even among traditionally more pro-asylum liberal newspapers, which are now are pressured to "help preserve liberal cultural heritage."

Pro-asylum campaigns also need to reflect on the colonial legacy of their own discursive acts. Indeed, their anti-racist efforts construct in many cases their discourses in similar racialized terms because of the "intervening" nature of NGOs and governments. Furthermore, the straightjacket imposed by institutional compromises constrains the potential of these campaigns to challenge prevalent discursive acts. It also limits their ability to question some of these discourses as implicit racism in a more radical and effective way. Most important, many of these campaigns dismiss critical discourses while embracing more traditional responses; hoping that marketing strategies will be enough to counterbalance anti-asylum campaigns. In so doing, they fail to recognize that powerful racist narratives are encapsulated in these discourses.

These pro-asylum campaigns do perform, nevertheless, an important function in changing the norm. In the case of Scotland, the reaction to dawn raids in which the police enter houses of asylum seekers in the middle of the night or early hours of the morning to place whole families under arrest have slowly been challenged by local communities and the Scottish Executive (which have no power, however, to intervene since it is still a prerogative of London). In 2005 about 200 campaigners gathered at immigration offices in Glasgow to protest over the treatment of refugees in the city (BBC 2005b). What is interesting about these protests is that they have questioned the fundamentals of anti-asylum discourses; both in terms of articulating a message and in terms of the nature of the protests. Not only are the participants from some of the poorest white working-class areas of Glasgow, who against all prevalent narratives about the class-location of racists, have identified themselves with the asylum seekers, but they have also gone on to question the morality of deportation and imprisonment. In so doing, the protesters have bypassed the complex set of devious legal paraphernalia often used to justify dawn raids. They have questioned the legitimacy, not only of the discursive acts justifying removals, but also of those who collude with them (newspapers and police). The protests have multiplied, despite initially been ignored by the London-based tabloid newspapers, who have recently had to bow to the reality of these grassroots movements and acknowledge their existence and power (to the point that now some media have embraced ant-raid protests as a legitimate cause). These protests have derived from anger and frustration of locals against the forcible removal of asylum seekers (who they see as their neighbors), show equally solidarity with people no longer lost in the anonymity of the term asylum seeker. These grassroots campaigns offer a new and distinctive way forward, one that I hope we all start paying more attention to.

Notes

1.   I am more than aware of the problematic nature of using such categories such as right, left, and center.
2.   For example, *The Scottish Sun* (The regional version of Rupert Murdoch's *The Sun*), replaced the local title *The Daily Record* as the leading newspaper in Scotland, by

cutting its retail price by a third. Despite the convergence with local content of other Scotland-based newspapers, it has nevertheless important implications in terms of the news agenda. MacMillan, A. (January 7, 2007). *New tune for the Record as PM title becomes freesheet.* http://scotlandonsunday.scotsman.com/business. cfm?id=31782007 (accessed on January 12, 2007).

3. The Rivers of Blood speech was a controversial speech delivered by the British politician Enoch Powell (1912-1998) about immigration and socialist anti-discrimination legislation on April 20, 1968. The central political issue addressed in the speech was not immigration itself. The speech focused on the introduction by the Labour government of anti-discrimination legislation that would effectively criminalize the expression of racial prejudice in certain areas of British life. Powell never held another senior political post, but gained considerable public support from the public.

4. The 1951 Convention relating to the Status of Refugees is the key legal document in defining who is a refugee, their rights and the legal obligations of states. The 1967 Protocol removed geographical and temporal restrictions from the Convention.

5. Interviews with two sub-editors of London-based tabloids in Glasgow in June 22, 2006 and June 28, 2006. Anonymity was granted.

6. There was a corollary to this episode. A year later the Labour government proposed to deny AIDS/HIV treatment to asylum seekers, something that was universally resisted and rejected by all medical bodies in the UK.

7. Created in 1985, the Scottish Refugee Council is an independent charity dedicated to providing advice, information and assistance to asylum seekers and refugees living in Scotland. It provides specialist services in areas such as housing and welfare, education and employment, family reunion, women's issues, community development, the media and the arts. The SRC plays a leading role in policy development and campaign on refugee issues.

8. Sally Daghlian, Chief Executive of the SRC, speaking at the event. Negative attitudes—meeting the challenge on September 19, 2005 in Glasgow.

9. Interview with Norma McKinnon, coordinator of OXFAM's Asylum Positive Image Campaign in Scotland on March 12, 2005.

10. Scotland was offered a referendum on devolution by the Labour Party in the build up to the 1997 election. This manifesto promise was honoured in 1997 just four months after the general election and a process of devolution began for Scotland which led to a Scottish Parliament based in Edinburgh coming into being in 1999.

References

Anderson, B. 1983. *Imagined Communities: Reflections on the Origin and Spread of Nationalism.* London: Verso.

Arterton, F.C. 1987. *Las estrategias informativas de las campañas presidenciales.* Caracas: Ateneo de Caracas, USIS.

Awkward, M. 1995. Negotiating Difference: Race, Gender, and the Politics of Positionality. Chicago: University of Chicago Press.

Backer, T. E., Rogers, E.M. and Sopory, P. 1992. *Designing Health Communication Campaigns: What Works?* London: Sage Publications.

Bailey, O. G. and Harindranath, R. 2005. Racialised 'othering'. In: Allan, S., (Ed.) *Journalism: Critical Issues.* pp. 274-286. Berkshire, England: Open University Press.

Baker, P. and McEnery, T. 2005. A corpus-based approach to discourses of refugees and asylum seekers in UN and newspaper texts. *Journal of Language and Politics.* Vol. 4, No. 2. Pages 197–226.

Barker, M. 1981. *The New Racism: Conservatives and the Ideology of the Tribe.* London: Junction Books.

BBC. January 22, 2007. *Tabloids defend asylum coverage.* http://news.bbc.co.uk/1/hi/uk_politics/6288539.stm (accessed on March 2, 2007).

BBC. May 25, 2006. *Home Office 'damaged' by scandals.* http://news.bbc.co.uk/1/hi/uk_politics/5017028.stm (accessed on July 21, 2006).

BBC. September 2, 2005a. *Racism campaign is 'ineffective'.* http://news.bbc.co.uk/1/hi/scotland/4206772.stm (accessed on March 12, 2007).

BBC. September 17, 2005b. Protest over refugee dawn raids. http://news.bbc.co.uk/1/hi/scotland/4254490.stm (accessed on March, 12, 2007).

Beaudoin, J. P. 2004. Non-governmental organisations, ethics and corporate public relations. *Journal of Communication Management.* Vol. 8, No. 4. pp. 66-371.

Beckford, M. July 12, 2007. Ban 'racist' Tintin book, says CRE. *The Telegraph.* http://www.telegraph.co.uk/news/main.jhtml?xml=/news/2007/07/12/ntintin112.xml (accessed July 12, 2007).

Bhavnani, R., Mirza, H. S., & Meetoo, V. 2005. *Tackling the Roots of Racism: Lessons for Success.* London: The Polity Press.

Blacklock, M. December 6, 2005. Now the cross is banned; No crucifixes but school allows Sikhs to carry daggers. *The Daily Express.*

Blain, N. and Hutchison, D. (editors). 2007. *The Media in Scotland.* Edinburgh: Edinburgh University Press.

Bulmer, M. and Solomos, J. 1999. *Racism.* Oxford: Oxford University Press.

Cobb, R. and Elder, C. 1983. *Participation in American Politics: The dynamics of agenda-building.* Baltimore: John Hopkins University Press.

Coombs, W. T.; Holladay, S.; Reynolds, F. 2006. *Public Relations a Critical Introduction.* London: Blackwell Publishing Limited.

Dearing, J. W. and Rogers, E. M. 1996. *Agenda-Setting.* London: Sage Publications.

Demetrious, K. 2002. Grassroots energy: A case study of active citizenship and public communication in risk society. *Journal of Communication Management.* Vol. 7, No. 2, pp. 148-155.

Essed, P. 1991. *Understanding Everyday Racism: An Interdisciplinary Theory.* London: Sage Publications.

Fairclough, A. 2001. *Better Day Coming.* New York: Penguin Books.

Fitzgerald, T. 2008. *Discourse on Civility and Barbarity.* Oxford: Oxford University Press.

Fowler, R. 1991. *Language in the News: Discourse and Ideology in the Press.* London: Routledge.

Fuller, J. 1996. *News Values.* Chicago: Chicago University Press.

Gale, P. 2004. The refugee crisis and fear. *Journal of Sociology.* Vol. 40, No. 4, pp. 321-340.

Gilroy, P. 1987. *There ain't no black in the Union Jack.* London: Routledge.

Glaser, J. 1996. *Race, Campaign Politics, and Realignment in the South.* New Haven: Yale University Press.

Grunig, J. E. 1992 Editor. *Excellence in Public Relations and Communication Management.* Hillsdale, NJ: Erlbaum Associates.

Hall, S. 1997. Racist Ideologies and the Media. In: Marris, Paul and Thornham, Sue, (Ed.). *Media Studies: A Reader.* Edinburgh: Edinburgh University Press.

Hall, S., Crichter, C., Jefferson, T., Clarke, J. and Roberts, B. (Editors). 1978. *Policing the crisis: mugging, the state, and law and order.* London: Macmillan.

Herman S. E. and Chomsky, N. 1994. *Manufacturing Consent. The Political Economy of the Mass Media.* London: Vintage.

Herman, S. E., & McChesney, R. 1997. *The Global Media, the new missionaries of corporate capitalism.* London: Cassell.

Hinsliff, G.a.R.A. December 18, 2005. Cameron: I'm the real voice of liberal UK. *The Observer.*

Irwin, A. 2007. *Reporting Asylum in Scotland.* Glasgow: Oxfam Scotland.

Jesuit Refugee Service (2007). *Detention in the context of forcible return of irregular migrants.* http://www.detention-in-europe.org/index.php?option=com_content&task=view&id=103&Itemid=132 (accessed on June 23, 2007).

Jones, N. 1999. *Sultans of Spin.* London: Victor Gollancz.

Kundnani, A. 2007. *The End of Tolerance.* London: Pluto Press.

L'Etang, J. and Pieczka, M. (editors). 2006. *Public Relations: Critical Debates and Contemporary Problems.* London: Lawrence Erlbaum Associates.

L'Etang, J. (2005). Critical public relations: Some reflections. *Public Relations Review.* Vol. 31, pp. 521-526.

L'Etang, J., & Pieczka, M. 1996. *Critical Perspectives in Public Relations.* London: Thomson Learning.

Law, I. 2002. *Race in the News.* London: Palgrave.

Lentin, A. 2004. *Racism & Anti-Racism in Europe.* London: Pluto Press.

Lewis, J., Inthorn, S. and Wahl-Jorgensen, K. 2005. *Citizens or Consumers? What the media tell us about political participation.* London: Open University Press.

Lloyd, H.M. 1973. *Standards and ethics of public relations practice: first report on the research study conducted for the Professional Standards Committee of the International Public Relations Association.* London: IPRA.

Lugo-Ocando, J. 2007. *A Tale of Donkeys, Swans and Racism.* Communication & Social Change. Vol. 1, No. 1. Pages 22-37.

Lynn, N. and Lea, S. 2003. A phantom menace and the new apartheid: The social construction of asylum-seekers in the United Kingdom. *Discourse & Society.* Vol. 14, 425-452.

McCombs, M. E. 1975. Mass Communication in Political campaigns: Information, Gratification and Persuasions. S. Chaffee (Editor). *Political Communication: Issues and Strategies for Research.* Beverly Hills (California): Sage Publications, Inc.

McNair, B. 1995. *An Introduction to Political Communication.* London: Routledge.

Mendelberg, T. 2001. *The Race Card. Campaign Strategy, Implicit Messages, and the Norm of Equality.* Princeton, USA: Princeton University Press.

Molero de Cabeza, L. 2002. *El discurso político en las ciencias humanos y sociales.* Caracas: Fonacit.

Murji, K. 2006. Using racial stereotypes in anti-racist campaigns. *Ethnic and Racial Studies* Vol. 29, No. 2. Pages 260-280.

Nicks, G. August 21, 2003. Police hunt rustlers after 9 are snatched; Asylum Seekers Eat Our Donkeys. *The Daily Star,* Page 14.

Office for National Statistics 2004. *UK population grows to 59.2 million.* http://www.statistics.gov.uk/CCI/nugget.asp?ID=1039&Pos=1&ColRank=2&Rank=224 (accessed on September 12, 2005).

Office for National Statistics. 2003. *National Statistics Omnibus Survey 1990-2003.* London: HMS Stationary.

OXFAM, NUJ, SRC, and AI. 2005. *Fair Play.* Edinburgh: OXFAM-Scotland.

OXFAN. 2006. UK Poverty Programme. Myth 8: "Asylum-seekers should be locked up." http://www.oxfamgb.org/ukpp/safe/myths8.htm (accessed on March 12, 2007).

Parkinson, M. and Ekachai, D. G. 2005. *International and Intercultural Public Relations: A Campaign Case Approach.* Boston, MA: Allyn & Bacon.

PCC. 2003. Report 65. Nuradin Dirie, Chair of the Somali Coordinating Committee. *Press Complaints Commission.* http://www.pcc.org.uk/news/index.html?article=MzMxNQ== (accessed on March 11, 2006).

Puchan, H., Pieczka, M. and L'Etang, J. 1999. Rethinking PR evaluation. *Journal of Communication Management.* Vol. 4, No. 2, pp. 164-175.

Reisigl, M. and Wodak, R. 2001. *Discourse and discrimination: rhetorics of racism and antisemitism.* London: Routledge.

Rice, E.R. and Atkin, C.K. 1989. *Public Communications Campaigns.* 2nd ed., London: Sage Publications.

Sallot, L. M., Cameron, G. T. and Lariscy, R. A. W. 1998. Pluralistic Ignorance and Professional Standards: Underestimating Professionalism of Our Peers in Public Relations. *Public Relations Review.* Vol. 24, No. 1, pp. 1-19.

Scottish Executive. 2001. *Population decline predicted.* http://www.scotland.gov.uk/pages/news/2001/11/p_SE4356.aspx (accessed on July 2, 2005).

Seib, P. and Fitzpatrick, K. 1994. *Public Relations Ethics.* New York: Wadsworth Publishing.

Schlesinger, P., Miller, D., and Dinan, W. 2001. *Open Scotland? Journalists, Spin Doctors and Lobbyists.* Edinburgh: Edinburgh University Press.

Sullivan, M. July 4, 2003. Asylum gang had 2 swans for roasting. *The Sun,* Page 1.

Theaker, A. 2001. *The Public Relations Handbook.* London: Routledge.

Threadgold, T. 2005. *Asylum Media Project in Wales 2003-04.* Cardiff: Comic Relief.

UNHCR. 2006. *The State of the World's Refugees 2006 —Chapter 2 Safeguarding asylum: Box 2.3 The Tampa Affair: interception and rescue at sea.* http://www.unhcr.org/publ/PUBL/4444d3c320.html (accessed on March 15, 2007).

Van Dijk, T. 1991. *Racism in the Press.* London: Routledge.

Waisbord, Silvio (2001). *Family tree of theories, methodology and strategies in development communication: convergences and differences.* http://www.comminit.com/strategicthinking/stsilviocomm/sld-1774.html (accessed on March 23 2005).

Ward, I. 2002. The Tampa, Wedge Politics and a Lesson for Political Journalism. *Australian Journalism Review.* Vo. 1, pp. 20-32.

Watt, N. January 28, 2005. The Guardian profile: Lynton Crosby. *The Guardian.* http://www.guardian.co.uk/guardianpolitics/story/0,,1400262,00.html (accessed on March 3, 2006).

Wilson, G. August 6, 2005. Deportation not fair, says extremist (on benefits). *The Daily Mail.* http://www.dailymail.co.uk/pages/live/articles/news/news.html?in_article_id=358382&in_page_id=1770 (accessed on December 12, 2006).

Wodak, R. and Meyer, M. 2001. *Methods of critical discourse analysis.* London: SAGE.

Wodak, R. et al. 1998. *The discursive construction of national identity.* Edinburgh: Edinburgh University Press.

Anti-Racist Campaigning and Nation-Building in Namibia

Ingrid A. Lehmann

Introduction

The United Nations' support for Namibia has had a long and varied history that is now, two decades after Namibian independence, fully ripe for evaluation. The UN's peacekeeping operation, which was deployed in Namibia in 1989-90, has generally been assessed by scholars and practitioners as one of the more successful UN missions, and it is often seen as a role model for other multi-dimensional peacekeeping operations.[1] UNTAG (United Nations Transition Assistance Group) was also the first UN peacekeeping operation in which a comprehensive information campaign was conducted, even though UNTAG had no explicit mandate for either nation-building *or* for conducting information campaigns.[2]

This chapter explores the development and practice of UNTAG's information program, i.e., the communication arm of this UN-run intervention in the long-standing civil and regional conflict in southern Africa, a conflict which had destabilized the region for several decades. UNTAG's third-party intervention transformed the territory of Namibia from an apartheid-dominated, externally-governed state to an independent, democratic government with constitutional guarantees of racial equality.

Notwithstanding the lack of a specific information mandate, the UN Secretariat, acting in the ad-hoc fashion so typical of many UN peacekeeping operations, conducted educational and information campaigns which were designed to persuade the Namibians of the value of independence, and to win their consent to the necessary political processes. In so doing, UNTAG introduced an impromptu but effective campaign against racism and for nation-building.

One of the many paradoxes of United Nations programs and policies is that in the field of anti-racism where the UN has one of its longest records due to the development of international human rights law, beginning with the International Convention on the Elimination of All Forms of Racial Discrimination in 1965, action in the practice of the world organization had been notably weak. The UN was continually frustrated by South Africa's decades of defiance and even the use of far-reaching sanctions against the apartheid-regime appeared to have little impact.

As Mark Alleyne has pointed out, the UN's anti-racist projects often remained ritualistic and consisted of the rote passage of General Assembly resolutions[3] and the designation of events, such as the International Year for Action to Combat Racism and Racial Discrimination in 1971, as well as three decades (1973-83, 1983-93, and 1993-2003) and three world conferences (1978, 1983, and 2001) dedicated to this theme. The UN also conducted extensive anti-apartheid propaganda campaigns from UN headquarters in New York, but those remained divorced from the project-at-hand, the independence of Namibia. Furthermore, the United Nations' bureaucratic compartmentalization had separated its anti-apartheid programs from the Namibian independence program,[4] a compartmentalization that prevented a comprehensive formulation of a broad-based anti-racist political strategy by the UN Secretariat.

For these reasons, the reopening of the Namibia negotiations in 1988 after a twelve-year hiatus, posed a great opportunity for the international community to make progress in southern Africa. Namibian independence can thus be seen as a first step in the fall of the apartheid regime, a fact that is recognized by many observers but still not adequately analyzed from a political communications perspective.

This chapter will analyze how, by injecting a multi-cultural and multi-racial presence in a society long dominated by apartheid and master-minded by South African occupiers, the UN applied its organizational credo of "cultural internationalism."[5] Akira Iriye's concept, which sees *internationalism* as "an idea, a movement, or an institution that seeks to reformulate the nature of relations among nations through cross-national cooperation and interchange,"[6] is applied in this study to the UN's anti-racist campaigns in Namibia. Information campaigns, in the context of discourse theory,[7] are seen as communicative practices that are used to construct internationalism. Following Alleyne's constructivist approach to UN peacekeeping,[8] which postulates that changes in identity politics between parties to a conflict can play a role in ending war and maintaining peace, it becomes clear that information campaigns are vital tools of the United Nations in the promotion of its goals of universal human rights values and racial equality.[9]

The Challenge of South West Africa/Namibia for the United Nations

The vast, sparsely settled, and mineral-rich territory previously known as South West Africa[10] was administered by South Africa under a League of Nations mandate, which was supposed to prepare the country for independence. However, in 1948 South Africa began its de-facto annexation of the territory by granting the South West African white population seats in the South African parliament. The UN General Assembly revoked South Africa's mandate in 1966, declaring its administration "illegal." A long tug-of-war between South Africa and the international community then ensued; this ended only in 1988 when South Africa agreed to a peace plan. That plan assigned to the United Nations a monitoring and supervisory role during a transitional period that would lead to independence.

For several decades, a long war between South Africa and the South West African People's Organization (SWAPO) was waged largely on Namibia's northern border with Angola. The conflict also engaged the Soviet Union, Cuba, and East Germany, as well as several Western countries that supported South Africa to varying degrees. The war along the border between Namibia and Angola became increasingly costly in terms of lives lost and resources spent, so that an internationally negotiated peace plan, named "435" after Security Council resolution 435 of 1978, laid the groundwork for the transition to independence under UN supervision.

In Namibia, a quarter-century of German colonial rule[11] was followed by South African apartheid-based administration,[12] which imposed divisive racial policies and racist mindsets. Consequently, mistrust, resentment and hatred were widespread among the eleven different ethnic and racial groups. Among whites, many shared the South African belief in "god-given" racial hierarchies that had for so long assigned them privileged social and economic positions. Namibians of mixed racial backgrounds, who often held service positions in South West African business establishments, caught as they were between rigid racial lines, tended to be cautious and quiescent.

Over the years, South Africa had developed a powerful propaganda machine that used the educational system and the media for its purposes. Pervasive apartheid laws governed all aspects of society, and were enforced by civilian South African administrators as well as the police and the military. Paramilitary units, particularly the notorious "Koevoet" (Crowbar), which formed counter-insurgency units in South Africa's war with SWAPO, were accused of numerous atrocities against the civilian population in the Namibian north. This led independent U.S. observers to conclude in mid-1989 that "a pervasive atmosphere of fear and terror hangs over Namibia."[13]

Enter the United Nations

There were several United Nations players acting in support of Namibia over the years:

- The UN Council for Namibia, which was composed of 31 Member States and the representative of the South West Africa People's Organization (SWAPO), conducted education and training programs for Namibian exiles abroad. It was seen by South Africa as a tool of SWAPO and was not allowed access to Namibia.
- A UN Commissioner for Namibia based at UN Headquarters in New York acted as an external advocate for the country, but was not recognized by South Africa. The last commissioner was Bernt Carlsson who died in the Lockerbie crash in December 1988.
- The UN Department of Public Information (DPI) planned and conducted, *inter alia,*
  - o   anti-apartheid information programs
  - o   Namibia-information programs
  - o   Peace and Security programs
- The United Nations Transition Assistance Group (UNTAG) was administered by the UN's Department of Peacekeeping Operations and became the main vehicle for implementing the task of leading Namibia to independence.

On April 1, 1989 UNTAG found itself on the ground in Namibia to conduct multiple tasks: It was to monitor a cease fire between SWAPO and South Africa, oversee the phased withdrawal of South African forces from Namibia, monitor the confinement of SWAPO to base and to supervise South African administrators in an election leading to the independence of the country. In addition, it had to ensure the elimination of discriminatory laws, supervise the law enforcement agencies and assist in drafting the country's constitution.

Upon its arrival, UNTAG was hailed by many black Namibians as a savior, and expectations of a speedy transition to democracy and black majority-rule ran high. Most, but not all, local whites saw the UN as an interloper and as an ineffective meddler, and the mission was frequently the object of their ridicule. Because of these diverse sentiments, UNTAG's communication challenge, that of persuading the population of this non-self-governing territory that independence and self-rule was in its own best interest, became a vital job. It has, however, not yet been thoroughly analyzed.[14]

The injection of a "third party" such as UNTAG, which employed at its peak over 8000 military, civilian and police personnel, was a major event in a country then populated by only a million and a half inhabitants. As UNTAG drew its personnel from over 120 countries coming from all regions of the world, it had a wide international base. Once these thousands of internationals were deployed in multi-racial teams all over the country, they quickly became symbols for multiculturalism in this emerging nation.

Racial Divisions in a Fragmented Territory

In 1989 Namibia was still generally known by its geographical location, i.e., South West Africa. Its white inhabitants referred to themselves as "South Westerners" and even the main liberation movement SWAPO had South West Africa in its name.

The South African administration had set up ten "ethnic and second tier representative authorities" in the territory in 1980,[15] which served to divide and fragment, rather than unite the country. Even though their powers, as part of the UN settlement plan, were transferred to the administrator-general in 1989, "the de facto administration is still divided along regional and ethnic lines until a new government is elected."[16] Most pervasive was the effect of South Africa's "homelands" policy in Namibia. In the capital, Windhoek, the native population was forcibly relocated from its "old locations" to outlying "townships." The black population was resettled to a township called Katutura, and the "Coloureds" to a separate area called Khomasdal. Within Katutura, the tribal groups were further separated, and tribally based schools and councils were set up. A curfew from sunset to sunrise was strictly enforced to keep nonwhites out of the center of Windhoek at night. While some features of what was termed "petty apartheid" had been abolished in the 1980s,[17] the country was still in an apartheid mindset, which affected all walks of life.

South Africa itself was at that time governed by emergency laws proclaimed by President P.K. Botha that permitted detention without trial. The detention period could be extended indefinitely by the minister of law and order. As a result, as Judge Richard Goldstone maintains, "some ten thousand South Africans were being held in prisons and police cells."

As late as 1994 Goldstone himself "appreciated the fearsome power that criminal elements in the South African security establishment had managed to build up not only in South Africa but also abroad."[18]

Another divisive factor was the sheer multitude of languages spoken in Namibia. Afrikaans was still the *lingua franca,* but English was slowly becoming more prevalent, and the latter eventually became the official language of Namibia following independence. The native languages spoken in South West Africa were Bushman, Herero, Kwanyama, Nama, and Ndonga, as well as dialects within each language. German was spoken by the influential community of German farmers and businessmen.

During the transition process, the UN staff was expected to work alongside the predominantly white South African administrators in Namibia, not to replace them. These Afrikaaners were a group of proud and self-reliant bureaucrats who felt that they had done a good job in administering the territory for decades: "Afrikaaners believed they were a superior but native African tribe whose territories had been encroached upon by warlike and primitive black tribes from the North."[19] Many of them expected that they would have to be repatriated to South Africa following black majority rule in Namibia. According to Robert Harvey, white South African negotiators who were holding secret talks with a number of exiled ANC leaders including Thabo Mbeki in the United Kingdom in 1988/89, expressed concern that, following the Namibian elections, they would have to resettle 60,000 whites from Namibia to South Africa and that they would need money to support this process.[20] The threat of a white exodus following independence was thus another source of insecurity affecting the transition process and adding to a mood of uncertainty and doom.

Information and Education: A Vital Task

It was clear that the South African propaganda-machine and the apartheid-dominated educational system, which had prevented the people of this territory from achieving self-determination, would be very difficult to countervail. Given the fact that most of the SWAPO activists and other political exiles only returned to the country in the later stages of the independence process, UNTAG was the major political counter-force to white South African rule in the transitional period. If UNTAG was to achieve a predominant role in the Namibian discourse it would require a major effort on the information front.

This was recognized from the outset by Martti Ahtisaari of Finland, the secretary-general's special representative. Ahtisaari had previously acted as commissioner for Namibia and had visited the country repeatedly.[21] When he authorized a UN preparatory mission to Namibia in February 1989, which was to fine tune plans for this most ambitious peacekeeping task, an information specialist was included in this team.[22] It was thus known to the UN planners that Namibia had an educational system dominated by the apartheid-system, and that about 75 percent of the Namibian electorate was illiterate. The country did not have institutions of higher learning except for vocational schools, and a nascent "academy." The intellectual elite had been either forced into exile, or had left voluntarily for university training abroad. There were no electoral rolls and the concept of free and fair elections based on racial equality was foreign to the population.

Jean Krasno describes the situation into which UNTAG entered in 1989:

> What continued to be misunderstood outside Namibia was the fact that while the South African government had agreed to independence, there were many South Africans and white Namibians who did *not* go along with this decision and tried to either sabotage the process in general, or manipulate it in order to attempt to maintain white control. This was done through intimidation, violence, and the assassinations by using the Koevoet special forces and the political party DTA (Democratic Turnhalle Alliance) to carry out the policy. The South African-controlled media, especially radio and television, continued to use systematic disinformation and biased reporting to manipulate the process.[23]

Radio and television were a governmental monopoly run by the South West African Broadcasting Corporation (SWABC). As few Namibians owned television sets at that time, radio was the most influential medium in the country. There were also several lively and independent privately owned newspapers available in Namibia,[24] which to some extent followed language and political divisions, but which nevertheless served as the main forum for political debate during the transitional period.

From the United Nations' point of view, the following information activities had to be carried out:

1. The local print media had to be well-briefed about the UN's intentions and activities, as well as about measures for voter education and democratic processes.
2. The SWABC broadcasts had to be closely monitored for their impartiality, and, if possible, forced to abandon one-sided positions.
3. The UN had to commence its own radio programs as soon as possible.
4. Visual means of communication had to be produced and distributed by the UN to convey its messages to the large group of illiterate voters.

While the first condition could be relatively easily achieved through daily press briefings by UNTAG's spokesman, the second, the lack of control of SWABC's political broadcasts, was, according to Ahtisaari's political director, Cedric Thornberry, the "principal failure" of UNTAG.[25] It therefore became of vital importance for UNTAG to develop its own voice through a regular UN radio program, Radio UNTAG. The fourth requirement, that of a strong visual presence, was best served by UNTAG's novel identity and voter education program, which used a multitude of visual tools to convey messages with a minimal use of words.

A Public Information Campaign without a Mandate Takes Off

Shortly after the UN Security Council had given the green light for the deployment of UNTAG in late December 1988, staff members of the recently formed Peace and Security Programmes Section of the Department of Public Information began to work out a comprehensive information program for that mission. A small *ad hoc* team, which included a graphic designer hired by the Department, developed a comprehensive information campaign that included the training of staff who volunteered for assignments in Namibia. The main aim of this program was to strengthen "the UN's ability to explain its mission in Namibia to the people of that nation-to-be as well as to the world press."[26] The program's objectives were detailed as follows:

a) To establish the identity of the UN and explain its role in the independence process;
b) To explain the process itself, both to those who will participate in it and to the outside world;
c) To promote the integrity and effectiveness of the UNTAG mission though timely responses to any misinformation that may appear;
d) To report regularly on the independence process as it unfolds, within Namibia and to the world press; and
e) To chronicle the principal events in print and on film for the historical record.[27]

This program then outlined the public information tasks that would need to be performed, the staff resources required and provided detailed budgetary estimates. The program was updated and expanded as the mission unfolded. An essential and novel feature was the UNTAG identity system which aimed "to present a consistent, uniform, positive image of UNTAG in Namibia and beyond."[28] This idea received strong support from Mr. Ahtisaari at an early stage as "offering a promising means of conveying a single and effective image of UNTAG within a huge and linguistically diverse territory."[29] The information program received the support from both Mr. Ahtisaari and Mrs. Therese Paquet-Sevigny, the under-secretary-general for public information, and production of information materials began in February 1989, first at UN headquarters and later in Namibia itself.

UNTAG's forty-two district centers, as well as its police stations and other civilian offices, were soon equipped with a great variety of visual information materials that were produced in Windhoek and distributed around the country. They were available in English, Afrikaans, and most indigenous languages. The slogans used on these posters, bumper stickers, decals, and wall sheets were derived from the settlement plan for Namibia "435" and were creatively adapted to convey confidence in the political process. The following list of slogans, while not comprehensive, provides an overview of the topics covered by these posters, wall charts, and decals:

> *UNTAG – Free and Fair Elections in Namibia*
> *Your vote is Secret – and your Ballot Is Safe*
> *It's Your Time to Choose for Namibia*
> *Vote in Free and Fair Elections*
> *UNTAG Supervises and Controls the Voting Process*
> *UNTAG Supervises and Controls the Counting Process*

While most of these slogans referred to the election process and were part of the intensive voter education campaign carried out in all major Namibian languages, they also helped to establish UNTAG's identity and explained the purpose of the organization's role in the country. As Jan Arnesen, the designer of most of these visual materials said, in many parts of Namibia, "this was the only physical evidence, other than the white UN vehicles marked with black 'UN,' that these 'outsiders' had come to their country, town or village for a more broad-reaching purpose other than to impose a foreign military presence."[30] A total of 590,000 separate information items were produced during the year of UNTAG's deployment in Namibia and its cost was estimated at around one million dollars.[31]

Suspicions and Intimidation: A Rocky Start

Prior to the unfolding of the UNTAG information campaign there were many and various rumors and suspicions among Namibians concerning the United Nations' presence in Namibia. Similarly, among the UN staff many had serious concerns and reservations about dealing with the white South African administrators.

In addition, even though the black population was generally most welcoming to the UN, the internationals and many locals were doubtful about SWAPO's peaceful intentions. Many of the civilians recruited by the UN for this operation had their first peacekeeping experience in Namibia and did not know what to expect. Others, such as I who had previously been to Namibia, had our own misgivings following encounters with skeptical or openly hostile individuals and "spoilers" of the peace process:

> The apartheid system, which had been in effect in South-West Africa for many decades, was still influencing attitudes and behaviour of the local population, black and white. It became clear to some of the UN personnel involved in the transition process that UNTAG itself was perceived as an actor on the political scene, and that its staff was scrutinized and observed and tested continuously for its impartiality and general approach to the country. Suspicions ran high, particularly among the white population, just as rising expectations led to an overestimation of the speed of the transition process among some blacks in the country. Most UNTAG staff were not prepared for this intensity of feeling, for and against the United Nations in Namibia.[32]

While some of these feelings of uncertainty on the part of UN staff were ameliorated through pre-deployment training programs in New York, Geneva and Vienna, as well as in-country briefings for the thousands of short-term staff who arrived in the fall of 1989 as election observers, the feelings of disquietude were hard to overcome. Marrack Goulding, under-secretary-general for peacekeeping, who chaired the secretary-general's task force on Namibia at UN headquarters in New York, described the dissensions within the UN leadership in New York over how to deal with South Africa:

> Everyone detested the system which existed in South Africa. Some in the Secretariat and in the delegations of member states were nevertheless ready to allow for the possibility that South African policies might be changing for the better and were ready to give the South Africans the benefit of the doubt. Others were reluctant to place any trust in them and always assumed the worst. This was the primary cause of dissension within the Task Force.[33]

But actions by members of the liberation movement SWAPO nearly caused the UN operation to abort at the very start. April 1, 1989 was the date when the ceasefire was to begin. The UN's advance party had only arrived a day before, due to lengthy delays in the decision-making about troop-levels and financing of the mission in the UN General Assembly. UNTAG did not yet have sufficient troops, vehicles, or communications equipment to monitor the ceasefire on the northern border when more than a thousand SWAPO fighters, in violation of the agreement, entered the country from Angola. South Africa demanded that the incursion be stopped, the UN reluctantly agreed, and intense battles ensued for about ten days between South African forces and SWAPO fighters, during which several hundred combatants were killed.

This period of fighting at such an early stage sowed much distrust, and the credibility of the United Nations suffered a severe blow. It also delayed the timetable for the implementation of the peace plan by about six weeks. Some of the UN staff already in the country at that time kept their bags packed throughout this dangerous period.[34] This understandably had serious repercussions for the UN in the months to come. It left deep feelings of insecurity, not least among UN staff operating in the country. Several instances of open hostility and attacks on UN facilities were recorded. For example, in September 1989 the UNTAG office in the town of Outjo was attacked by machine guns and grenades, killing a civilian security guard. UN cars had tires slashed and graffiti displayed such as: "UNTAG = United Nations Terrorist Assistance Group."

On September 12, 1989 a prominent white SWAPO member and lawyer, Anton Lubowski, was murdered in front of his house in Windhoek. This showed, according to Cedric Thornberry, "that the tiny minority of extremists who opposed the Namibian settlement were becoming desperate."[35] The purported assassin, an Irish contract killer, was caught, but had to be released months later for "lack of evidence." It was widely believed that the murder was part of a campaign to disrupt SWAPO's participation in the elections,[36] as graffiti appeared the day after the Lubowski assassination threatening Sam Nujoma, the SWAPO leader who was to return to Namibia from years of exile on 14 September, with a similar fate.

Nervousness ran high in Namibia during those days and the UN's Cedric Thornberry himself was evacuated to New York for reasons of personal safety in early October: "That there was a truly amazing amount of South African skullduggery in the months before the Namibian elections cannot be seriously disputed, and we were in some respects very fortunate to have been able to pass through it with only slight damage to ourselves."[37]

Political Tools

What helped greatly in calming tempers and creating a more rational political environment was the adoption, by all political parties in Namibia, of a "Code of Conduct" which consisted of a series of principles and standards for political debate and election campaigning. The code of conduct was initiated and negotiated by UNTAG, and prescribed sixteen points to which all nine political parties committed themselves: to respect each others' party symbols and campaign materials; to decline intimidation of and by party workers; banning weapons at political rallies; avoiding language that might incite to violence; and agreeing to a process of appealing to UNTAG in case of violations of the code. UNTAG publicized the code throughout the country by distributing about 20,000 copies of the text in poster-form through its more than forty district centers.

UNTAG also began to hold fortnightly meetings with the major political parties in its district centers to discuss all matters of concern relating to the election campaign. These meetings brought face-to-face political antagonists who had fought each other during the war, thus serving as significant confidence-building measures that helped greatly in improving the political climate. They also helped UNTAG district offices and their staff gain a much higher political profile in the communities in which they worked. Meetings were often held in community halls, churches, schools, or in open-air gathering places and underneath trees.

Despite continuing turbulence in the north of Namibia, in most communities around the capital, Windhoek, and in the south of Namibia, things became quieter by early summer 1989. In districts such as Khomasdal, the mixed-race township of Windhoek where I headed the UNTAG District Center from May 1989, people were generally shy, but were not unfriendly to the United Nations. Once we had established contacts with community leaders and explained our mission, the holding of free and fair elections and the independence of Namibia from South Africa, discussions became more open and lively, as was reported by Special Representative Ahtisaari to UN headquarters in New York on 18 June 1998:

> An UNTAG public meeting was organized at Khomasdal, the so-called "coloured" township of Windhoek, on 13 June. Despite the cold mid-winter evening, a crowd of more than 300 participated actively in a two-hour session of statements, questions and answers. It was a lively meeting, but the tone is now noticeably different than even a month ago—still critical, but becoming buoyant, more optimistic, essentially supportive...[38]

An important development for the country was the return of large numbers of refugees, i.e., exiled Namibians who had lived for many years during the liberation struggle in over forty countries worldwide.

Eventually, about 43,000 returnees were repatriated by the United Nations High Commissioner for Refugees (UNHCR), who assisted them with the provision of food, shelter, education and special care for vulnerable groups. The largest number of exiles returned from Angola and Zambia, where many of them had fought for SWAPO. Initially, they were the cause of many suspicions and resentments among their compatriots—black and white—who had stayed at home. Many of the exiles had received an excellent education abroad and would eventually become the new elite in an independent Namibia. Some, such as a group of several hundred children and young adults who had been raised and educated in communist East Germany for many years, were well schooled, but many faced adjustment problems.[39]

Radio UNTAG

A very effective and popular information tool of the peacekeeping mission in Namibia was its radio program, which was broadcast five days a week in English, and translated and rebroadcast in the various Namibian languages. Lena Yacoumopoulou, of DPI's radio section in New York, was the producer/presenter of a total of 200 programs that focused on current political issues related to the various stages of the independence process, from aspects of voter registration to mine clearance. Usually, Lena or her colleagues interviewed UN staff on aspects of their work, which proved a very popular format and made UNTAG personnel and their activities widely known among the population who, in many cases, remained perplexed about UNTAG's activities. The radio programs, while not focusing on racial themes, touched on issues of decolonization and multi-racial societies, as the following excerpts show:[40]

Interview with Cedric Thornberry on 23 June 1989:
"435 is essentially a decolonization, a self-determination process and all the functions of UNTAG are geared to support that basic push for the people of this country to have the opportunity of taking a decision about their own political future."[41]

Interview with Brigadier Daniel Opande, the Deputy Force Commander on 30 June 1989:
"Naturally, we Africans have had years of colonial domination, and when another country is going to be independent, we all rejoice. So I feel very much more committed to seeing that this process succeeds...I personally have hopes that Namibia, being the last in Africa to achieve independence, is in a better position to learn from the mistakes of other African countries.... My message for all the Namibians, regardless of

their background – race, colour, creed or whatever – is that they have a role to play in ensuring that transition to majority rule becomes a reality this year."[42]

Interview with Blandina Negga, regional director in Gobabis on 7 August 1989:

"I was told that Gobabis was a very difficult area, but coming from Antigua and Barbuda, or the West Indies, where our motto is live and let live, and everyone is a person, I never took it seriously, and when I went in I met everyone and I held out my hand and said I am Blandina Francis Negga, and I am the Regional Director of UNTAG for Gobabis, and not once has anyone refused to shake my hand. I think being a woman and being black has been somewhat of a plus for me, because I was an object of curiosity in Gobabis...in that way I never felt my gender or my colour was a handicap."[43]

These excerpts give a good feeling for the atmosphere and the attitude of some of the UNTAG officials. They also show the impact the mere presence of multicultural teams of UN staff from over 100 countries had on a country like Namibia. Striking is, however, the absence of any references to apartheid[44] in the two hundred radio programs broadcast by UNTAG. This reflected not so much the personal choice of editors or producers of these programs, but was a result of the overriding political imperative of the need for UNTAG's "impartiality." An "impartiality package," negotiated painstakingly with all political parties in the early 1980s, had come into effect on April 1989, which required that the UN, as well as the other political actors, refrain from any activities that might reflect negatively on its impartiality.[45]

Bread-and-butter issues dominated the daily radio programs along with specific questions related to the November elections and the democratic transition process. The UN as an inter-governmental organization representative of "cultural internationalism" presented itself and its staff in non-racial terms in those broadcasts, as in all its information products. Namibians saw dozens of UNTAG's multi-national and multi-racial registration and election teams work together on an equal footing, criss-crossing the country for several weeks. In some of the remoter places they were often met with amazement and disbelief, like Martians. A typical mobile election team, for example, might consist of a civilian policeman from Barbados and a Japanese election monitor, an international Secretariat staff member from Western Europe, along with a Namibian driver/interpreter. Often, initial disbelief and disquietude among the locals about these international teams turned into respect and even admiration: May be these foreigners could teach us something after all?[46]

A week prior to independence, Radio UNTAG interviewed Namibian school children and their teachers in St. George's School, the first integrated school in Namibia, about their perceptions of this international body in their country (12 March 1990):

Student: "When I think of UNTAG, I think of how they left their countries and came to our country and help us make it an independent country"

Student: "The UNTAG, they stop some countries from fighting other countries and try to make peace so other people can have foods and houses instead of just having bombs."

Student: "[B]ecause they came here to our country to give peace."

Student: "I like to listen to their languages, I like hearing them on the radio and I like watching the news when they are on television and usually when I think of UNTAG I think of an UNTAG number plate."[47]

The "Independence" Discourse

The UN's political success in Namibia was possible because several factors fortuitously coincided: the peace plan "435" proved viable; the strong support of the major powers involved in the Namibia peace negotiations did not falter after the debacle of 1 April 1989; and South Africa, for its own reasons, had decided to cooperate in the venture for Namibian independence. Namibia had become a testing ground for multi-racial democracy in southern Africa.

The election results, with a two-thirds majority for SWAPO, did not give the liberation movement an absolute majority, forcing it to compromise with other political parties and instituting a parliamentary democracy with an established opposition. It allowed the whites to remain in the country and to make a contribution in independent Namibia, which many of them cherished.

During the transition, UNTAG became a bureaucratically self-contained operation with one main goal: supervising the Namibian self-determination process. The UN's main message in this apartheid-dominated territory was that the political process leading to independence was the most important goal and the first step towards national self-determination. It was assumed by both Namibians and internationals, although rarely openly discussed, that majority rule would automatically put an end to apartheid and the most blatant racist divisions. The independence discourse thus became the dynamic force propelling the movement for self-determination, majority-rule and anti-racism.

How the country would transform itself from apartheid-reign to a multi-racial society following the UN's departure, with the accompanying complexities and tensions, was also unclear. As discussed above, post-independence nation-building was not in the UN's mandate at that time and the UN proudly announced that it was able to leave the country ahead of schedule, clearing it from the often-voiced charges of maintaining peacekeeping operations such as those in the Middle East or Cyprus for many decades without resolution.

Nation-building as such was then left to the Namibians,[48] and although many of those celebrating Namibia's independence in 1990 hailed the arrival of "a new nation,"[49] the formation of a new state was probably a more accurate description of the process witnessed here. The United Nations' work in Namibia from 1990 onwards focused on economic development projects administered by the United Nations Development Programme and other UN agencies. Nevertheless, the UN left a strong legacy of democratic decision-making and multi-racial cooperation in Namibia and helped set the country on a path that, to this day, appears durable.

Lessons Learned?

The United Nations Secretariat conducted post-mission assessments of its Namibia-operation from various angles, political, military, logistical, administrative, and informational. A summary of that analysis is contained in its major reference work, *The Blue Helmets—A Review of United Nations Peacekeeping*.[50] Susan Manuel, the current chief of the Peace and Security Section at DPI Headquarters summarized the major lesson learned in the following way, "Since its late 1980s mission in Namibia, UN peacekeeping has used civic education and its own forms of media to promote awareness among the general public of its mandate and the peace process."[51] One of the most visible organizational manifestations of this was the issuance, in November 1997, of "Provisional Guidelines for Public Information Components in United Nations Peacekeeping and other Field Missions," a small handbook prepared jointly by DPI and DPKO. Another indication of lessons learned is that information specialists are now routinely included in the start-up phase of UN field operations. Moreover, training sessions are regularly held by both Departments for staff dealing with information issues in the field.

Unfortunately, the United Nations did not apply the positive lessons learned from its Namibia operation uniformly to all its subsequent peacekeeping missions. While the UNTAG information experience became a model for several of the operations which immediately succeeded it, such as those in Central America, Cambodia, and Mozambique, the lessons were not consistently applied.

For example, the radio program of the UN's peacekeeping operation in Rwanda was deployed 18 months after the genocide occurred and was therefore not available to counteract racist propaganda. In the Congo-operation (MONUC), Radio Okapi, a joint UN-NGO project was launched in 2002, and is seen by some observers as the most popular radio station in the country. According to Dan Lindley, it demonstrates that the UN and other international actors can use information campaigns to "defang hate mongers"[52] whose propaganda manipulates ethnic histories and politics. It was, however, striking that some of the senior information and political officers involved in the Namibia operation were unable, for a variety of reasons, to apply the lessons from Namibia in UNPROFOR (UN Protection Force in the former Yugoslavia) in Croatia and Bosnia only two to three years later.[53] There is no guarantee that an intergovernmental organization such as the United Nations can necessarily apply the lessons learned in one operation to another in a different political and military environment.

Assessment

The highly visible, year-long presence of the UN in Namibia, with thousands of staff—military, civilian police and election monitors—working in multi-racial teams, had a confidence-building effect on many in Namibia. The UN's network of political offices, dispersed throughout the country, played an important part in the reconciliation of political adversaries, and in establishing a democratic code of political conduct. The transparency of the electoral process itself set high standards for future free elections in Namibia and, four years later, in South Africa itself.

Looking back at the information campaign accompanying this operation we can now begin to explain how an ad-hoc information program masterminded by UN Secretariat officials could be carried out without an explicit mandate from the Security Council. I can offer at least three explanations:

First, the political primacy of the independence discourse was UNTAG's strength, rather than a weakness, in that all other developments, including the end of apartheid and the building of a multiracial democratic society, flowed from it. The success of this process resulted from a strong third-party intervention by the UN, which was backed up by the international community, including all major powers.[54] This strategic support enabled the Mission to conduct an effective campaign of cultural internationalism.

Secondly, the UN's Namibia operation proved the importance of leadership for the conduct of information campaigns and mission-internal communication. When the head of a peacekeeping mission decides that an information component is vital to the success of the operation, experience shows that the resources will usually be found to create it and carry it out. While UNTAG's information campaign "was a case of brilliant, but eleventh-hour, improvisation at the operational level,"[55] it also represents one of the last times when the "ad-hocism,"[56] so symptomatic of early UN peacekeeping, succeeded so well. Leaders of successive UN operations in the first half of the 1990s in Somalia, Rwanda, and the former Yugoslavia, largely ignored the requirements for effective communication programs in their missions, and did so at great cost to the image of the United Nations.

Thirdly, UNTAG reconfirmed the creative power of the UN Secretariat in shaping peacekeeping missions. Studies conducted by Leon Gordenker in the 1960s had already shown "that secretariats have great weight in the policy process of international, as of other, organizations," and he judged that the much-criticized Office of Public Information had proved "enduring and resilient."[57] Thomas Weiss has identified international secretariats as "a group of persons whose commitment is not to the status quo, but to the creation of a more just world order,"[58] and Michael Barnett has stated that "international organizations can become, first, a site for new political identities and definitions of interests that are inconsistent with their original intent, and, second, a locus of authority far removed from those whose lives they affect and in whose name they operate."[59] The experience of UNTAG proves Barnett's first point, and underlines the importance of information campaigns in curbing the risks associated with his second point.

The United Nations' information campaign in Namibia thus assisted the UN in promoting "cultural internationalism" in two ways: On the one hand it helped UNTAG in Namibia to create an identity for itself in its third-party intervention, thus acting as a role model for other UN peacekeeping operations at work in conflict environments. On the other hand, it helped the Namibians to reinvent themselves after decades of apartheid-rule. The construction of a national identity in racially divided countries following civil and ethnic conflicts remains one of the great challenges for those countries and the international community alike. UNTAG in Namibia made significant contributions to both goals.

Notes

1. See James Dobbins, Seth G. Jones, Keith Crane, Andrew Rathmell, Brett Steele, Richard Teltschik, Anga Timilsina, *The UN's Role in Nation-Building – From the Congo to Iraq* (Rand Corporation, Santa Monica, 2005); Roland Paris, *At War's End – Building Peace After Civil Conflict* (Cambridge University Press, 2004), Chapter 8; and Virginia Page Fortna, "United Nations Transition Assistance Group," in: William J. Durch (ed.), *The Evolution of UN Peacekeeping, Case Studies and Comparative Analysis* (New York, St. Martin's Press, 1993), pp. 353-375 and Jean Krasno, "Leveraging Namibian Independence," in: Jean Krasno, Bradd C. Hayes, Donald C.F. Daniel (eds.), *Leveraging for Success in United Nations Peace Operations* (Westport, Ct., Praeger), pp. 25-54, and Fen Osler Hampson, *Nurturing Peace – Why Peace Settlements Succeed or Fail* (U.S. Institute of Peace Press, Washington, D.C., 1996), Chapter 3: Namibia.
2. Dobbins et al., p. 34 state correctly that "its nation-building mandate was minimal." In the late 1980s, nation-building was not yet a widely accepted concept. It received some level of acceptance with the publication of Secretary-General Boutros Boutros-Ghali's *Agenda for Peace* in 1992.
3. Mark D. Alleyne, *Global Lies? Propaganda, the UN and World Order* (Palgrave, Macmillan, New York, 2003), pp. 111-120.
4. The two programs were managed by different Secretariat offices and in the public information field, as well, staffing, budget and work program were maintained and operated separately.
5. Akira Iriye, *Cultural Internationalism and World Order* (Johns Hopkins University Press, Baltimore and London, 1997) defines cultural internationalism as a world order in which "individuals and groups of people from different lands have sought to develop an alternative community of nations and peoples on the basis of their cultural interchanges" (p. 2). Others, such as Michael Barnett have identified the concept of "cosmopolitanism" as the "secular religion of the international community and its cathedral, the UN." See Michael Barnett, "The UN Security Council, Indifference, and Genocide in Rwanda," in: *Cultural Anthropology* 12 (4), 1997, pp. 570 and 575.
6. Iriye, p. 3.
7. David Howarth, Aletta J. Norval & Yannis Stavrakakis (eds.), *Discourse Theory and Political Analysis: Identities, Hegemonies and Social Change* (Manchester and New York, Manchester University Press, 2000, see esp. Chapter 1.
8. See Mark Alleyne's chapter on the UN in Guatemala in this book.
9. For an early expression of the UN's understanding of the concept of race as a "myth" see United Nations Economic and Security Council, Statement by Experts on Problems of Race, communicated by A. Metraux, in *American Anthropologist*, New Series, vol. 53, no. 1 (Jan.-Mar., 1951), pp. 142-145.
10. Namibia is bordered in the north by Angola, in the south and south-east by South Africa, on the east by Botswana; the narrow Caprivi strip extends 300 miles eastward and shares borders with both Zambia and Zimbabwe.
11. German colonial rule only lasted from 1884 to 1915, but this period was marked by uprisings, of the Herero and Nama tribes, in particular. In 1904, the Herero uprising was put down by the German colonial rulers—approximately 65,000 Hereros were killed.
12. Stephen R. Ratner defines apartheid:
    Apartheid was the system of racial discrimination and separation that governed South Africa from 1948 until its abolition in the early 1990s. Building on years of discrimination against blacks, the National Party adopted apartheid as a

model for separate development of races, though it served only to preserve white superiority. It classified persons as either white, Bantu (black), colored (mixed race), or Asian. Its manifestations included ineligibility from voting, separate living areas and schools, internal travel, passes for blacks, and white control of the legal system (in: Roy Gutman and David Rieff, *Crimes of War, What the Public Should Know* (New York, Norton, 1999, p. 26).

13. Commission On Independence for Namibia, "Report of the First Observer Mission of the Commission on Independence for Namibia," New York, July 1989, pp. 3-12.

14. In my book *Peacekeeping and Public Information—Caught in the Crossfire* (Frank Cass, London, 1999), I dedicated a chapter to the UN information campaign in Namibia. Dan Lindley's book, *Promoting Peace with Information – Transparency as a Tool of Security Regime*, (Princeton University Press, 2007) contains a chapter on Namibia, and Cedric Thornberry, in *A Nation Is Born—The Inside Story of Namibia's Independence* (Gamsberg Macmillan, Windhoek, Namibia, 2004), gives prominence to his own role in the information campaign.

15. *Namibia Handbook and Political Who's Who* (edited by Pütz, Von Egidy and Caplan), (Windhoek, The Magus, 1989), pp. 420-424 lists ten second-tier administrations: Caprivi, Coloured, Damara, Herero, Kavango, Nama, Owambo, Rehoboth, Tswana, White.

16. Ibid., p. 402.

17. In 1983, P.W. Botha announced a 12-point plan which allowed for a gradual dismantling of "petty apartheid": segregation in public places and buses, the Mixed marriages Act, and the law prohibiting sexual intercourse between blacks and whites was repealed in 1985, the Pass Laws were repealed in 1986.

18. Richard Goldstone, *For Humanity—Reflections of a War Crimes Investigator* (Yale University Press, New Haven, 2000), p. 56 (italics added).

19. Robert Harvey, *The Fall of Apartheid, The Inside Story from Smuts to Mbeki* (Palgrave Macmillan, New York, 2001), p. 24.

20. Ibid., p. 152.

21. In 2008, Ahtisaari was awarded the Nobel Peace Prize, *inter alia,* for his role in the Namibian peace process.

22. Having been part of the 1978 survey mission as a member of the Secretary-General's office. I was asked to perform this task. In 1989 I headed a newly created unit called the Peace and Security Programmes Section of DPI that provided the liaison between DPI and DPKO. The information gained during the February 1989 survey mission was essential in designing the information program for UNTAG and reviewing important technical details such as printing establishments etc.

23. Jean Krasno, op. cit., p. 41.

24. *Namibia Handbook,* pp. 351-354 lists seventeen daily or weekly papers and two news agencies in 1989.

25. Cedric Thornberry, op. cit., p. 287.

26. Information Programme for the United Nations Transition Assistance group in Namibia" (revised proposal submitted to Mr. Ahtisaari on 31 January 1989). This program became the basis for all public information work, inside Namibia and internationally. The UN Controller at that time, Luis M. Gomez, called this program "an excellent showcase of a full-blown, thought-through information program, on a world-wide scale, overlapping two budget periods and drawing from more than one source of funding." (Memorandum from Luis M. Gomez to Martti Ahtisaari dated 8 February 1989. These internal communications, copies of which are in my possession, show that Cedric Thornberry's contention in his book *A Nation Is Born* that the UNTAG information program was not supported by DPI is factually incorrect and misleading.

27. United Nations Information Programme on Namibia, Section II.
28. Proposal for an UNTAG Identity System" (rev.1) by Ingrid A. Lehmann, dated 27 January 1989.
29. Memorandum from Mr. Ahtisaari to Ms. Therese P. Sevigny, under-secretary-general for public information, dated 27 January 1989.
30. Jan Arnesen in a letter to the author dated 25 January 1997.
31. *The Blue Helmets – A Review of United Nations Peacekeeping* (Third edition, United Nations Department of Public Information, New York), p. 220. The cost estimate is my own and very difficult to reconstruct, as many information items were not budgeted for in advance and had to be paid for out of related budgetary sections, such as "miscellaneous supplies and services. See Lehmann, *Peacekeeping and Public Information,* op. cit., pp. 49-50 (n.44). Cedric Thornberry maintains that the information campaign was partially self-funded though the sale of T-shirts. *A Nation Is Born*, op. cit., p. 190.
32. Ingrid Lehmann, *Peacekeeping and Public Information*, op. cit., p. 35.
33. Marrack Goulding, *Peacemonger* (John Murray, London, 2002), p. 175.
34. In *A Nation Is Born,* Cedric Thornberry dedicates Part Two: "The Tragedy of April" to this critical phase, in which he put the blame elsewhere. See Thornberry, pp. 87-141. *The Namibian* (7 April 1989) reported: "The Director of the Office of the Special Representative, Mr. Cedric Thornberry, yesterday admitted that the United Nations were presented with an ultimatum to either allow the deployment of South African troops or have UNTAG kicked out of the country." (p. 2).
35. Ibid., p. 265.
36. Molly Lubowski and Marita van der Vyver, *Anton Lubowski—Paradox of a Man* (Queillerie Publishers, Strand, S.A., publication undated) tell the story of one of the earliest white Namibian SWAPO-members in the context of the atmosphere of intimidation and hatred that prevailed throughout the 1980s. The perpetrators of the Lubowski-murder were, as outlined by Lubowski and Vyver, linked to the South African death squads that operated in the apartheid days in Namibia as well. In the daily newspaper *The Namibian* (20 October 1989) a story appeared "SA's Covert Team" which was based on the allegations of an ANC operative, Sue Dobson, who claimed she was part of a covert operations team of the South African "Bureau of Information" which ran a campaign "to discredit SWAPO and the UN" with a budget totalling 3.5 million South African rand.
37. Thornberry, p. 305. Thornberry sees his enforced three-week evacuation as a result of a New York-based intrigue against him (ibid., pp. 295-304).
38. United Nations Transition Group in Namibia, *UNTAG in Namibia, A New Nation Is Born* (United Nations, Windhoek, p. 15). In Khomasdal, with its approximately 30,000 residents, political sympathies lay predominantly with the more conservative Democratic Turnhalle Alliance (which received about 25 percent of the votes in the elections in November nationwide).
39. The psychological problems that some of the "GDR kids" face to this day are well described in Constance Kenna (ed.) *Homecoming – The GDR Kids of Namibia* (New Namibia Books, Windhoek, 1999).
40. I am grateful to Lena Yacoumopoulou for making available transcripts of 201 radio programs broadcast by Radio UNTAG between June 1989 and March 1990. All the excerpts cited here are taken from the transcripts.
41. UNTAG radio program no. 10: "An overview of UNTAG compared to previous missions, with Cedric Thornberry."
42. UNTAG radio program no. 15: "Monitoring the demobilization of territorial forces and the handing in of their weapons; the role of the soldier in a peacekeeping force. Gen. Prem Chand and Brig. Opande."

43. UNTAG radio program no. 41: "UNTAG Regional Directors of Gobabis and Mariental – Negga and Rahim – discuss the reaction to UNTAG's presence."

44. Similarly, the UN's main reference book documenting its own work against apartheid, *The United Nations and Apartheid, 1948-1994* (New York, United Nations Department of Public Information, 1994) is 544 pages long and consists of a compendium of 221 documents related to apartheid. However, it contains only eight documents that mention Namibia, and most of those relate to South Africa's exploitation of Namibia's national resources.

45. *The Blue Helmets,* op. cit., p. 208 and Thorberry, op. cit., pp. 271-273.

46. When I revisited Namibia in the spring of 2004, I told several people we encountered that I had worked with UNTAG fifteen years earlier. This elicited positive responses, along the lines of what a middle-aged black man working in Caprivi told me: "You brought us peace."

47. UNTAG radio program no. 195: "The first integrated school in Namibia (St. George's). Students and teachers discuss their views on UNTAG."

48. David Horwarth, "The difficult emergence a democratic imaginary: Black Consciousness and non-racial democracy in South-Africa," in *Discourse Theory and Political Analysis-Identities, Hegemonies and Social Change* (ed. by David Horwarth, Aletta Norval and Yannis Stavrakis, Manchester University Press, 2000, pp. 168-192) analyzes the evolution of the non-racial, populist discourse in South Africa. It would be interesting to extend Horwarth's analysis, which shows how a non-racialist agent, "the people," became the agent of historical change, to Namibia's own post-independence developments from the point of view of discourse theory.

49. As for example in the salutary title of Thornberry's book *A Nation Is Born.*

50. *The Blue Helmets,* op. cit., Chapter 11: United Nations Transition Assistance Group (UNTAG), pp. 201-229.

51. Susan Manuel, "UN media and post conflict peace-keeping," article prepared for UNESCO-seminar, May 3, 2004, http://www.unesco.org/webworld/wpfd/2004.

52. Dan Lindley, *Promoting Peace with Information – Transparency as a Tool of Security Regimes* (Princeton University Press, Princeton, N.J., 2007), p.195.

53. See Lehmann, *Peacekeeping and Public Information,* op. cit., Ch. 7.

54. Fen O. Hampson's concept of "ripeness" best explains the fortuitous circumstances which allowed the Namibia operation to succeed, in: op. cit. (Fn1).

55. Lehmann, op. cit., p. 148.

56. Brian Urquhart, one of the fathers of UN peacekeeping, recently assessed the UN Oil-for Food Programme and summarized well the underlying operational rationale for the ad-hoc activities of the Secretariat:
    "The UN was not originally set up to run complex operations, but almost from the outset it steadily developed programs in the field, especially in peacekeeping, without ever providing adequate permanent structures to support them. Instead, the programs were subject to bureaucratic rules not designed for emergency field operations. *The Secretariat thus often had to rely on a large degree of improvisation*" (emphasis my own).
    Brian Urquhart, "The UN Oil-for-Food Program: Who Is Guilty?," *The New York Review of Books*, vol. LIII, no. 2, February 9, 2006, p. 50.

57. Leon Gordenker, "Policy Making and Secretariat Influence in the UN General Assembly: The Case of Public Information," in: Robert W. Gregg and Michael Barkun (eds.), *The United Nations System and its functions* (Princeton, NJ, 1968), p. 136.

58. Thomas G. Weiss, *International Bureaucracy, An Analysis of the Operation of Functional and Global International Secretariats* (Lexington, MA, 1975), p. 42.

This contrasts with more recent studies of international organizations, such as the one by Michael Barnett cited above (fn. 3), who criticizes the indifference at the UN during the Rwanda crisis of 1994.

59. Barnett, op. cit., p. 576.

Celebrating Multiculturalism:
European Multicultural Media Initiatives
as Anti-Racist Practices

Karina Horsti

Looking back on 20 years of European media policy, which reflects issues of ethnic minorities and immigrants there are significant developments in both policy and implementation. There are a variety of diversity toolkits, books of guidelines, journalism education projects, diversity projects, and policies to increase "cultural diversity" in both media content and workforce. In addition, more minority media have emerged in the context of new migration and technological and demographic changes. The mediascape (Appadurai 2003) where new immigrants and ethnic minorities operate in Europe is therefore increasingly transnational; representations, media productions and media consumptions circulate between localities and create new ideas of belonging. Nevertheless, we need to recognize that national and regional European regulation and resources do play a role in the ways minority media and majority media operate in an increasingly diverse mediascape. For instance, minority media are very much influenced by politics and policy shifts at the national and European levels (Camauër 2003, 84).

Multicultural initiatives within mainstream media and ethnic minority media are interlinked, and the field can be defined as a multi-ethnic public sphere following Charles Husband's (1996) conceptualization. The initiatives to develop a multi-ethnic public sphere in Europe can be analyzed as anti-racist campaigns since the basis of these initiatives lies in multicultural policies, and more deeply in the anti-fascist tradition in Europe. Unlike in the more market-oriented media field and laissez-faire orientation to new immigrants in the United States (Stratton and Ang 1994), northern European media policies of cultural and ethnic diversity in particular have been interventionist and multiculturalist (Awad 2008; Horsti & Hultén forthcoming). However, in the current social setting in Europe, it is difficult to analyze racism—or anti-racism—since public discourse avoids using both concepts. In the early 1990s racism appeared as a general concern among European societies, although racism was often limited to neo-Nazism, rise of right-wing parties, and racist personal attitudes (such as those of Jörg Haider of Austria) rather than treated a structural problem of society as a whole.

Multicultural policies faced "a backlash" in the early 2000s in Europe. Les Back (2007, 133) observes that terrorist attacks in Britain were portrayed as the "end of multiculturalism." Similarly, Peter Hervik (2008, 64) argues that in Denmark a new neo-nationalistic rhetoric signaled an understanding of immigrants, refugees, and their descendants as being incompatible with Danish values and that raw uncompromising intolerance would be the only language the newcomers understand. In this environment, multicultural policies that recognize minority needs would no longer be acceptable. Similarly, Ellie Vasta (2007) argues that the Netherlands has moved from a multiculturalist ethnic minority policy toward an assimilationist majority policy since the turn of the century. Although these countries are perhaps the most extreme examples of shifts in integration and immigration policy in northern Europe, similar discursive changes have taken place elsewhere.

It is a new discourse of "realism" that claims multiculturalism is too "idealistic." Racism became deleted from the public vocabulary in Europe, and cultural diversity discourse took over in situations where plurality and difference are addressed with a more "enlightened" attitude. In contemporary Europe, it is more favored to be "for diversity" than "against racism." Nevertheless, I will be talking about racism and anti-racism in this chapter, particularly to stress the roots and connections to discourses of multiculturalism, assimilation, segregation, racism, and anti-racism, and to treat discourses as shaping and being shaped by current politics in Europe.

This chapter discusses the differences and similarities between multicultural discourses and cultural diversity discourses. Furthermore, it will position these discourses in relation to older anti-racist discourses and movements.

These discourses are further analyzed through the cases of *A Diversity Toolkit* and *The Diversity Show*, which are European collaborations of public service broadcasters to provide tools to implement cultural diversity policies. The toolkit was published in 2007 by the European Union

Fundamental Rights Agency (FRA) in collaboration with the European Broadcasting Union (EBU). The *Diversity Toolkit* is distributed free of charge to anyone interested, and is used in journalistic training in media organizations and journalism schools. There is a DVD with good and bad examples of news and current affairs programs from various European countries and a toolkit with questions that guide training sessions. In addition, there are ethical guidelines and links to relevant websites. *The Diversity Show* was put together mainly by the Dutch public service broadcaster NPS and took place in Hilversum, the Netherlands, on November 6, 2008. It was the third event in a series of seminars organized by the EBU and national broadcasters that focus on multicultural programming. In the show European broadcasters presented their successful formats and shared "good practices" of operating in multi-ethnic societies.

Initiatives such as the *Diversity Toolkit* and *The Diversity Show* are produced to address a certain problem in the changing society and media field. I ask how these initiatives define problems in mainstream media, and what type of policy and implementation these initiatives offer as a prognosis.

Public Service Broadcasting in Multi-Ethnic Societies

Public service broadcasters are particularly important in developing and implementing multicultural media policy since their licenses are based on the "serve all" principle. For instance, the conditions for active membership in the EBU (European Broadcasting Union) are laid down in Article 3§3 of the Union's Statutes,[1] which includes the following paragraph:

> (b) they [members] are under an obligation to, and actually do, provide varied and balanced programming for all sections of the population, including programmes catering for special/minority interests of various sections of the public, irrespective of the ratio of programme cost to audience.

This statement requires a strong commitment from the broadcasters to include minority rights to communication "irrespective of the ratio of cost to audience." However, public service broadcasters who are at the core of this union have traditionally been nationalistic and protective, aiming to cultivate the national imagination and contribute to nation building. Their particular role is to provide national programming to balance international and transnational media flows (Horsti and Hultén forthcoming). Due to strong public service broadcasting in most European countries, the minority axis in programming has been more mission oriented, compared to, for instance, the United States where market orientation has dominated minority issues (Awad 2008).

European collaboration, particularly through European Broadcasting Union (EBU) and/ or European Union (EU) funding takes inspiration and ideas from national experiences and disseminates "good practices" throughout Europe, and provides experience to national broadcasters. Measures are also taken to implement and monitor these policies. New monitoring tools and sanctions are created—the *Diversity Toolkit* being one recent example.

The analysis in this chapter draws on critical discourse and policy analysis (Fairclough 1995, Richardson 2007, Stevens 2003, McGuigan 2002) and asks, how these Europe-wide initiatives define and understand cultural diversity, multiculturalism, and anti-racism. The toolkit and show event are particularly relevant since they attempt to provide concrete tools for implementing diversity policy at the European level.

Fairclough (1995, 56) defines discourse as a language used in representing a given social practice from a particular point of view. Anti-racist, multicultural and cultural diversity discourses are schemes for managing the diverse and changing society. Political, economic, cultural, and social contexts influence the text, its production, and consumption. The text also contributes to the contexts. Critical discourse analysis focuses on the social, political, and economic needs and interests of these discourses.

Critical policy analysis has developed methods to identify problems in policy within various fields such as education, health care, administration, and culture. The aim of this research field is not only to critically discuss the policies but also to improve policy design and implementation. Multiple research methods and data are generally used such as policy documents and interviews with policy actors (see e.g., Stevens 2003, McGuigan 2002). Critical policy analysis examines the purpose, fruition and other aspects of policy and focuses on the complex questions of inducements, rules, facts, rights, and powers. Policy can simultaneously limit options and open up possibilities (Stevens 2003, 662-3).

Multicultural media policy can be analyzed as a crossroads of various more established policy fields. It connects more general law and policy of integration, discrimination, communication, and culture. As policy-making is a dynamic process, multicultural media policy not only is being influenced by these more general policies but also is contributing to their development.

Anti-Racism, Multiculturalism, and Now Cultural Diversity

Anti-racist discourses were used to unite Europe after World War II. Anti-colonialism, anti-slavery, anti-apartheid and anti-fascism were considered to be crucial European values and fundamental basis for politically, economically, and socially unified Europe. Anti-fascism particularly between the 1930s and 1950s was important for recovery from the Nazi trauma. The more recent forms of anti-racism since the 1960s have focused on the position of new immigrants, refugees, asylum seekers, undocumented migrants, and ethnic minorities (Anthias and Lloyd 2002, 6; Lloyd 2002, 64).

Multiculturalism that emerged particularly in northern Europe in the 1970s through the 1980s as a state policy similar to the Canadian multicultural policy could be understood as a form of anti-racism. However, there are also several conflicting points in the intersection of these two discourses that I will discuss later.

Multiculturalism emerged criticizing assimilation policy that was accused of being racist just like the segregation policy that, for instance, Nazi Germany used in its strategy to manage (and finally destroy) ethnic differences. In the 1970s and 1980s, many European countries began to recognize minority languages and cultural rights that had previously been prohibited or ignored during the nation-building process. In the late 1800s and early 1900s, there had been a concern that minorities would threaten the homogeneity of the imagined national community.

This "anxiety of incompleteness" (Appadurai 2006, 8-10) bothered nation-states well into the 1970s when differences began to be treated as something positive and consumable. However, as Appadurai (2006) shows in his studies, the anxiety that majorities often have about minorities is still alive globally, and Europe is no exception. Recent shifts to assimilationist policies and discourses in Europe are one demonstration that nationalism is still there although differently packaged.

Multicultural discourses have been ambivalent and it has not been clear how multiculturalism is defined. First, we should differentiate between multicultural and multiculturalism (Hall 2003, 233-4). If a community is described as multicultural, the understanding is descriptive; multicultural refers to a community with several distinctive "mono" cultures and ethnicities. Sometimes multicultural also refers to individuals who consume these cultures, and thus live a multicultural life (Yack 2002, 109). Multicultural therefore is used as an adjective to illustrate the social characteristics of a society or lifestyle.

Multiculturalism refers to a policy and strategy that nations, the European Union (EU), and other communities and institutions use to manage plurality and social problems related to diversity. The main essence is to make a distinction between the majority and minorities and establish a social system in which minority needs such as language and cultural and religious particularities are recognized. The majority society is determined to protect its minorities' right to practice their own culture. The difficult and most debated section of this policy of course is the limits of multiculturalism and "tolerance." Multicultural euphoria often dismisses the fact that there always is a majority that decides what is tolerated and what is not, what is "too particular," and what is an acceptable difference. Ghassan Hage (2000) criticizes multiculturalism in Australia by claiming that both racist discourse and multicultural discourse share a conception of a nation in which "whites" dominate either through logic of racism or through logic of multiculturalism. "White belief in one's mastery over the nation, whether in the form of a White multiculturalism or in the form of a White racism, is what I have called the White nation fantasy. It is a fantasy of a nation governed by White people, a fantasy of White supremacy" (p. 18).

Although multicultural policies and discourses have roots in anti-racism, the two discourses have had their conflicts. Recent anti-racist movements, such as pro-asylum movements, have also criticized multicultural discourses for their celebration of cultural differences. The British anti-racist movement of the 1980s, for instance, stressed structural and institutional forms of racism, and criticized the focus on individual prejudice, therefore contrasting the movement's politics with multiculturalism (Anthias and Lloyd 2002, 6).

The discursive landscape in Europe changed at the turn of the millennium when multicultural policies became severely criticized in public debate. The argument was that a number of events, such as terrorist attacks in Madrid and London, disturbances in French suburbs, the Prophet Mohammed cartoon crisis in Denmark, and a number of other "crisis" stories related to Muslims such as wearing hijabs in schools, "honor killings," and "forced marriages" all were proof that multicultural policies had failed and produced a lack of social cohesion. Thus, multicultural discourse lost some of its power as an anti-racist tool. Instead, discourse highlighting social cohesion and more vaguely "cultural diversity" came to replace the multicultural approach.

However, all these discourses discussed here can be defined as sets of polycentric, heterogeneous, and overlapping discourses and practices that combine a response to assimilation, racism, and segregation (both biological and cultural logics of racism) (Anthias and Lloyd 2002, 16). I will now discuss the more recent discourse of cultural diversity that has, to a large extent, replaced multiculturalism, for instance, in European public service broadcasting policies where addressing multiethnic societies is set out.

Cultural Diversity Discourse

There are various discursive debates, "diversity politics," on how to solve the problem of non-recognition and misrecognition of ethnic minorities and immigrants. Lentin and Titley (2008) argue that "diversity has become a ubiquitous and widely adopted notion and framework not because it synthesises and furthers an array of political projects and critiques, but because it provides a gently unifying, cost-free form of political commitment attuned to the mediated, consumer logics of contemporary societies" (p. 13). They see the increased use of "diversity" as a fluid phenomenon, which is prevalent in the socio-political work of various international institutions and nongovernmental organizations (NGOs). As multiculturalism has received criticism from various directions, and has gained a negative connotation, diversity is an attempt to re-brand multiculturalism. Nevertheless, the discursive shift is not just re-naming but stresses certain aspects more than others.

First, the diversity paradigm attempted to take a wider scope than multicultural paradigm, treating ethnic and racial differences similar to disability, gender, and sexual orientation. This means that diversity politics could create greater pressure on the dominant "majority" groups as there are also many "natives" in disadvantaged positions. However, the weakness of this unitary position is that the minority front is so diverse that more marginalized and less consumable differences are easily ignored.

Second, diversity politics aim at mainstreaming whereas multicultural policy typically was interested in preserving separate "cultures." Diversity is celebrated to the ultimate extent that people should realize they are different from one another, highlighting the increasingly individualized consumer culture of contemporary European societies. What is different enough to count as "diversity," and what is the limit of diversity, generally remains vague.

Third, diversity is more clearly an issue of competence: everyone's duty and opportunity. Diversity is treated as a fact of life, something inescapable everyone needs to cope with. Whereas multicultural was generally a quality people were born with or gained through practicing multicultural activities, diversity is particularly a skill people should learn.

The discursive shifts are not empirically clear, but should be analyzed as overlapping processes in time and space. The recent shift does not solve the main weaknesses of the multicultural paradigm. The recognition of ethnic/racial identities took place at a time when unequal positioning and marginalization still continue to exist. Although the Council of Europe anti-racist campaign says, "all different all equal,"[2] multicultural policies as well as cultural diversity policies are managed by a group, typically the majority ethnic group within a nation. Diversity discourse attempts to deal with the equality aspect by embracing everyone (to recognize his or her own uniqueness), but in so doing fails to acknowledge the hierarchy and power structures within societies, and thus may end up depoliticizing anti-racism.

Development of Multicultural Media Initiatives in Europe

The mainstream media in Europe has reacted to the demographic and social changes since the 1960s—earlier in larger countries with a colonial past, such as France, Britain, and the Netherlands. The reactions vary from country to country. Generally speaking, the motivation for the recognition of ethnic minorities, migrants, and immigrants in the media has shifted from assimilationist and integrationist positions toward pluralist, multiculturalist, and anti-racist positions (Cottle 1998, 297).[3] In the 1960s, broadcasters aimed at educating new immigrants in the host society's customs in the spirit of assimilation policies and later less obviously in the spirit of integration policies. This is what Sarita Malik (2002, 57) calls classic "public service broadcasts" designed to help integrate the newly arrived immigrants. Furthermore, some broadcasters wanted to present news from the countries of origin to maintain ties with the previous locations. This demand, however, ceased since access to satellite television increased in the 1980s.

The European situation in multicultural media production differs significantly from the situation in the United States where market logic has been the major force in increasing diversity. However, this might be changing in the near future as Isabel Awad (2008) suggests in reference to general media commercialization, privatization, and concentration of ownership—trends that are currently getting stronger in all European countries. Multicultural media policies that particularly public service broadcasters began to implement in the 1980s demonstrated strategies for increased recognition of migrants through a focus on genre, guidelines, and recruitment.

First, initiatives have directed attention to the conventions of journalism and elaborated more flexible genres to give access to minority views, sources, and professionals. Second, all EU countries have codes of ethics, which give more or less specific guidelines for reporting on immigrants and ethnic minorities. Journalists' associations or NGOs generally prepare these codes. In addition, legislation prohibits aggressive racist reporting. Third, recruitment has aimed at solving one of the main problems of minority relations in the European media—the access to the media profession. Training journalists with immigrant or ethnic minority backgrounds has been one of the most important attempts to facilitate access to the profession. Though there are multicultural media initiatives that use at least one of these strategies in most European countries, there is an obvious lack of research in this area (Horsti 2007, Horsti and Hultén forthcoming). Some studies focus on multicultural television and specifically on the producers and editors' viewpoint (see, e.g., Cottle 1998 and 2000; Sreberny 1999; Malik 2002; Leurdijk 2006).

A new tendency appeared this century: the time of specific programming or publishing is passing. In Britain, black-specific programming gradually began to decrease in the mid-1990s, and programming has taken on ethnicity and race in a more playful way. The programs embrace new multiculturalism based on broad-based socially inclusive "cross-cultural" appeal. Similar shifts have taken place, for instance, in Sweden, Finland, and the Netherlands. (See, e.g., Horsti and Hultén forthcoming; Leurdijk 2006; Malik 2002, 71.) Arguments are that the separate slots marginalize the topics and professionals and that these programs do not attract large audiences. The present trend of broadcasters is to extend multicultural policies into all programming and recruitment. In addition, policy documents on cultural diversity have become a necessity in public service broadcasting in the 2000s. However, as public service broadcasting itself is facing economic difficulties, new recruitment policies are more talk on paper than actual practice (Hultén 2009).

Discursive Transitions from Multiculturalism and Anti-Racism to Cultural Diversity Discourse

The European Broadcasting Union (EBU) has been influential in shaping multicultural policies and initiatives at the national level. The multicultural discourse of the 1990s that claimed special rights for minority audiences has passed. Moreover, racism and anti-racism are no longer mentioned. For instance, *Diversity Toolkit* and information material about *The Diversity Show*,[4] avoid using the terms "racism" and "anti-racism." Another recent example in which the European public service broadcasting union EBU was involved with is the *UNESCO Convention on Cultural Diversity*, which entered into force in March 2007. It stresses protection of cultural values in trade agreements, and the worry is this document is focused more on the majority "national" cultures than ethnic minority or diaspora cultures. These recent discourses were not present in the 1990s when, for instance, the EBU was much more concerned about the rise of neo-Nazism and racism than losing "national" cultures. Statements such as the following example are rather difficult to find in documents produced in the 2000s.

In 1994, the EBU adopted a *Declaration on the role of public service broadcaster in a multiracial, multicultural and multifaith Europe* that states the following:

> We public service broadcasters, noting that freedom of expression, including the freedom of the media, is one of the fundamental conditions of a genuine democratic society, are fully aware of the important role that we have to play in a multiracial, multicultural and multifaith Europe. ...
>
> We, as broadcasters, should ensure that our services defend the equal rights and dignity of all human beings, reject trivialization of violence and *act against xenophobia, racism and destructive nationalism*. ...
>
> In concert with the 1993 Vienna declaration of the heads of state and government of the member states of the Council of Europe, we are *concerned at the rise of racism and fascism in Europe and believe it is our duty to combat these attitudes*[5] (emphasis added).

In this declaration, the EBU declares its role in recognizing the rights and needs of minority populations: [...] *are fully aware of the important role*. In this sense, this is an example of pluralist and managed multicultural discourse. This position is legitimated through 1) freedom of expression, 2) democracy, and 3) the public service principle. The EBU is explicitly taking an anti-racist stand: [...] *reject trivialization of violence and act against xenophobia, racism and destructive nationalism, [...] we are concerned at the rise of racism and fascism in Europe and believe it is our duty to combat these attitudes.*

This statement offers a standing point from which I will now analyze in detail the discourse of 2007-2008 as it appears in the *Diversity Toolkit* and *The Diversity Show* website.

Diversity Toolkit and Diversity Show:
Depoliticization of Anti-Racism

As described and analyzed above, media policies and initiatives in many European countries began with a clearly anti-racist position aiming to develop public broadcasting output and production toward a more inclusive public sphere regarding new immigrants in particular. In addition, the aim was to offer experience and knowledge for general audiences to relate to the cultural and demographic changes in their society. Therefore, the aim was to recognize minority identities, avoid misrecognition and construct multicultural self-presentation of the societies.

However, the discourses have changed. The most recent example is *The Diversity Show*, a continuation of two preceding large meetings focusing on cultural diversity among European public service broadcasters. These meetings offer a gateway to the thinking of ethnic minorities and multiculturalism in the current European context. First, why do the broadcasters see diversity policy and practice as important? Behind every policy, there is a need—often a socially shared perception of a problem. What is the perceived problem, and how are the broadcasters solving it? And, more importantly, why has this policy area become increasingly relevant among those in leading positions in the early 2000s?

The problem definition is stated in the information sheet of the 2007 event organized by France Télévisions and UNESCO in Paris: *Migration and Integration, Europe's Big Challenge: What Role Do the Media Play?*[6]

This title presupposes that migration poses challenges to Europe, more precisely the integration of new immigrants. Furthermore, the title suggests that media play a key role. Integration is often described as a "two-way process" in which the immigrant and the receiving society need to change. This thinking is bound to the idea of the national, and does not adequately identify transnational life worlds and the increasing mobility of people, between, to, and out of European countries. Furthermore, the increasing concern of non-integration has brought assimilationist arguments back to the public sphere. Various citizenship and language tests in many European countries try to measure the ability to integrate or assimilate into majority values.

The *Diversity Toolkit* refers to particular key events in Europe to make its argument for the need for cultural diversity policies. Fritz Pleitgen, the director general of the German public service broadcaster WDR and the president of the European Public Service Broadcasting Union, refers to "disturbances in the French suburbs, the Danish cartoon row and terrorist attacks in several European countries" as "clear warning signals showing us that integration, equal rights and a peaceful dialogue between cultures do not happen automatically." These events are brought into discussion as signs of the perceived failure of multicultural policies. More integrative and selective policies are claimed to be the answer. The constructed problem therefore is the immigrants and their lack of integration and sharing of European values—not segregative policies and practices in societies.

These extracts illustrate that the problem is defined as lack of social cohesion, lack of collective identity (particularly European identity), and lack of integration. Since the problems are perceived to be recent, the assumption is that previously (before the rise in immigration) Europe had cohesive and integrated societies, overlooking the heterogeneity of the societies that has always existed but has been marginalized. Although events are presented in a positive and celebrative light, they socially construct and define a certain problem. For instance, *The Diversity Show* ad on the website claims: "So let's face it, media makers. Multiculturalism is a fact of life. Let's get on with it."

Cultural diversity policies are therefore predominantly a response to a disruption in (national) harmony, a fact that needs to be addressed and corrected. The answer is twofold as stated in both the *Diversity Toolkit* and *The Diversity Show*: Diversity should be visible on the screen and part of the newsroom. Such a stress on diversity in media practitioners is a step, which has become clearer in the last few years compared to the earlier phase of the 1980s and 1990s. However, as Gunilla Hultén (2009) points out in the Swedish case, clear statements and policies for culturally diverse newsrooms do not translate into a reality in which journalists with migrant backgrounds would have an equal share of the profession. Sweden, one of the most supportive of such policies in Europe and holding the highest number of prizes delivered at the European Prix Iris event for the best multicultural programming (Horsti 2009), still has a significant divide between the minority population and the share of journalists with a minority background in the journalistic profession.

According to this two-fold policy addressed in both initiatives analyzed here, the aim is to recognize the cultural diversity—or multiculturalism—of European societies in both media texts and productions. If this aim is not met, *The Diversity Show* claims that "this absence creates feelings of indifference or rejection" (retrieved July 15, 2008, from http://www.diversityshow.nl/).

The *Diversity Toolkit* offers practical tools for journalists to deal with multicultural themes, such as coverage of immigration, visibility of ethnic minorities, extending source networks to minority communities, and paying particular attention to balance and perspective. The *Diversity Toolkit* is structured as a DVD collection of examples from different programs broadcasted in different European countries. Each program is accompanied by an introduction to the particular country and case related to the example. There are more general and more exact questions to guide interpretation.

The first most important area where the questions direct attention is the personal mindset of professional journalists. The toolkit encourages journalists to recognize their own attitudes. For instance, there are questions such as "How far does your own mindset influence your choice of stories to cover?" (p. 43). "To what extent do you use music and sounds to achieve a certain impact on the audience?" (p. 19).

Second, the toolkit guides attention to professional skills, standards, and newsroom composition. The toolkit poses questions such as "Do you actively try to recruit colleagues who will bring a diversity of perspective into the newsroom?" (p. 51). "Do I consult more experienced colleagues—and those from different backgrounds—when necessary?" (p. 61).

The first focus stresses the personal level, and therefore builds on the conception that racist discourse is a result of distorted individual attitudes. The second focus recognizes structural racism by giving attention to the recruitment and background of practicing journalists. Nevertheless, an individual definition of racism remains stronger since individuals bring "diversity" into the newsrooms. Practices and structures are not directly addressed.

In the first focus, the problem is identified to exist in personal attitudes; therefore, the solution is education of journalists. Cultural diversity is perceived as competence gained through learning. Therefore, the goal is an enlightened journalist with an anti-racist agenda. As an example of this type of reasoning, I quote Frans Jennekens, chairman of the Eurovision Intercultural and Diversity Group: "In my view diversity is something between the ears. It has to do with opening the mind to other opinions and taking one's own background into account" (p. 6).

As some journalists can be benchmarked as having "cultural diversity competence," it might justify other journalists not having such competence but specializing in other areas (economics, foreign affairs, home, and gardening). Ghettoization, which was one critique against multicultural orientation in media policy, is still not resolved in the new cultural diversity paradigm.

The second focus stresses the recruitment of journalists with minority backgrounds. Therefore, the competence is gained not through learning but through living in a particular position in society. This goal of the *Diversity Toolkit* and *The Diversity Show* approaches an understanding of racism as a product of persistent patterns, practices, and structures rather than distorted personal attitudes. Still, the focus is on the individual, and structures and practices do not play such an important role.

Both objectives, the education of journalists and the recruitment of a more diverse workforce, boil down to the same results: more competent individuals needed in media practice.

Conclusions

The recent European initiatives to increase cultural diversity in the media at a high institutional level stress that ethnic minorities and new immigrants should get access to both the screen and the newsroom. The increased policies and activity in this domain are a result of the perceived threat of the non-integration of the minority population in Europe. Signs of "lack of social cohesion" are interpreted from key events that have been heavily aired in the media: disturbances in French suburbs, the Danish cartoon crisis, and terrorist attacks in Europe. In particular, the public service broadcasters are now taking responsibility for social cohesion in terms of "cultural diversity." This is not just a mission-oriented policy but increasingly a market issue, since public service needs to attract audiences from the increasingly relevant minority population. However, the new discourse of cultural diversity, which has emerged to replace multiculturalism in many ways, tends to depoliticize ethnic minority rights. As cultural diversity is used in a more extensive and vague fashion than multiculturalism, the discourse loses all political power. While everyone has the right to be different, and is claimed to be unique in his or her own one-of-a-kind way, the discourse overlooks power relations and continues to contribute to the marginalization of ethnic minorities.

The analyzed cases see problems at the level of 1) the integration of new migrants and ethnic minorities and at the level of 2) the personal perceptions and attitudes of individual journalists. Therefore, the aim is to educate journalists about minority cultures and customs, and integrate journalists with minority backgrounds into the newsrooms. These policies support a position in which social conflicts are perceived to originate from a lack of communication and understanding.

Social responsibility is increasingly transferred to the migrant: suitability is measured, and difference is managed. At the same time, the diversity discourse has increased. However, it still remains unclear what counts as diversity. Current initiatives, such as the *Diversity Toolkit* and *The Diversity Show*, skirt this issue as much as they can. It seems that suitable difference is preferred, and too radical difference is excluded to reach "social cohesion."

During the past 20 years, the European media have become more aware of minority issues, and this has become an area of expertise within media and communications. However, exclusion of many migrants and ethnic minorities still persists. Cultural diversity and social cohesion are discourses that reflect the latest incarnations of mechanisms to manage difference but fail to recognize power relations and thus continue to reproduce the marginalization of minority groups.

Notes

1. EBU Membership conditions retreived September 30, 2008, from http://www.ebu.ch/departments/legal/activities/leg_membership.php.
2. http://alldifferent-allequal.info/ (referred July 15, 2008).
3. Cottle characterizes the political shifts in the history of the BBC's multicultural programming with these positions. Similar results can be drawn from the report on the Swedish televisions' (SVT) multicultural programming (Andersson, 2000).
4. http://www.diversityshow.nl/ (referred July 15, 2008).
5. EBU declaration on the role of public service broadcasters in a multiracial, multicultural and multifaith Europe, adopted by the EBU television programme committee at its 66th meeting in Geneva on October 25 and 26, 1994. The declaration was reprinted in Diffusion EBU. 2001/4 https://www.ebu.ch/CMSimages/en/publications_automne_2001_tcm6-12444.pdf (referred October 9,2007).
6. The French website of the event, retrieved August 7, 2008, from http://www.integration-media2007.com/ News from UNESCO retrieved August 7, 2008 from http://portal.unesco.org/shs/en/ev.php-URL_ID=11668&URL_DO=DO_TOPIC&URL_SECTION=201.html.

References

Andersson, M. 2000. *25 Colourful years in television.* Stockholm: SVT.
Anthias, F. and Lloyd, C. 2002. Introduction. Fighting racisms, defining the territory. In *Rethinking Anti-racisms. From theory to practice*, ed. Floya Anthias and Cathie Lloyd, 1-21. London: Routledge.
Appadurai, A. 2006. *Fear of small numbers. An essay on the geography of anger.* London: Duke University Press.
Appadurai, A. 2003. Disjuncture and difference in the global cultural economy. In *Theorizing Diaspora. A Reader,* ed. Jana Evans Braziel and Anita Mannur. Oxford: Blackwell.
Awad Cherit, I. 2008. Cultural diversity in the news media: A democratic or a commercial need? *Javnost—the Public*, 15(4): 55-72.
Back, L. 2007. *The art of listening.* Oxford: Berg.
Camauër, L. 2003. Ethnic minorities and their media in Sweden: An overview of the media landscape and state minority media policy. *Nordicom Review* 24(2): 69-88.
Cottle, S. 1998. Making ethnic minority programmes inside the BBC: professional pragmatics and cultural containment. *Media, Culture & Society* 20(2): 295-317.
Cottle, S. 2000. Between rock and a hard place: Making ethnic minority television. In *Ethnic minorities and the media*, ed. Simon Cottle, 100-17. Buckingham: Open University Press.
Fairclough, N. 1995. *Media discourse.* London: Edward Arnold.
Hage, G. 2000. *White nation. Fantasies of white supremacy in a multicultural society.* London: Routledge.
Hall, S. 2003. Monikulttuurisuus. In *Erilaisuus*, ed. Mikko Lehtonen and Olli Löytty, 233-78). Tampere: Vastapaino.

Hervik, P. 2008. *Original spin and its side effects. Freedom of speech as Danish news management.* In *Transnational media events. The Mohammed cartoons and the imagined clash of civilizations*, ed. Elisabeth Eide, Risto Kunelius and Angela Phillips, 59-78. Göteborg: Nordicom.

Horsti, K. 2009. Anti-racist and multicultural discourses in European public service broadcasting: Celebrating consumable differences in Prix Europa Iris media prize. *Communication, Culture & Critique.* 2(3): 339-360.

Horsti, K. 2007. Managed multiculturalism in Finnish media initiatives. *International Journal of Multicultural Societies*, 9(1): 113-130.

Horsti, K. and Hultén, G. (forthcoming) Directing diversity: Managing cultural diversity media policies in Finnish and Swedish public service broadcasting. *International Journal of Cultural Studies.* (Accepted for publication.)

Hultén, G. 2009. Diversity disorders. Ethnicity and newsroom cultures. *Conflict and Communication Online*, 8(2): 1-14.

Husband, C. 1996. The right to be understood: conceiving the multi-ethnic public sphere. *Innovation: European Journal of Social Sciences*, 9(2): 205-16.

Lentin, A. and Titley, G. 2008. More Benetton than barricades? The politics of diversity in Europe. In *The politics of diversity in Europe*, ed. Gavan Titley and Alana Lentin. Strasbourg: Council of Europe Publishing.

Leurdijk, A. 2006. In search of common ground; strategies of multicultural television producers in Europe. *European Journal of Cultural Studies*, 9(1): 25-46.

Lloyd, C. 2002. Anti-racism, social movements and civil society. In *Rethinking Anti-racisms. From theory to practice,* ed. Floya Anthias and Cathie Lloyd, 60-77. London: Routledge.

Malik, S. 2002. *Representing black Britain. A history of black and Asian images on British television.* London: Sage.

McGuigan, J. 2002. Cultural policy studies. In *Critical cultural policy studies,* ed. Justin Lewis and Toby Miller, 23-42. Oxford: Blackwell.

Richarson, J. E. 2007. *Analysing newspapers. An approach from critical discourse analysis.* New York: Palgrave Macmillan.

Sreberny, A. 1999. *Include me in. Rethinking ethnicity on television: audience and production perspectives.* London: Broadcasting Standards Commission in conjunction with the Independent Television Commission.

Stevens, L. P. 2003. Reading first: A critical policy analysis. *Reading Teacher*, 56(7): 662-9.

Stratton, J. and Ang, I. 1994. Multicultural imagined communities: Cultural difference and national identity in Australia and the USA. *Continuum: The Australian Journal of Media & Culture*, 8. (9 December 2003), http://wwwmcc.murdoch.edu.au/ReadingRoom/8.2/8.2.html

UNESCO 1976. Background paper II of the Committee of governmental experts to prepare a draft declaration on race and racial prejudice, 26-30 January 1976. (5 October 2007), http://unesdoc.unesco.org/images/0001/000156/015642eb.pdf

Vasta, E. 2007. From ethnic minorities to ethnic majority policy: Multiculturalism and the shift to assimilationism in the Netherlands. *Ethnic and Racial Studies.* 30(5): 713-740.

Yack, B. 2002. Multiculturalism and the political theorists. *European Journal of Political Theory*, 1(1): 107-19.

The Myth of Racial Democracy: Music and Performance as Interventions into the Public Discourse on Race in Brazil

Nakisha T. Nesmith (Niva Ayodele Flor)

Introduction

Brazil has long been renowned as a "racial democracy." However, the myth of racial democracy starkly contrasts with the realities of a pernicious racial inequality that permeates Brazilian culture and social structure. Yet, with dominant classes perpetuating the false notion that class rather than "race" was central to Brazilian social circumstance, black activists and consciousness movements that attempted to shed light on racial injustice and systematic oppression were viewed by the mainstream as being "racist" and "un-Brazilian." The re-emergence of Afro-Brazilian *blocos afros* (afro blocks)—carnival and cultural-based music groups in the late 1970s marked a major turning point in Brazilian public racial discourse. Using the stage as their platform, these groups began to use "race" to fashion alternative and positive self-images as a means of resistance. This chapter examines *Amulherada,* an all-female carnival group in Salvador, Bahia and the ways in which they use their music to create a space for crafting, negotiating and resisting racial and gender subjectivities.

Salvador, Bahia hosts the largest *festa da rua* or street celebration in the world. In 2006 there were an estimated 2 million attendees, 471,000 of which were tourists, 231 carnival organizations, and 100 trio elétricos (Correio da Bahia 2006, 7). Concentrated in the Central District—Campo Grande, Barra and Ondina neighborhoods, the city practically transforms overnight into a massive six-day street celebration. In theory, carnival is "free" and open to the public. But who and what constitutes "public" is a problematic and recurring theme in Brazil's history—explaining both the permanence of public discourses that reinstitute racism and the anti-racist struggle of activists, leaders, musicians, and socio-cultural organizations seeking resistance to oppression and racist denial.

Discourse theory enables us to consider how dominant structures present limited situations for social change and how subaltern groups resist the ideas and interests of the dominant classes as a basis for political resistance, independence and consciousness (Wodak and Reisigl 1995, 176). The potential for inquiries centered in oppressed cultures and music in particular, offer us a bridge between race, class, and gender, showing us that this type of inquiry is not bound to one specific culture or set of experiences. In this chapter, I examine the particular contributions of Amulherada, an all-female carnival group based in the Centro Historico, Pelourinho. I begin with a brief discussion on race and black activism in order to articulate the dynamics of identities in Brazil, whether they are racial, gender, and/or class. I then address how racism and racist denial inspired cultural-political movements created by and oriented towards Afro-Brazilian communities. I conclude by exploring Amulherada's use of Afro-Bahian popular music, *samba reggae*, and drum performance as a means of reclaiming their voice, and advancing and empowering women, particularly women of color an even more vulnerable group in Brazilian society. A textual analysis of their music reveals how their songs not only offer a reflection of contemporary Afro-Brazilian culture, but illustrates how music and performance can in turn be a tool for liberation, equality and power. This is not to suggest that Afro-Bahian music is a *social movement*, but rather illustrates the creative *use* of music in the struggle for social and political justice.

Race and Black Consciousness

"...Brazilian racism is like a gun at the back of the head rather than one pointed between the eyes"
—José Vicente, president of Afrobras[1] .

Confronting the deeply entrenched structures of race, racial identity, racial categorization, and racism in Latin America is no simple task. For centuries, these questions have provoked intense debates and conflicts, particularly in Brazil—disputes over civil rights, the particularities of race relations and the position of people of African and Indigenous descent and the construction of racial identities in a so-called "non-racialized" society. Scholars of race have devoted great attention in trying to alter Brazil's self-image of a multicultural, non-racist society. They have done this because they were convinced that despite its celebration of racial and ethnic mixture in official as well as popular discourse, racism and racial discrimination in Brazil did exist. As more and more studies began to explore the social and economic positioning of blacks in society, and the dimensions of power between blacks and whites (Fontaine 1985, 58) they found that internalization of mainstream white culture reflected a reality where overt and subtle racism could co-exist, leading to new sensibilities in terms of what it meant to be black and Brazilian (van Dijk 2005). In the modern, urban context, what it means to be black Brazilian has given a new impulse to contemporary formations of black culture, identity, and consciousness that is increasingly present in Brazilian race relations in a variety of powerful and influential ways.

Black Mobilization and Activism

Despite government insistence of racial democracy, Brazil has a long history of black activism and anti-racist movements. The first wave of black activism emerged during the time of slavery with the development of the *quilombos*—autonomous, self-sustaining societies created in the hills of northeast Brazil by former enslaved Africans, free blacks, and Indigenous people. The most famous quilombo is Palmares, led by black leader Zumbi, who for decades headed the resistance against Portuguese invasion. The second wave took place during the period 1914-37 with the rise of the Black press (Nascimento 2007, 122) and Frente Negra Brasileira (Black Brazilian Front), which existed between 1931 and 1937 (Hanchard 1999, 6). Advocating racial equality for Brazilians of color, the Frente Negra was the largest black organization in São Paulo with groups in Rio de Janeiro and Bahia[2] (Marchant 2002, 1). The third wave of black political organization came about in the 1970s as a response to outright discrimination in education, housing, distribution of resources, political power, and social and economic mobility. As a consequence of their subordinate position in society, black consciousness groups began to construct public spheres of their own that challenged Brazil's societal and political norms (Hanchard 1999, 61). In exposing racial ideologies of the Brazilian state and governing elite, many of these political organizations like Movimento Negro Unificado Contra a Discriminação Racial (United Black Movement Against Racial Discrimination) were labeled "un-Brazilian" and racist. This was partly due to the prevailing image of "racial democracy," formulated by sociologist Gilberto Freyre and maintained by the Brazilian elite.[3] This view was also accompanied by an equally ardent faith in *branquemento* or cultural whitening[4]—the belief that importing European literature, music, architecture, music, and emphasizing ethnic/racial mixing would eventually eliminate the non-white population thereby erasing the marks of a primitive past and creating a new and modern "Brazilian" culture. By the mid-1970s, however, working mostly from census data and quantitative studies, scholars were openly critiquing racial democracy. Race and racism, sociologists Nelson do Valle Silva (1978) and Carlos Hasenbalg (1979) argued, no longer needed to be treated like matters of circumstance, but as a day-to-day reality in Brazilian society.

The resurgence of the black movement in the 1980s brought many new voices to the forefront. Cultural activists and political leaders began to take on issues with regard to black awareness and consciousness-raising, marking what I consider to be the fourth wave of black activism. Black workers had more time and money to invest in organizing community and social activities and started to demand equality and show more interest in black pride and in black organizations (Sansone 2003, 25). Patterning themselves after the civil rights and Black Panther movement in the United States, as well as liberation movements in Portuguese-speaking colonies in Africa, blacks began to devise new strategies for self-awareness that were distinctively Afro-Brazilian. At the centennial of the abolition of slavery in 1998, Afro-Brazilian activists protested against it, choosing instead to celebrate November 20th, the day of the death of the Afro-Brazilian liberation leader Zumbi, which today is known as Dia da Conscienca Negra (Black Consciousness Day). Followers of the Movimento Negro Unificado (United Black Front) used statistics to show that blacks had poorer educational facilities, lower incomes, and worse housing than white Brazilians (Butler 1998). They pushed that the color or race *negro* be put on the census to further research about the marginalization suffered by black Brazilians. These actions however, were seen as anything but anti-racist, but rather as racist disruptors to an evolving and more increasingly "modern" Brazil.

Gente de Cor (People of Color)

An in-depth exploration of race, race relations and racial terminology in Brazil and how they have evolved throughout history reveal shifting patterns and meanings over time. In 1991, the census reported that blacks and mestiços make up over 82 percent of the inhabitants of the Salvador metropolitan area, making the percentage of whites in Salvador considerably lower than in other parts of the country (Neves 2002, 4). Only 5 percent of that population however, identified as black.[5] One argument is that blacks are less likely to identify as *negro/a* and more likely to self-identify as *mestiço/a* because of the low value placed on being black. Additionally, many darker skin blacks marry lighter skin or white to improve the chances of their offspring (Sheriff 2001).

In *Shades of Citizenship* (2000) Melissa Nobles examines how color categories used in the Brazilian census helped to support *ideologies* of whitening among Brazilian elites. Her work is important because it highlights how the state can create color or racial categories that may or may not be in line with how citizens understand or interpret these categories (Mitchell n.d.).

European immigrants were accepted into Brazil to supply cheap labor and African immigration was legally barred from 1890 to 1907 (Nobles 2000,100). In the late twentieth century, color choices were limited to white, black, yellow, and the mixed category *pardo*, an ambiguous category connoting the colors white and black and brown.

In Brazil, the self-definition of color defines groups of individuals with similar social and cultural characteristics. Racial terms and/or categories that people use to indicate their own color can also indicate their social position and cultural awareness (Sheriff 2001). When classifying others, these terms do not always refer to physical appearance but is a combination of factors such as hair style, mannerism, educational level, and income. Social whitening occurs when a black or brown person reaches a high economic class level or a certain status of fame. In both instances, whether it is cultural whitening, miscegenation, or social whitening, to be of African descent and/or *negro* is to be significantly valued less.

The Illusion of Inclusion

In 2002, new affirmative action policies mandated that several state universities establish quotas for black students. Two years prior statistics revealed that of the 6000 professors at the University of São Paulo, the largest state university in the country, only 10 were black. Statistics further illustrated that among the 5.8 million Brazilians who completed college 82.8 percent identified themselves as white; 12.2 percent as mixed race; 2.3 percent as Asian; 0.1 percent as Indigenous; and 2.1 percent as black (IBGE 2000).

Critiques of affirmative action argue that such quotas will change the ways in which Brazilians view themselves, especially in the case where race is not determinable by physical appearance (*The Economist* 2003, 32). The promulgation of the Law 10.639/03 that obliged the inclusion of "History and Afro-Brazilian Culture" in the official curriculum of the public system of teaching was monumental in that it was the first time in the nation's history that the government formally addressed the racist exclusion of blacks in the social, economic, and political development of Brazilian history in schools. Many activists and black leaders, however, are not too quick to jump on the bandwagon for fear it will create false hope and false expectations. "I think that the law is necessary," says Carlos Eduardo Santana, former director of education at the Malê Debalê cultural headquarters, "but who is going to teach the teachers who are supposed to be teaching our history?" (Carlos Eduardo Santana, personal interview, February 15, 2006). In 2004, a business college in São Paulo named Zumbi de Palmares University of Citizenship (Lloyd 2004) opened as a response to low admittance and acceptance rates of blacks in colleges and universities. Founded by activist José Vicente, the university reserves 50 percent of its seats for black students. The first university in Latin American history designed for blacks, it offers four-year programs in business administration, and degree programs in law, transportation, urban planning, and education. They have adopted measures to attract students who would otherwise be unable to attend college. For example, classes are held at night for students who have full-time jobs, and the university offers subsidized tuition at half of what students are paying at private colleges.

Education is not the only arena where blacks are left dangling in the social and political balance (Twine 1997, 59). Negative connotations of blackness and acts of violence against blacks are rarely portrayed as such, but rather framed as violence against the poor in combating drugs (Mikevis and Flynn 2005, 1) aiding in the criminalization of blacks in the media. The first ever study of its kind, conducted by SEMUR, Secretaria Municipal da Reparação (Municipal Secretary of Reparation), evaluated the treatment of black workers during Salvador carnival in 2006. The study revealed that the workers worked long hour shifts, earning a mere R15 per night (roughly US $7.50) and were fed and treated poorly by carnival staff and the police. The study also revealed that acts of violence against black parade participants in general were higher than that of whites. Over the course of three days, they recorded 126 accounts of racial discrimination against blacks (Verônica 2006, 3).

Racist Denial and the Public Sphere

There is no denying that Salvador, Bahia has cultural roots in Africa. On almost every street corner are "bahianas"—female street vendors adorned in white lace and colorful beads and jewelry—selling Afro-Brazilian foods and sweets. African-inspired figurines and statues are sold as novelties in shopping malls and local shopping centers. Still, blacks remain underrepresented in practically all sectors of Brazilian society, with the exception of sports and entertainment, the only two sectors where blacks have managed to achieve partial acceptance. Even in these sectors, they are met with resistance by the mainstream that ignores and underestimates the cultural politics that lie at the core of most black Brazilian music (Dunn 1999, 11). Over 100 years after the abolition of slavery, Afro-Brazilians continue to live in poverty and suffer from unemployment and poor healthcare. The irony of Salvador's *hyper-Africanity* is that it paints a portrait of a society that not only embodies black culture, but embraces and valorizes black heritage. In reality, *elements* of Afro-Brazilian culture are selectivity woven into mainstream culture and/or the public domain. Thus, "public" is a contradictory space that remains open to some and closed to others.

For the Brazilian elite, the public sphere has been upheld as the yardstick for modernity, and political and socioeconomic development that did not include blacks.[6] Moments of partial admittance into the public sphere by blacks came only as a consequence to their political struggle and self-motivation. One method in which Afro-Brazilians have been able to address as well as raise serious questions about their denial into the public sphere, as I will point out, has been through music and cultural performance. For Amulherada, music has been the most provocative and effective way of addressing a wide range of contemporary social and political issues, and providing important information to black and non-white poor communities that have little access to media and other print resources.

Cultural Groups and Performance-Based Activist Movements

Cultural groups emerged in Bahia in the 1940s as carnival entities called *afoxés*. They were groups made up mostly of men of the same Candomblé terreiros or temples who gathered in public to perform the music and rhythms of the *orixás,* African deities in the Yoruba pantheon (Dunn 1999). The most famous afoxé was Filhos de Gandhi (Sons of Gandhi) founded in 1949 in homage to the human rights activist Mahatma Gandhi. Early afoxés like Filhos de Gandhi however, did not have a political agenda, but rather a cultural one. Their aim was to gain visibility and reinsert black culture into carnival, at which time was still dominated by white carnival groups and trio eléctricos. Despite their pacifist ideology, Filhos de Gandhi, along with other afoxés were oppressed and persecuted by the local authorities and government.

In sketching the history of race in Brazil, Michael Hanchard (1999) argues that until the 1970s, Afro-Brazilian participation and capitalization of Afro-Brazilian cultural practices were key to the construction of a Brazilian nation. The black cultural movements of the 1980s and 1990s however, began new explorations of *blackness* that drew from international symbols. Deeply rooted in the afoxé tradition, but with an emphasis on the Diaspora and not on Brazil, these contemporary groups sought to connect blacks to a world experience that could not be distinctly Brazilian but Afro-Brazilian, unlike the samba schools, and capoeira schools that had been deemed national symbols. In many instances, these organizations used cultural practice as ways to create a "safe" space for black comfort, as an alternative to the white public sphere. Young Brazilians began to shift their gaze away from Europe and towards the black Diaspora—namely the newly independent nations of Guinea-Bissau, Cape Verde, São Tomé, Angola, Mozambique, the Commonwealth Caribbean, and the United States (Dunn 1999, 8). Cultural groups called blocos afros branded a style known as *samba reggae*, a principal product in the Afro-Bahian movement. Samba reggae is characterized by its percussive style and mixture of Afro-Brazilian samba, Jamaican reggae, and African American soul music (Guerreiro 2000, 57). It differs from any other Brazilian popular music in that it does not incorporate harmonic instruments, such as guitar or piano and is made up of various types of drums, (i.e., surdo, timbau, tarol, timbales, repique) called the *banda* (band) or *bateria* (Guerreiro 2000, 57).

The founders of the first blocos afros were influenced by a political movement out of Rio de Janeiro known as Black-Rio (Dunn 1999, 7). Natural hairstyles and afros known as *bleque pau* or black power, braids, and African dashikis became apart of their newfound blackness, a consciousness that was becoming more increasingly present in the music and performance. Blocos afros were not, as was sometimes presumed, inherently racist in either their design or intent. Rather, drawing from local and national black cultural forms and symbols, these cultural organizations attempted to refashion distinct and organic styles of their own by using their music, dance, and religion, as organizing principles around

Afro-Brazilian identity formation. Many Brazilians, however, still view black consciousness movements as increasing racial polarization. This heightens tensions between Brazilian intelligentsia that has historically claimed Afro-Brazilian cultural practices as Brazilian and activists who seek to devise safe spaces within their own public sphere.

In addition to purely socio-political groups in Brazil, the emergence of cultural groups mainly in Salvador was as equally important to the mobilization of blacks. Black identity movements have typically emerged in the Americas during periods in which the exploitation and oppression of blacks is socially highlighted by political struggle (Walcott 1993; Morris 1984). These movements fostered oppressed group solidarity, linked local exploitation to larger struggles of black peoples, and created a cultural space to articulate anti-hegemonic counter narratives (i.e., new histories, new genealogies, and new links with time and place). Amulherada represents an Afro-centric vision of Brazilian identity among the working class segment of Brazilian society, by continuing to create a new black public sphere in Arjun Appadurai's terms, what we might call Afro-Latin ethnoscape or landscape of identity (Appadurai 1991, 191). Such ethnoscapes are always sites of plurality, where the transnational movement of goods, people, and ideas intersects with localized identities. Amulherada attempts to communicate with and take part in a cultural African Diaspora that reaches far beyond their national borders. Their music, though grounded in a concrete local history, emphasize themes like racism, sexism and resistance that are common in the experience of the entire hemisphere's African population. At the same time however, their music celebrates the survival of black difference in a localized manner, emphasizing a particular musical tradition as the victory over local and national forms of oppression. Thus "blackness" is expressed through music as a cultural ideology that not only unites Afro-Brazilians with a Diasporic inter-culture, but also encourages their disengagement from an oppressive government.

Amulherada

The Amulherada Cultural and Carnival Community Guild first appeared in 1992 under the auspices of the Kallundu Cultural Space, a local community organization aimed at producing social activities in and around Salvador. In 1994 the women's ensemble Kallundu and the Kallundetes was formed, and four years later in 1998 they created the youth bloco Kallundinhos which paraded in the Batatinha Circuit (small carnival route near Salvador's Central District). In 2001, Amulherada was formed under the directorship of Monica Kalile, taking two things from the original ensemble—women drummers and a rhythm invented especially for the group, *muana*, which means "black child." The muana is based upon the foundation of Candomblé (ageré de Iansã) and samba. Beyond muana, the bloco also utilizes funk, meringue, samba reggae, reggae, and afoxé. In 2002, Amulherada marched in carnival joining together with thousands of women from various organizations such as Forum das Entidades Negras, Unegro, Pastoral Afro, CEAO, CEAFRO, Coletivos de Mulheres Negras, Escola Luza Mahin, and the Associação de Lavadeiras do Abaeté (Monica Kalile, personal interview, April 12, 2006). In addition to working with youth and women's advocacy organizations, Amulherada partners with various community based organizations as well as gives performances and workshops in dança afro (afro dance) and capoeira.

Music as Activism

"To sing words is to elevate them in some way, to make them special, to give them a new form of intensity"

—Simon Frith[7]

The transformative quality of music is undoubtedly one of the most powerful and influential forms of expression in humankind. Many scholars have explored the effectiveness of music as a tool for social commentary and political activism. Their findings placed music at the heart of bridging communication gaps within communities, mobilizing social protest, promoting activism and group solidarity, raising consciousness, spreading awareness and hope and generating resources, financial and otherwise (Baraka 1963; Moore 1997; Baer and Singer 2002; Adams 2002; Keyes 2004; Reed 2005; Peddie 2006; Salime 2008). A sense of powerlessness and the desire to want to effect change within oppressive governments has led many communities to seek ways to express their discontent through and by music. Derek Walcott in this discussion of national development, black resistance, and identity formation argues:

The history of black music enables us to trace something of means through which the unity of ethics and politics has been reproduced as a form of folk knowledge. This sub-culture often appears to be the intuitive expression of some racial essence but is in fact an elementary historical acquisition produced from the viscera of an alternative tradition of cultural and political expression which considers the world critically from the point of view of its emancipatory transformation. In the future, it

will become a place which is capable of satisfying the (refined) needs of human beings that will emerge once the violence—epistemic and concrete-of racial typology
is at an end. Reason is thus reunited with the happiness and freedom of individuals
and the reign of justice within the collectivity (Walcott 1993, 137).

Simon Frith points out that the relation between text and song has been
explored in African American music because song was both "culturally
important for so long as a means of expression of all sorts, and because,
for the same oppressive historical reasons, oral culture (rather than print)
for so long remained the source of social identity" (Frith 1996, 174).
The politics of music and cultural resistance practiced by Afro-Brazilians points specifically to the formation of community. For Amulherada,
music is a vehicle for addressing pertinent social and racial issues, not
just as Afro-Brazilians, but as Afro-Brazilian women. Music is therefore
the means of achieving two attainable goals: 1) cultural preservation
and community building and 2) gender equality and advancement of
women's rights.

Songs for Social Protest

More than a carnival group, Amulherada is also a non-governmental
organization (NGO) that works for women's rights and for the rights of
Afro-Brazilians. According to Monica Kalile, Amulherada uses carnival
as a platform to discuss the exploitation and discrimination of black
women. In 2006, there were only two all-female percussion ensembles
in Salvador. Goli Guerreiro suggests the lack of women percussionists
is due to percussion's origins in the ritual space, which historically
did not permit women (Guerreiro 2000, 197). Amulherada's theme for
2006 carnival was *Capoeira—Herança Africana* (Capoeira—African
Heritage). They attempted to demonstrate the role of capoeira, an African Brazilian martial art that for centuries has been used as a form of
resistance against slavery. In tribute to capoeira and capoeira master
teachers in Salvador, Amulherada invited various capoeira groups to
parade and perform with them, one of the only groups during carnival
to have capoeira as an integral part of their performance.

One out of many self-composed songs Amulherada performed during
carnival included "Anjos do Tambor"[8] (below), by Monica Kalile, Juci
Pereira, Itamar Tropicália, and Welington Epiderme Negra. In this song,
they carve out their space in the historically male-dominated world of
percussion by proclaiming that women are not the weaker sex, but are
strong and powerful. They later go on to refer to themselves as the "anjos

do tambor," or angels of the drum playing in Pelourinho, the historic center of Salvador and home to nationally and internationally known carnival groups Olodum, and Filhos de Gandhi:

Elas são mulheres	They are women
Da cabeça aos pés	From head to toe
Tocam percussão	They play percussion
Não devem nada a ninguém	They don't owe anything to anyone
Me dizem que é sexo frágil	They tell me that it is the weaker sex
Quem disse se enganou	Who said that is mistaken
Hoje as mulheres	Today women
Estão mostrando seu valor	Are showing their worth
Me dizem que é sexo frágil	They tell me that it is the weaker sex
Quem disse se enganou	Who said that is mistaken
Hoje as mulheres	Today women
Estão tocando no tambor	Are playing the drum
Tocando no tambor	Playing the drum
Tocando no pelô	Playing in Pelo
Anjos do tambor	Angels of the drum

In "Zumbi + 10 Do Norte" (below), by Sérgio Participação and Monica Kalile, they proudly affirm the role of women as warriors and their struggle against prejudice and racism. This song demonstrates the blurred lines between race and gender struggle. In the case of Amulherada, the struggles are interconnected. In other words, they see their struggle for gender equality very much linked to their struggle for racial equality. Testifying to the experience of black women, they locate the black experience of oppression back to the gender oppression of women, calling attention to the particular struggle of the oppressed black woman.

Do Nordeste	From the Northeast
Do Centro Oeste	From the Central West
Do Sul	From the South
Mulheres negras que lutam	Black women who fight
Pelo seu espaço	for their space
Na luta	In the struggle
Na batalha	In the battle
Seu suor derramado	Their spilled sweat
Autoridade máxima	Maximum authority
Preste bem atenção	pay close attention
Deixa de preconceito	let go of prejudice
Somos todos irmãos	We are all brothers and sisters

Preconceito não!	No Prejudice!
Racismo não!	No Racism!
Somos mulheres guerreiras	We are women warriors
A vitória está em nossas mãos	The victory is in our hands.

"Guerreiras Invenciveis" (below), by Valdinei Riosand Roque Carvalho, brilliantly addresses women and their role in the creation of humankind. This song is novel because is suggests that the black movement cannot exist without acknowledging and celebrating women as essential players in its creation. This kind of song raises serious questions about women's involvement and total inclusion in the Brazilian black movement.

Somos feras indomáveis	We are wild animals
Honra e gloria da nação	Honor and glory of the nation
Por uma causa africana	For an African cause
Lecionamos a lição	We teach the lesson
Somos guerreiras invencíveis	We are invincible warriors
Se inflamar pode haver confusão	If you mess with us there will be problems
Pra manter ordem no mundo	To keep order in the world
Estamos para o que der e vier	We are here for anything
Estamos pra Desmon Tutu	We are Desmond Tutu
Jessy Jackson e Mandela	Jessie Jackson and Mandela
Marcus Garvey e Pelé	Marcus Garvey and Pelé
Estamos em Salvador	*We are in Salvador*
Kingston e Yaundé[9]	*Kingston and Yaundé*
Despetalando a negra flor	Deflowering the black flower
No coração de uma mulher	In the heart of the woman
No coração de uma mulher	In the heart of the woman

Finally, "Encanteira" (Enchanted), by Valmir Britto and J. Batista, echoes the importance of black women's role in the movement by linking the Bahian experience to the interdiasporic struggle of African women.

Mulher gera o mundo e faz girar	Women generate the world and make it go round
Menina, Mulher, Mulherada	Girl, Woman, All Women
A Mulherada Baiana Africana	African Bahian Women
Me Chama	Call me
A Mulherada Baiana Encanta	African Bahian Women enchant
E Sabe Amar	And know how to love

Mulher Rendeira	Seamstress woman
Mulher Lavadeira	Launderer woman
Cheia de graça	Full of grace
Cheia de amor no coração	Full of love in the heart
Veio ao mundo fazer gerar	Came to the world to create life
É luz na escuridão	They are the light in the darkness
Razão	Reason
Que a emoção pode ver	That emotion can see it
Cantando pra não chorar	Singing to not cry
Sorrindo pra não sofrer	Smiling to not suffer
Saber viver a vida	To know how to live life
No mundo inteiro	In the whole world
Sou baiana sou guerreira	I am Bahian, I am warrior
com meu canto de primeira	With my prime song
eu sou África eu sou África	I am Africa, I am Africa
No mundo inteiro	In the whole world
Sou Baiana	I am Bahian,
Genitora da beleza	Progenitor of beauty
Eu sou África, eu sou África, mama Africana	I am Africa, I am Africa, Mother Africa[10]

Conclusion

While racism, racist denial, and discrimination are very much part of Brazilian society, Amulherada constitutes a channel for expression and rebellion, and a social critique by means of collective manifestation (Caldas-Coulthard 1996). Creating spaces for the performance of black music, Amulherada appropriates spaces and symbolic forms in order to create objective and collective forms of dissent. The mass appeal of *samba reggae* brought this new form of music to the attention of the government and the music and entertainment industry, giving black artists and black music more visibility and economic mobility than ever before. As I demonstrated, Amulherada's song lyrics range from local to global, and traditional to contemporary, evoking personal sentiments and experiences. Interestingly enough, social messages behind the music often do not go further than that to critically analyze the society that creates this level of disparity and frustration. In this regard, the black cultural movement has failed. This failure to create a dialectical approach between racism and prejudice in Brazilian society and samba reggae place many groups like Amulherada at risk of becoming just another popular music commodity as the mainstream tries to normalize and silence their subjected and oppressive experience of Afro-Brazilians. Still,

Amulherada continues to draw attention to the social ills and problems that plague Brazilian society by highlighting the complex, overlapping concepts and challenges of race, gender and sexuality. These challenges are key to understanding the socio-political struggles and the historical trajectory of racism and oppression against blacks in Brazil.

Notes

1. Out of eden: Race in Brazil. 2003. *The Economist* 368 (8331): 32-34. http://www. economist.com/printedition/displayStory.cfm?Story_ID=1897546 (accessed April, 2009).
2. In 1935, the Getúlio Vargas regime put an end to the organization by outlawing all political organizations based on racial affiliations. Attempts were made to rekindle the black movement, but black organizations during the Second Republic, 1946-1964, refrained from direct political participation. Among the most successful was the Black Cultural Association which worked in conjunction with the Black Experimental Theater and the Brazilian People's Theater (Puerto, n.d.).
3. In his most noted work, *Casa Grande e Senzala*, Freyre's principal concern was not to affirm African culture, but rather examine its impact on the formation of the Brazilian family, which in turn affected Brazilian society as a whole.
4. Much of the literature of the 1940s echoed Freyre's conceptualization of racial democracy. In *Negros in Brazil: A Study of Race Contact at Bahia* (1942), Donald Pierson argued that there was a cordial relationship between races, because slavery was more "humane" and Portuguese colonizers were more accepting of religion, cuisine, and other cultural beliefs practiced by blacks. In the late 1950s, The United Nation Educational, Scientific, and Cultural Organization (UNESCO) developed a research project that enabled Brazilian scholars to conduct investigations of their own. In contrast to Freyre's assertions, these scholars found evidence of racial inequality.
5. The 2000 census showed that the number of people that self-identified as black increased to 6.2 percent. At the same time, there were less people calling themselves pardo, preferring instead to identify as white. Brazilian Institute of Geography and Statistics, http:// www.ibge.gov.br.
6. In *The Structural Transformation of the Public Sphere*, Jürgen Habermas (1962) defined the bourgeois public sphere as an imaginary community "made up of private people gathered together as a public and articulating the needs of society with the state" (176).
7. Simon Frith, *Performing Rites: On the Value of Popular Music* (Cambridge, MA: Harvard University Press, 1996), 174.
8. Lyrics from Anjos do Tambor, Zumbi + 10 Do Norte, Guerreiras and Invenciveis Encanteira may not be reproduced without permission from the copyright holders.
9. Capital city of south-central Cameroon.
10. Songs are author's translations.

References

Adams, Jacqueline. 2002. Art in social movements: Shantytown women's protest in Pinochet's Chile. *Sociological Forum* 17 (1): 21-56.

Appadurai, Arjun. 1991. Global ethnoscapes: notes and queries for a transnational anthropology. In *Recapturing Anthropology: Working in the Present*, ed. R.G. Fox, 191-210. Santa Fe, NM: School of American Research Press.

Baraka, Amiri. [1963] 1988. *Blues People: Negro Music in White America*. Westport, CT: Greenwood Press.

Bear, Hans, and Merrill Singer. 2002. *African American Religion: Varieties of Protest and Accommodation*. Knoxville, TN: University of Tennessee Press.

Butler, Kim D. 1998. *Freedoms Given Freedoms Won: Afro Brazilians in Post Abolition São Paulo and Salvador*. New Brunswick, NJ: Rutgers University Press.

Caldas-Coulthard, Carmen Rosa and Malcolm Coulthard, eds. 1996. *Texts and Practices: Readings in Critical Discourse Analysis*. London: Routledge.

Dia da Consciência Negra: Retrata Disputa pela Memória Histórica. *Com Ciência*, October 11, 2003. http://www.comciencia.br/reportagens/negros/03.shtml (accessed April 4, 2010).

Dunn, Charles. 1992. Afro-Bahian carnival: A stage for protest. *Afro-Hispanic Review* 11(1-3): 11-20.

Fontaine, Pierre-Michel. 1985. Blacks and the search for power in Brazil. In *Race, Class, and Power in Brazil,* ed. Pierre-Michel Fontaine, 58-73. Los Angeles: Center for Afro-American Studies, University of California Los Angeles.

Frith, Simon. 1996. *Performing Rites. On the Value of Popular Music*. Cambridge, MA: Harvard University Press.

Guerreiro, Goli. 2000. *A Trama Dos Tambores: A Musica Afro-Pop De Salvador*. Editora: São Paulo, Brazil.

Habermas, Jürgen. [1962] 1991. *The Structural Transformation of the Public Sphere*. Cambridge, MA: The MIT Press.

Hanchard, Michael. 1999. Black cinderalla? Race and public sphere in Brazil." In *Race Politics in Contemporary Brazil,* ed. Michael Hanchard, 56-76. London: Duke University Press,

Hasenbalg, Carlos. 1979. *Discrimacão e Desigualdades Raciais*. Rio de Janeiro: Edições Graal.

Hasenbalg, Carlos and Nelson do Valle Silva. 1999. Notes on racial and political inequality in Brazil. In *Race and Politics in Contemporary Brazil,* ed. Michael Hanchard, 34-45. London: Duke University Press.

Instituto Brasileiro de Geografia e Estatística. http:// www.ibge.gov.br.

Keyes, Cheryl L. 2004. *Rap Music and Street Consciousness*. University of Illinois Press.

Kalile, Monica. 2006. Personal Interview. Salvador, Bahia Brazil. April 12.

Kraay, Hendrik. 1998. The politics of race in independence-era Bahia: The black militia officers of Salvador, 1970-1840." In *Afro-Brazilian Culture and Politics,* ed. Hendrik Kraay, 89-213. London: M. E. Sharpe.

Lloyd, Marion. 2004. In Brazil, a different approach to affirmative action Latin America's first university for black students opens amid a countrywide debate about quotas." *Chronicle of Higher Education*, October 29. http://chronicle.com/article/In-Brazil-a-Different/24399 (accessed May 10 2009).

Marchant, Elizabeth. 2002. An interview with Fernando Conceição." *Callaloo* 25 (2): 613-619.

Margolis, Mac. 2003. Brazil's racial revolution: Affirmative action has finally come of age. *Newsweek.* November 3. http://www.newsweek.com/id/60298 (accessed May 9, 2009).

Mikevis, Dayanne and Matthew Flynn. 2005. Brazil's Black civil rights activists achieving overdue policy reform. Americans Program, Center for International Policy. http://americas.irc-online.org/amcit/731 (accessed May 30, 2009).

Mitchell, Gladys. n.d. Whitening, color identification, and support for affirmative action in Brazil. Masters Thesis, University of Chicago.

Moore, Robin. 1997. *Nationalizing Blackness: Afrocubanismo and Artistic Revolution in Havana, 1920-1940*. Pittsburgh, PA: University of Pittsburgh Press.

Moraes, Christina De and Eder Luis Santana. 2006. Carnaval de Salvador atrai mais turistas. *A Tarde*. Salvador. February 23.

Morris, Aldon. 1984. *The Origins of the Civil Rights Movement: Black Communities Organizing for Change*. New York: The Free Press.

Nascimento, Elisa Larkin. 2007. *The Sorcery of Color: Identity, Race, and Gender in Brazil*. Philadelphia: Temple University Press.

Neves, Franscesco. 2002. Two Brazils. *Brazzil*. http://www.brazzil.com/cvrmay02.htm (accessed May 5, 2009).

Nobles, Melissa. 2000. *Shades of Citizenship: Race and the Census in Modern Politics*. Stanford, CA: Stanford University Press.

Números do circuito. 2006. *Correio da Bahia*. Salvador. March 17.

Out of eden: Race in Brazil. 2003. *The Economist* 368 (8331): 32-34. http://www.economist.com/printedition/displayStory.cfm?Story_ID=1897546 (accessed April, 2009).

Peddie, Ian, ed. 2006. *The Resisting Muse: Popular Music and Social Protest*. Burlington, VT: Ashgate.

Puerto, Alexandra. n.d. The Brazilian black movement in the twentieth century: A middle-class mulatto monopoly. http://userwww.sfsu.edu/~epf/1997/puerto.html (accessed April 1, 2010).

Reed, Thomas Vernon. 2005. *The Art of Protest: Culture and Activism from the Civil Rights Movement to the Streets of Seattle*. Minneapolis, MN: University of Minnesota Press.

Salime, Zakia. 2008. Mobilizing Muslim women: Multiple voices, the sharia, and the state. *Comparative Studies of South Asia, Africa and the Middle East* 28 (1): 200-211.

Sansone, Livio. 2003. *Blackness without Ethnicity: Constructing Race in Brazil*. New York: Palgrave Macmillan.

Santana, Carlos Eduardo de. 2006. Personal Interview. Salvador, Bahia Brazil. February 15.

Sheriff, Robin E. 2001. *Dreaming Equality: Color, Race, and Racism in Urban Brazil*. New Brunswick, NJ: Rutgers University Press.

Silva, Nelson Valle do. 1978. White non-white income differentials: Brazil. PhD diss., University of Michigan.

Twine, France W. 1997. Racism in a Racial Democracy: The Maintenance of White Supremacy in Brazil. New Brunswick, NJ: Rutgers University Press.

Van Dijk, Teun. 2005. *Discourse and Racism in Spain and Latin America*. Amsterdam: John Benjamins Pub.

Verônica, Sylvia. 2006. Sai o balanço do preconceito na folia. *A Tarde*. March 3: 3-4.

Walcott, Derek. 1993. "It ain't where you from, its where you're at: The dialectics of diaspora identification." In *Small Acts: Thoughts on the Politics of Black Culture*, ed. Paul Gilroy, 120-145, London: Serpents Tail.

Walker, Sheila, ed. 2001. *African Roots/American Cultures: Africa in the Creation of the Americas*. Lanham, MD: Roman and Littlefield Publishers Inc.

Winant, Howard. 1999. Racial democracy and racial identity: Comparing the United States and Brazil." In *Race and Politics in Contemporary Brazil*, ed. Howard Winant, 45-61. London: Duke University Press.

Wodak, Ruth and Martin Reisigl. 1999. Discourse and racism: European perspectives." *Annual Review of Anthropology* 28: 175-199.

British Asians and the Cultural Politics of Anti-Racist Campaigning in English Football[1]

Daniel Burdsey

Introduction

In October 2004, the *Guardian* newspaper reported that Aston Villa, an English Premier League football club, was in negotiations with a production company about making a television series. Taking advantage of the contemporaneous public popularity of so-called "reality" shows, such as *Big Brother*, *Hell's Kitchen*, *X Factor* and *I'm A Celebrity ... Get Me Out Of Here!* on British television,[2] the program would focus on a promising young British Asian footballer and follow his attempts to progress from the club's academy (youth section) to the first-team squad (MacInnes 2004). Whilst the use of mass communication media has become an increasingly common feature of anti-racist campaigning, this project would have represented a truly unique contribution towards the aim of overcoming one of English professional football's most inveterate social problems—its widespread failure to recruit and include players from its British Asian communities.[3] However, from the outset such an approach appeared ill-considered, tokenistic, and inevitably ephemeral, ignoring or trivializing the racial prejudice and discrimination, and the repercussions of white privilege, habitually experienced by British Asian players.

Whether it was due to amendments to the original idea, or the fact that the newspaper report was inaccurate, a television show of this description never materialized.[4] Instead, in February 2005, Aston Villa launched a different program: *Villawannabee*. This competition involved local young players battling it out to win a six-week trial with the club. Open to players from all ethnic backgrounds, it appeared far-removed from the "reality" show described above. Nevertheless, if the wider repercussions of the competition are considered, the club's potential motives and desired outcomes may well have been the same.

Villawannabee was screened for nine weeks on the Asian Television Network (ATN), a South Asian entertainment channel available in Britain on digital satellite television. ATN has a predominantly (if not exclusively) British Asian audience and the show was co-presented by Tasmin Lucia Khan of the BBC Radio Asian Network.[5] This suggests that the project was strongly underpinned by a commercial imperative and was perceived as a way of promoting the club and its brand to British Asian communities, especially the large number in the city of Birmingham, where the club is situated.[6] Out of 2500 contestants, the competition was, somewhat predictably, won by a British Asian teenager, Pavitar Randhawa. Whilst any suggestion that British Asian viewers would only vote for a British Asian player is both simplistic and reproduces the ethnic absolutism that Gilroy (1992) criticizes, the club were surely aware that such a result was not unlikely. The probability of *Villawannabee* being used by the club as a marketing tool to attract British Asian supporters is increased when one considers that in the succeeding months the club announced its plans to repeat the competition in India. The belief that marketing and development work in the Indian subcontinent will help to overcome the exclusion of *British* Asians represents a truly misguided and essentialist logic, but it is becoming increasingly common in English professional football (Burdsey 2007).

While *Villawannabee* initiated a tentative and partial connection between Aston Villa and its local British Asian communities, it would be naïve to believe that it will have significant repercussions in overcoming the latter's exclusion from the game. Any strategy that revolves around novelties and popular cultural fads rather than challenging football's power structures and the procedures, behaviors, and attitudes that discriminate against, and exclude, minority ethnic groups from the professional game is going to be inexorably unstable, transient, and ineffective. However, as this chapter demonstrates, the former approach often dominates and, as such, reduces the effectiveness of many attempts to increase the inclusion of British Asians in English professional football.

Outline of the Chapter: Standpoint and Content

Before outlining the standpoint and content of this chapter, it is important to first provide some brief portraiture of the topic under investigation.

Football has become an increasingly popular and socially significant leisure activity for many young British Asians (Bains and Johal 1998; Burdsey 2006). However, despite the fact that they comprise over three percent of the population in Britain, only six British Asians were on the playing rosters of the 92 professional league clubs during the 2009-2010 season.[7] This state of affairs has been created and sustained by a number of imbricating factors. First, the pervasive influence of racism, the marginalizing effects of hegemonic whiteness, and (post)colonial discourses that have emasculated the South Asian body, have combined to exclude British Asians from the game. Second, the historical absence of British Asians from professional football as players, coaches, managers, administrators, and directors has meant that young players continue to be excluded from the contact networks that have facilitated white, and to a lesser extent African-Caribbean, participation. In other words, their limited social and cultural capital in the game means that the necessary re-cruitment processes remain unfamiliar or inaccessible (Burdsey 2004b). Thirdly, racism in amateur football has forced many British Asian clubs to compete in ethnically segregated leagues and tournaments which, for a number of reasons, are seldom scouted by professional clubs in their search for talented young players (Burdsey 2004a).[8] In this sense, the chapter builds from a belief that racism is not just ideological; rather, it permeates the *structures* of the English game.

From the late 1990s, the paucity of British Asians in professional football began to attract substantial attention from a number of agencies, both inside and outside the game. In particular, it has become a prominent issue on the agenda of the anti-racist football movement, i.e., the loose coalition of national and regional organizations, club-based initiatives, and governing bodies that seek to eradicate racism from, and promote racial equality in, English football. Such interventions are very timely and extremely welcome. However, this chapter argues that, despite the largely well-meaning intentions of these organizations, it has become apparent that their effectiveness in increasing the participation of British Asians in professional football is limited. Whilst they have helped to challenge some of the stereotypes about British Asians and their involvement in football, they often inadvertently utilize and reproduce outdated, culturalist interpretations of their lifestyles and identities as well. As a result many policies and strategies fail to reflect and represent the interests, attitudes and aspirations of young British Asian players and supporters.

The following analysis argues that there is a pressing need to rethink the nature and practical implementation of certain aspects of current initiatives. Such critical reflection will not only elucidate the theoretical complexities surrounding issues of race and ethnicity in football, but in a more pragmatic sense it also enables us to evaluate which aspects of anti-racism are "working," which are not, and why. This is a crucial procedure as we strive to challenge and eradicate racism, and to improve the efficacy of racial equality strategies in English football. Academic analyses have often been divorced from the work of activists and practitioners (Alexander and Alleyne 2002), whilst the *politics* involved in undertaking research in ethnic and racial studies is not always given adequate attention (Alexander 2006). Yet challenging racism (amongst other forms of discrimination) requires an appreciation of the mutually beneficial relationship between theory and practical implementation. As Miles (1989: 5) states, "as has been said on countless occasions concerning the unity of theory and practice, if the analysis is wrong, then it is likely that the political strategy will not achieve the intended objectives."

Accordingly, this chapter embodies a commitment to critical social research in that it "is characterised by a concern to interrogate and expose relations of social power, not merely as a disinterested academic exercise, but as part of a broader project of progressive social transformation" (McDonald 2002, 100). In other words, this paradigm represents a political struggle against oppressive social structures (Harvey 1990). More specifically, this chapter is underpinned by the principles of Critical Race Theory (CRT). CRT necessarily involves a commitment to the pursuit of social justice for it facilitates "resistance to the passive reproduction of established practices, knowledge and resources that make up the social conditions that marginalise 'race' logic and racialised processes as core factors in the way we manage and experience our sport and leisure" (Hylton 2009: 23).

CRT also emphasizes the importance of centering marginalized "voices" and, in this instance, those of British Asian players themselves. Their attitudes, aspirations, beliefs and experiences are intrinsic both to the generation of knowledge in this area and to constructing pragmatic responses to fighting racism. As Lentin (2004, 250) identifies, "often in anti-racism, representation has been constructed on the basis of assumptions by white anti-racists, made without consulting the populations whose interests they feel themselves to be representing." The research on which this chapter is based therefore utilized a life story/oral testimony approach as a means of trying to overcome the "silencing" of marginalized groups. Empathetic understanding arguably cannot substitute experiential knowledge of racism, however, and it is recognized that attempting to promote counterdiscourses can actually elide oppressed voices and simply reconstruct an alternative master narrative.

The position adopted here is one that is unequivocally supportive of the need to continually and actively challenge racism in English professional football, yet is critical of some of the procedures and strategies through which race equality and anti-discrimination measures are implemented in the game. More specifically, issue is taken with some of the intrinsic components of schemes that seek to promote the inclusion of British Asian players and supporters in professional football. These include the hegemony of white, middle-class men, and the related failure to engage and consult with young British Asian players; and the tendency to adopt Eurocentric frameworks and approaches that essentialize ethnic identities. In this regard, this chapter draws particularly on the work of Paul Gilroy and the radical critique of anti-racism espoused in his essay "The End of Antiracism" (Gilroy 1992).

Bell points out that "one of the main problems of writing "the End of Antiracism" was of course that Gilroy ran the risk of his critique being cast back into the lines of the debate itself: how could he take a stand that was both sympathetic to the intent of the anti-racist campaigns and be critical of them?" (2002: 511). However, as Gilroy and others have demonstrated, for anti-racism to be effective it needs to undergo continual critical evaluation. Put simply, it is "necessary to take a hard and perhaps painful look at the terms under which [it has] operated so far" (Rattansi 1992, 11). This process is crucial as we—as scholars, activists and/or supporters—strive to map and eradicate contemporary racisms.

The content of this chapter can be divided into five broad sections. First, the chapter briefly traces the historical development of anti-racism in English football and locates current trends in the wider socio-political context. Second, it critically analyses the way that British Asians, and their exclusion from the professional game, are represented within dominant discourses. This section introduces the concept of "positionality" as a means of challenging "commonsense," essentialist assumptions about race and racism. It also examines the positioning of (particular) British Asians as a "model minority" and assesses the ramifications for professional football. Building on this analysis, the third section provides a critique of the ways that British Asian footballers and supporters are often represented in anti-racist discourses and policies. It combines theoretical reflections on the application of concepts such as ethnicity, culture and community with empirical interview material. Fourth, the chapter assesses the implications of prioritizing "official multicultural-ism" in attempts to increase British Asian inclusion. Finally, a framework is outlined for trying to contextualize these players' experiences and challenge the discrimination that they face.

Anti-Racism in English Football: The Policy Context

The introduction of a visible, co-ordinated and proactive anti-racist movement was one of the most welcome advances in English football in the late twentieth century. Whilst football stadia have been frequently used as sites for the articulation of racist discourses and manifestations of racist violence since the 1930s, a discernible *anti*-racist movement did not emerge until much later. Embryonic *ad hoc* responses occurred in the late 1970s in opposition to the pernicious and increasing influ-ence of far right groups, such as the National Front (NF), who sought to canvass support amongst fans at certain clubs. However, it took another decade—and significant wider developments in supporter organization, resistance and empowerment—before a more formalized movement be-gan to develop. Initiatives tended to be organized on an individual club basis and it was often at those clubs previously targeted by the NF that the most prominent campaigns were formed (Thomas 1995).

The relative successes of these disparate, localized initiatives created a conducive climate for a project to be designed and undertaken on a bigger scale. This was provided by Let's Kick Racism Out of Football, the first organization to implement a national, "umbrella" anti-racist football campaign. The scheme was launched in 1993 by the Com-mission for Racial Equality (CRE).[9] In 1997 it became independent and adopted the title it currently holds: Kick It Out.[10] It is undoubtedly because of the influence and assiduous lobbying of Kick It Out that the game's governing bodies have finally started to acknowledge racism and many professional clubs (both in the UK and continental Europe) are now initiating their own anti-racist projects. By the start of the twenty-first century the anti-racist football movement was arguably the most prominent popular cultural anti-discrimination initiative in Britain. Anti-racist projects in other areas, such as Love Music Hate Racism (which has attempted to revitalize the Rock Against Racism movement of the late 1970s), are much less developed and have a considerably lower public and media profile. In football itself, anti-racism dwarfs attempts to eradicate other forms of discrimination, such as homophobia—a problem that continues to receive perturbingly little acknowledgment in the game.

The anti-racist football movement can be conceptualized of as a "cycle of protest" in that its diverse member organizations are inextricably interconnected within the same configuration: the pioneering groups provided the social and political spaces for succeeding members of the movement to work within; and different groups and initiatives share personnel, strategies and tactics, both historically and contemporarily (Williams 2004, 85). It is also important to locate the movement's growth within a wider socio-political climate in which issues surrounding race and racism have been rapidly imbued within both political and public consciousnesses. This is particularly the result of the Macpherson Report (the inquiry into the 1993 racist murder of black teenager Stephen Lawrence and subsequent bungled police investigation) (Macpherson 1999); the introduction of new anti-discrimination legislation, primarily the Race Relations (Amendment) Act 2000, which states that public authorities have a statutory duty to promote racial equality; and a shift by the Labour government towards promoting social inclusion in sports policy (Spracklen 2003). Furthermore, in sport itself, partnerships have been forged between the CRE and Sport England (the quasi-autonomous, non-governmental organization responsible for the strategic development of sport) to promote racial equality within national governing bodies and key sports organizations (Long et al. 2005; Spracklen et al. 2006).

Lloyd (2002: 62) suggests that "as a political movement anti-racism may be best understood as occupying different points on a continuum between well-organized, bureaucratic organizations, pressure groups and protest or social movements which challenge dominant social practices and preconceptions." All of these types are represented in football. The game's anti-racist agenda thus represents a "crowded policy space" (Houlihan 2000), involving a plethora of imbricating sectors, operating at different levels of the policy process. Participating agencies include those with a national remit for trying to eradicate racial discrimination and social exclusion, such as central government and the CRE; those involved in more localized sport development and neighborhood renewal programs; and those projects actually working within and alongside professional football clubs. These agencies therefore constitute an "issue network" (Rhodes 1997, 45). Directly opposed to the concept of a "policy community," an issue network includes a large number of participants; encompasses a range of interests; involves fluctuating interaction between, and access for, members; possesses a level of consensus, but also an ever-present degree of conflict; and is characterized by unequal power relationships, access and resource allocation.

The anti-racist football movement has raised awareness of racism in the game and has been successful in challenging aspects of racial discrimination, disadvantage and inequality. However, whilst it has been able to construct and articulate opposition to issues of overt racism, such as spectator abuse, it has been far less successful in challenging institutionalized barriers relating to the exclusion of specific groups, where the influencing factors and potential solutions are far more difficult to establish. Indeed, as Back et al. (2001) point out, it has been easier for people in football to see racism as the preserve of supporters as it can be compartmentalized as another aspect of anti-social fan behavior and enables issues of racism within clubs, associations and governing bodies to be ignored. As a result, the paucity of British Asians as professional players, along with other issues, such as the marked absence of African-Caribbeans in coaching and managerial positions (King 2004), still remain strikingly problematic. In summary, following Cohen (1992: 62-3), it can be argued that the anti-racist football movement has been more successful in constructing opposition to and combating what it is "against," but less effective in establishing and achieving what it is "for."

Positionality, the "Model Minority" Myth, and Dominant Interpretations of British Asian Exclusion from English Football

Before examining empirical examples of how British Asian footballers are represented within anti-racist discourses, it is necessary to provide a degree of context. It is important to outline the respective racialization of British Asian and black British bodies in relation to sporting participation, and to consider how wider social stereotypes influence dominant interpretations about their involvement in the professional game.

Dominant beliefs about the inclusion of minority ethnic groups in English professional football are characterized by (at least) three major assumptions. First, that the presence of black British players, together with increasing global recruitment from Africa, South America, and the Far East, signifies the erasure of localized racisms. Central to this perception is the idea that football is meritocratic and that processes of selection are "color-blind" (Bonilla-Silva 2006). As black players have achieved significant representation in the game, it is believed that this is equally (and easily) achievable for all other minority ethnic groups. The latter's under-representation is consequently not widely regarded as a particular problem because it is not perceived to be a consequence of racism. Second, that the footballing experiences of all minority ethnic groups are identical. All issues and problems are regarded as common, and so British Asians will eventually, it is assumed, replicate the path of black players into the game. This belief posits that a major break-through by British Asians is simply "a matter of time"—their level of progress is comparable to that of black players during the 1970s and so they will have achieved a similar presence within the next two or three decades. Both of these assumptions adhere to black/white binaries and reproduce the essentializing tendencies of such models (Kim 2004b). Third, that inclusion and exclusion are absolutes. The high numerical representation of black *players* is seen to signify that this group can be described, universally and unequivocally, as "included."[11] All of these postulations are erroneous but remain the hegemonic, accepted dogma within the game.

One way of demonstrating the misguided nature of this logic is through the concept of "racial positionality." According to Kim (2004a: 999) positionality "refers to the location of groups in the collective imagination, which is powered in the first instance by dominant white opinion-makers. This collective perception influences (and is influenced by) but does not wholly determine groups' social structural outcomes, which are mediated by other factors."

She points out that racism is contextually specific and this cannot be accounted for within the dominant notion of a vertical ethnic and racial hierarchy. Instead, positionality provides a more dynamic model for un-derstanding the experiences of minority ethnic groups. It recognizes the situational nature of identity, and allows for the fluidity and complexity of ethnic relations and trajectories, i.e., the fact that groups can shift their position relative to others across time and within different institutions and social settings. Positionality therefore reminds us that dominant discourses around ethnicity are continually changing. Through a process of "racial redistricting" (Gallagher 2004) certain groups can become part of categories from which they have historically been excluded (see e.g., Ignatiev 1995 on the Irish in the United States). Individual and group subjectivities are similarly prone to modification. For example, Pakistanis in Britain have seen themselves variously as Mirpuri, Kashmiri, ethnic minorities, black, Asian, Pakistani, and Muslim, depending on the tem-poral and socio-political context. Another advocate of the approach is Song (2004) who argues that positionality represents a more appropriate framework, not only at a conceptual level, but also in terms of subverting the political unacceptability of hierarchical models of oppression.

Fundamentally, positionality proclaims both the specificity of minority ethnic groups' experiences and the relationship between them, whilst also emphasizing how disintegrating structures of racial difference and white privilege benefits all minority communities (Kim 2004a). Whilst its application in the British context is underdeveloped in comparison to the United States, positionality has considerable use in analyzing ethnic relations in English football. It helps us to understand patterns of differential and fluctuating inclusion (both between and within different ethnic groups) and simultaneously challenges uncritical, overly benign views on the effects of racism.

As outlined at the beginning of this section, the issue of inclusion has traditionally been characterized by a racial dualism, i.e., viewed simply as a "black/white" issue. This position was arguably able to remain unchallenged in football for longer than in other social spheres because, until relatively recently, the only minority ethnic group significantly represented as professional players were African-Caribbeans. Furthermore, an emphasis on racism in *professional* football within the anti-racist football movement meant that little attention was given to the diverse ethnic groups participating at *amateur* level. The "invisibility" of British Asians in the professional game meant that their specific interests and identities were not acknowledged, and the issue of racism was interpreted solely in relation to the experiences of African-Caribbeans. Locating the experiences of minority ethnic groups as particular and fluctuating, as well as an interrelated "field of racial positions" (Kim 1999, 106), highlights the simplistic and essentialist nature of the dominant approach.

The positionality framework is of further benefit in explaining why football's central institutions—clubs and governing bodies—and the media have not historically viewed the exclusion of British Asians as an especially noteworthy phenomenon. Primarily, this is due to widespread support for the notion that British Asians represent a "model minority." The model minority appellation is employed more frequently in the United States and usually in conjunction with Asian American communities. Yet, while in North America the term "Asian" refers to very different communities than to what it does in Britain—predominantly those of Chinese, Filipino, Japanese, Korean, and Vietnamese rather than Indian subcontinental backgrounds—the criteria on which the concept is predicated are similar on both sides of the Atlantic. Of course dominant associations drawn between British Muslims and religious extremism/terrorism post 7-7 mean that this group has become increasingly excluded from the "model minority" category, but it is still regularly applied to Hindus and Sikhs.

According to the model minority thesis, these communities prioritize cultural values of diligence, family solidarity, respect for education and political conservatism, and possess a self-sufficiency that propels them towards economic success (Kundnani 2002). However, the positioning of Asian Americans and British Asians as model minorities does not do justice to the realities of socio-economic diversity within these groups. It homogenizes their complex and multifaceted identities, exaggerates their overall prosperity, and perhaps most importantly, downplays or ignores their experiences of racial discrimination (Kibria 1998; Kim 1999). For this reason, in practice, the idea of a model minority represents a myth rather than an actuality. It continues to serve an important dominant political purpose though, which has severe implications for *all* minority ethnic groups, not simply those designated as the model. By focusing on the putative achievements of one group, the injustices of others are silenced (Kim 2000-2001). Those that fail to achieve are seen to have only themselves to blame, through poor decision-making, indolence, or the absence of appropriate cultural values (Zhou and Sao Xiong 2005). The model minority thesis therefore supports the fallacy that racism has been eradicated and replaced with equality of opportunity for all. In reality, it is part of the ideological apparatus that creates and sustains the marginality of minority ethnic groups (Kibria 1998).

What are the implications of the model minority myth for football? The most significant problem is the way it has tended to reduce concerns about British Asian exclusion from the game. As Zhou and Sao Xiong (2005) point out, when a community is represented as a model minority, their under-achievement in certain spheres does not generate as much popular concern as it would with other groups. For example, because British Asians have been perceived as over-represented in other professional roles, such as doctors and lawyers, and in remunerative trades and businesses, their absence from what is seen as merely a sport has traditionally caused little anxiety. The fact that, like all ethnic groups, such professional positions are only available to a particular class stratum of the British Asian population is completely ignored, as is the large number of British Asians who have longed for the opportunity to make a career out of playing professional football (Burdsey 2007).

The final issue to raise with regard to positionality is the way that the differential inclusion of minority ethnic groups in professional football is influenced by biological racism. Biological racism continues to pervade sporting discourses and practices through the belief that an individual's intellectual or physical (in)abilities are directly related to her/his ethnic or racial background (St. Louis 2003). Accordingly, some groups are believed to be more organically suited to participation in specific sports than others. In Britain, (post)colonial stereotypes have emasculated the South Asian body and purported that it is not sufficiently conditioned for participation in contact sports. In contrast, African-Caribbeans have traditionally been regarded as possessing the necessary physical attributes—strength, power, and aggression—for such activities. Despite their lack of scientific credence, these corporeal classifications are extremely pervasive. Again, they serve to position the exclusion of British Asians as a result of a "racial" genetic defect, rather than issues of stereotyping and racism in football and the wider society.[12]

Representations of British Asians in Anti-racist Football Discourses: One Step Forward, One Step Back?

In recent years, the exclusion of British Asians has begun to be recognized as a problem by those inside the professional game, and increasing time and resources are being dedicated by a variety of agencies towards remedying the issue. Notwithstanding this, whilst the sentiments underpinning them are most welcome, many of the strategies designed to facilitate the involvement of British Asians in professional football have been hampered by a number of problematic characteristics. These can be grouped into two main categories: the reproduction of stereotypes (discussed in this section) and a failure to appreciate the entrenched, structural nature of racism in the game (addressed in the following one).

It is evident that in trying to implement policies that focus on the perceived needs of British Asian footballers, many club schemes and anti-racist football organizations actually reproduce stereotypical representations of, and assumptions about, their communities. Murji (2006) identifies that stereotypes are complex and contradictory constructions, and that there is a need to move away from dichotomous, absolutist interpretations that see stereotypes as unequivocally either "good/positive" or "bad/negative." Nonetheless, in dominant discourses there is a tendency to perceive British Asians as ghettoized in hermetically sealed units that deny them access to "western" practices and commodities. Their lives are interpreted as being structured predominantly (even exclusively) by the cultures, traditions and religions of the subcontinent, thus not only denying their roles as determining agents, but also ignoring their position as members of a dynamic, eclectic diaspora that is influenced by (and increasingly influences) British and wider global consumer cultures. For example, the Community Affairs manager at a Premier League football club described their work with British Asians, as follows:

> What we're doing at the moment is looking at ways that we can further attract Asian people onto our coaching programs, by producing our literature in a range of languages, by delivering the coaching more local to where they live so they don't have traveling obstacles to overcome and by using key people in the communities who are already established there and working with them … If they have an individual need, we will work with that. For example, if there's a dinner going on or if there's an awards ceremony and there's food we'll make sure that the food will be suitable for all tastes and maybe a vegetarian menu as opposed to a meat menu. If you're looking at language barriers then again we will try and work around that in the best way we can. If you're looking at uniform or suitable attire for people to play in, we will obviously operate with whatever religious constraints we have to work with.

Such provisions are hugely important in destabilizing the hegemonic whiteness that permeates the structures of professional football clubs (Long and Hylton 2002) and trying to facilitate the inclusion of a diverse range of ethnic groups. Furthermore, one can partially appreciate the dilemma faced by people involved in organizing and implementing such projects. For example, referring to an example from commercial advertising, Murji (2006: 266) cites the testimony of an individual who claims that his agency is often in a "no-win" situation: if a minority ethnic community is depicted as overtly "traditional," the portrayal is criticized for failing to account for the sensibilities of living in the UK; if the image appears too westernized, the advertisement is accused of failing to sufficiently acknowledge the cultural attributes of minority groups.

Nevertheless, any interventions need to be undertaken in a way that reflects the specific groups they are aimed at. The problem with representations of British Asians in English football is their failure to recognize the heterogeneity of the population under focus, and the fluidity of individual and group subjectivities, not just in relation to ethnicity and religion, but also to age, class, generation and gender. Taking the reference to language in the above transcript, it is illogical to suggest that young, second- and third-generation British Asians are unable to speak fluent English (Modood 1997). Furthermore, the Community Affairs manager also mentions problems perceived to be caused by certain items of clothing. Not only is it difficult to establish exactly how these would inhibit participation in football, but such beliefs also show little appreciation of the style and consumption patterns of young, British Asian players. A cursory glance around the pitches and playgrounds of

Britain's urban landscapes reveals that these players are just as likely to be dressed in the replica team jerseys and branded sportswear as their contemporaries from other ethnic backgrounds.

This example demonstrates the essentialist nature of representations of British Asian footballers in that they refer implicitly to *the* British Asian "community," portraying it as a homogenous, monolithic entity. They reflect a wider tendency whereby portrayals of minority ethnic communities "are too quick to draw closure, to capture in their frame a wide range of people assumed to share a culture in common" (Alleyne 2002, 617). Representations also embody what has been referred to as "false universalism" (Eisenstein 1984) and the "mark of the plural" (Shohat and Stam 1994), whereby the traits or behaviors of one individual are seen to be emblematic of those of all members of her/his community. In particular, there is a failure to acknowledge the specific identities and lifestyles of *young* British Asians. Representations tend to be based on images of older generations, for whom hybrid, diasporic identities may be less significant, and whose cultural habituses are more strongly connected to the subcontinent. Of course it is incorrect to talk of a British Asian youth identity or experience in the singular but, as Malik points out, "why should cultural differences be viewed as more salient than, say, class or age differences? In what way is a sixteen-year-old British-born boy of Pakistani origin living in Bradford of the same culture as a fifty-year-old man living in Lahore?" (2005: 362). The formulation of more representative and effective anti-racist strategies in English football needs to be based on an acknowledgment of internal differentiations in the British Asian population, together with an appreciation of the dynamic, fluctuating and porous nature of cultures, and the implications of progressive generational difference.

One way of working to achieve this would be through greater engagement and consultation with the young people at whom the strategies are targeted. However, evidence suggests that such channels of communication are currently underdeveloped (Burdsey 2007). Instead, any consultation that is undertaken with British Asian communities tends to be done through dominant religio-cultural institutions, such as mosques, temples, and community centers. Due to the stereotypical portrayals of British Asians outlined above, these institutions are seen to represent most authentically the lives and interests of these communities. Furthermore, the dominance of a "bureaucratic managerialist" approach to anti-racism (Carrington and McDonald 2003) means that organizations are increasingly directed towards these formalized methods of communication and discussion. It has become increasingly apparent though that community leaders and the institutions within which they operate are unable to represent the heterogeneity of the communities that they claim to speak for (Bunting 2005). In particular, it is evident that the voices of young people are being marginalized (Werbner 2002).[13] Therefore, engaging with dominant institutions and personnel is arguably not the most effective method for dealing with issues and problems related to football in British Asian communities, for it increases the likelihood that young people's interests and experiences are marginalized from decision-making processes.

Overcoming British Asian Exclusion: Bhajis and Bhangra or Breaking Down Barriers?

Policies directed towards overcoming the exclusion of British Asian players are usually labeled anti-racism. In reality, they often represent simply a form of multiculturalism. In making this distinction, it is important to point out that the two ideologies should not be dichotomized. Instead they should be positioned along a continuum of eradicating discrimination and prejudice, and celebrating ethnic and cultural diversity. As Anthias and Lloyd (2002, 2) point out, there needs to be a theoretical shift away from a binary position of "multiculturalism versus anti-racism," and a pertinent question to ask is, "what type of politics and theory can help to transcend the vacuum that currently exists?" Nevertheless, there are important differences between them that have significant implications for attempts to challenge racial discrimination and inequality in professional football.

In the wake of the 7-7 London transport bombings, the rhetoric of municipal multiculturalism has come under stringent attack from all sections of the political spectrum in Britain. Civic celebrations of difference are believed to have taken place at the expense of identifying and building on the commonalities between different ethnic groups. This absence of shared "core values" is (mistakenly) believed to be responsible for the social exclusion experienced by many minority groups and the growth of religious extremism in Muslim communities. These polemical critiques of multiculturalism have served to mask its historical successes and contemporary benefits in British "race relations," primarily the disruption of biological notions of race, the celebration of diversity in areas ranging from education to sport, and the placing of minority rights on policy agendas.

Embracing and celebrating ethnic and cultural diversity remains a vitally important element in combating discrimination in professional football. However, problems can arise when multiculturalism becomes "official," institutionalized and supportive of, rather than challenging to, the status quo (Kim 2004a). For example, Carrington and McDonald (2003) point out that one of the main paradoxes with the "doctrine of official multiculturalism" is the tendency for discourses to reify and essentialize notions of race, ethnicity, and culture. They argue that whilst the focus on ethnicity within multiculturalism was intended to overcome the static and objectifying category of race, it actually re-employs some of the very interpretations that make this concept problematic. Consequently, multicultural discourses often purport the absolute nature of ethnic categories and imply that the boundaries between the different cultures and experiences of these ethnic groups are fixed and impervious. Analogous to articulations of race, ethnicity becomes "an imposed, fixed and immutable category, a prison from which those it embraced [can] rarely escape" (ibid., 128-9).

These static models of ethnicity and culture are reflected in the strategies employed by professional football clubs: selling South Asian culinary delights, such as onion bhajis or spicy balti pies at refreshment kiosks; and inviting South American samba, South Asian bhangra, or African drum bands to perform at matches (usually, and somewhat unsurprisingly, those that fall within the annual National Week of Anti-racist Action at the end of October) and/or "community days." These initiatives attempt to increase the number of British Asian (as well as other minority ethnic) supporters attending matches, revolving around the idea that professional clubs can become more welcoming environments simply by celebrating ethnic diversity and offering items that are perceived to make British Asians feel more comfortable. However, as the following testimonies make clear, there is a fine line between meeting the desires and requirements of different groups, and being seen as patronizing and tokenistic. For example:

> I don't want to go to a football match for an onion bhaji! I want to go to a football match to see good football! I've been to games but I like to, you know, go for the atmosphere and the football and not for an onion bhaji! (Interview with member of a British Asian football federation).

> To say, well, we need to introduce onion bhajis or we need to have this, by all means if they're having a cultural awareness [day] and there is a particular theme behind it, fair enough, but if they think that by doing that you're going to bring more Asians into football, I don't think that's the case. (Interview with British Asian ex-semi-professional player).

At one level, the problem with such strategies is their reproduction of a primordialist, reified interpretation of British Asian "culture" (in the singular) and stereotypical assumptions about preferred food tastes. Equally problematic is the interpretation of culture as meaning "values, beliefs, knowledge, and customs that exist in a timeless and unchangeable vacuum outside of ... racism" (Razack 1998, 58). Racism is consequently marginalized from the analysis, ostensibly purporting the belief that discrimination and oppression can be eradicated simply by generating knowledge about and facilitating interaction with other cultures. The reasons why British Asians are not present in the first place—factors such as racism in the stadium and surrounding streets, rather than the absence of certain food products or particular half-time entertainment (Conn 2006)—are completely ignored. Gordon and Newfield (1996: 79) point out that "the most severe problem with multiculturalism's culturalism is that it can be satisfied with bracketing or avoiding institutional and structural determinants of inequality." As Sivanandan (2006) argues, "the fight for multiculturalism and the fight against racism go hand-in-hand: anti-racism is the element that makes multiculturalism dynamic and progressive." The use of multicultural practices instead of, rather than in conjunction with, more radical anti-discrimination measures and practices thus severely hampers the degree to which progress is being made towards eradicating inequality in professional football.

Indeed, the effects of these provisions are arguably more significant for white supporters than their British Asian counterparts. For example, Baringhorst (2000: 173) argues that participation in multicultural events "becomes a form of public confession or political statement, a demonstrative action of solidarity that combines self-related with solidarity action motives. At a time when the society's moral resources seem to be even more scarce than its material resources, taking part in public solidarity events represents a cost-effective way of easing a guilty conscience about one's political inertia and passivity."

As one British Asian player states, "for the white [football] community it is quite nice, you know, to hear a bhangra band or have a bhaji. It saves you from going to the curry house after the game really!" [Interview with British Asian amateur player]. However, instead of facilitating meaningful cross-cultural interaction, these events arguably simply provide a contrived and sanitized environment for a contingent and ephemeral engagement by white supporters with their local ethnic "Other," further perpetuating the western, neo-Orientalist gaze and desire for experiencing the exotic (Hutnyk 2000). Such provision fails to appreciate that difference is created through dominance and therefore it harmonizes with, rather than disrupts, triumphalist narratives (Kim 2004a). As a result, there is no significant increase in equality of opportunity in the occupational culture for the minority groups whose cultures are appropriated and commodified, nor any substantial subversion of the privileges held by white communities in the game.

British Asians and the Cultural Politics of Anti-Racist Campaigning in English Football: Some Lessons for the Future?

The final section of this chapter returns to the concept of positionality. The following discussion argues that not only does it represent the most adequate framework for understanding the experiences of British Asian footballers, but it also provides a route map for challenging the discrimination that they face.

Dialectics surrounding sameness and difference, division and solidarity have characterized anti-racist politics and campaigning for over thirty years. For example, the shifting emphasis from multiculturalism to anti-racism in Britain during the 1980s was premised on a perceived need to focus on the commonalities between all minority ethnic groups rather than to celebrate their diversity. Reflecting a belief that forming pan-racial coalitions was less politically divisive than focusing on ethnic difference, terminology shifted so that "ethnic minorities" became "black." "Political blackness" consequently became the hegemonic concept in "race relations" discourse. It was seen to acknowledge common experiences of racism and a shared history of colonialism, and therefore facilitated a new politics of resistance between diverse, oppressed minorities (Hall 1996).

This shift in nomenclature "demonstrated a process in which the objects of racist ideology reconstituted themselves as subjects of social, cultural and political change, actively making history, albeit under circumstances not of their own choosing" (Mercer 1994, 271). However, the cultural turn in "race relations" thinking during the 1990s, the (re)emerging focus on ethnicity in the academy, and recognition that the category "black" was essentially a politically and culturally constructed category that covered a huge range of subjectivities, identities and experiences, all contributed to "political blackness" losing support (Hall 1996). As Alexander (2002, 555) points out, with the benefit of hindsight, "'[b]lack' as a symbolic unity now seems naïve and anachronistic, at once idealistic and reductively undesirable."

One of the earliest, and subsequently most vehement, critics of the category "black" was Tariq Modood. He argued that the term marginalized and alienated British Asians, due to both its inherent essentialism and the fact that it has tended to be associated predominantly with groups who trace their ancestry to the Caribbean and sub-Saharan Africa. In particular he has been critical of the fact that it equates racial discrimination with *color* discrimination. He argues that any form of anti-racism that emphasizes skin color above other aspects of identity is likely to exclude British Asian groups because it ignores the significance of a *cultural* component in constructions and manifestations of anti-Asian prejudice (Modood 2005). To illustrate his argument he focuses on Muslims, demonstrating both the fact that they are more likely to see themselves in terms of their religious, rather than ethnic, identities and the marked rise in Islamophobia in the early twenty-first century. However, it has been argued that in attempting to differentiate British Asians from other minority ethnic groups, Modood actually essentializes British Asian ethnicities and identities (Solomos and Back 1996). Furthermore, critics have pointed out that although anti-Muslim prejudice is undoubtedly particularly prevalent at the moment, this does not mean that racism towards other groups has decreased, whilst privileging the oppression of one group can also be interpreted as disregarding the existence of shared problems or pan-ethnic solidarities (Song 2004).

What, therefore, are the implications of these debates for anti-racism in English football? The previous sections have highlighted the need to focus on the specific experiences of British Asian players (both in general and in relation to the heterogeneous groups that comprise this category). However, in addressing their issues and problems, there must also be an appreciation of those that they experience commensurably with other minority ethnic groups. The aim here is not to rehearse debates around constructionism and essentialism, and the advantages and disadvantages of minority ethnic groups using race as a political resource for resisting oppression (Kim 2004b; Nayak 2006). Instead, building on the above discussion on positionality, it is to argue that an effective anti-racism must simultaneously take into account particular group experiences and possess an appreciation of the wider racial dynamics in the game.

It is clear that discrimination towards British Asian footballers is based on, and experienced in relation to, not only skin color but also their ethno-religious identities. Stereotypes about British Asians and racist epithets directed towards them often include specific referents, based on perceptions about both racialized notions of physicality, and religious and cultural practices. Furthermore, as is the case with many other nations in the West, Britain has seen a marked rise in Islamophobia in recent years, particularly in the aftermath of 9-11 and 7-7 (Abbas 2005). There is increasing evidence of distinct anti-Muslim discourses within supporter racism in English football (Burdsey 2007). Accordingly, "antiracism begins (i.e., ought to begin) by accepting oppressed groups on their own terms (knowing full well that these will change and evolve), not by imposing a spurious identity and asking them to fight in the name of that" (Modood 2005, 104-5).

Nonetheless, it is important to locate these patterns of prejudice within the broader racial dynamics in British sport and society (both historically and contemporarily) and to not lose sight of the experiential commonalities of British Asian and other minority ethnic players in the game. All have been subjected to racism—and the perpetrators have not always sought to distinguish, or been concerned about, their specific ethnic backgrounds—and they have similarly experienced patterns of discrimination and exclusion with regard to, for example, the absence of minority ethnic people in management positions or the hegemonic whiteness that permeates the game's structures. Furthermore, the importance and potential of multiracial solidarities and coalitions in fighting racism in football must not be ignored, where mobilizing around a broader, symbolic "black" identity has been a significant facet of anti-racism campaigns. The most significant example of this was the "Stand Up, Speak Up" wristband initiative, pioneered by Barcelona's French star Thierry Henry in 2005 (Müller et al. 2008).

Collins (1998, 149) argues that "for oppressed groups, diluting difference to the point of meaninglessness comes with real political danger." Omi and Winant (1996) acknowledge the political advantages of panethnic blocs, but also highlight the desirability of mobilizing along particular ethnic lines at certain times. Alexander (2002: 567) states that "perhaps what we need is a third space, but one that is more than notional. This is one that holds on to the recognition of diversity within Britain's black communities but does not lose sight of the commonalities of experience, socio-economic, spatial, cultural, even emotional, which exist." While her proposal refers to social theory, it has practical relevance for the situation in English football. Positionality arguably represents this third way. It helps to understand that "group racialization trajectories are both distinct from one another and mutually constitutive" (Kim 2004a, 996), acknowledges the complexity of racial power relations, and lacks political divisiveness without necessarily reproducing essentialist racial blocs.

Conclusion

This chapter has raised three main issues in relation to overcoming the exclusion of British Asians from the professional game: the need to establish more accurate interpretations of British Asian youth lifestyles and identities, and to elevate young people's voices to a more central position in the development of anti-racist strategies and policies; the importance of not simply relying on discourses and practices of "official multiculturalism" and the necessity of implementing more radical anti-racist measures that actually challenge institutional barriers and structures; and to appreciate both the specificity and commonality of minority ethnic experiences in the game. What links these points together is the belief that any form of anti-discrimination discourse and practice must include minority groups not just culturally but also politically (Gordon and Newfield 1996). Otherwise, attempts to promote cultural diversity and fight discrimination within football's institutions will lack any progressive value, for existing power structures and sites of white privilege will be left unchallenged.

Notes

1. I am extremely grateful to Mark Alleyne for his inspiration, enthusiasm, friendship and leadership of this project. I hope this chapter lives up to his expectations. Thanks also go to the other authors involved in this collection for their suggestions on this chapter, together with those who provided valuable feedback at conferences where earlier versions of this chapter were presented: *P.E.A.C.E. Project International Conference: Creating a Global Civilization for Dialogue and Peace*, *TODA Institute for Global Peace and Policy Research Annual Conference*, Madrid, May 2005; *Anti-racist Discourses: Theory and Comparison—An International Conference*, Georgia State University, Atlanta, February 2006; and *Networking Communication Research: International Communications Association Annual Conference*, Dresden, June 2006.
2. These shows consist of members of the public and/or (minor) celebrities competing each against other in a variety of pursuits: *Big Brother* involves the contestants living together in a specially constructed house; *X Factor* is a competition between budding singers and songwriters; *Hell's Kitchen* revolves around teams of staff working for celebrity chefs; and *I'm A Celebrity...Get Me Out Of Here!* follows groups of celebrities trying to survive after being stranded in the Australian jungle. Each show takes the form of a series, with unsuccessful/unpopular contestants being voted out on a weekly basis, either by elected judges, other contestants or the general public.
3. In the British context, the term "Asian" is used to refer to those people who trace their ancestries to the Indian subcontinent. Thus, in contrast to the USA, for example, it does not include people from other parts of Asia. The category refers

to an extremely heterogeneous population that is stratified by ethnic, religious, regional, class, caste, and generational differences. Unless specifically stated as being a political signifier, and thus also referring to other ethnic groups, the term "black" describes African-Caribbean and African populations in the UK. The prefix "British" is employed to emphasize the hybrid identities of young second- and third-generation migrants who were born in Britain and/or possess British citizenship. For a discussion on the potentially problematic nature of this prefix, see Burdsey (2007).

4. In 2009 and 2010, Chelsea FC initiated a number of trials specifically for British Asian players with its *Search for an Asian Star* event.

5. The other presenter was former England international footballer, Terry Fenwick.

6. The West Midlands region, in which Birmingham is situated, is home to one-fifth of the 747,285 Pakistanis, eleven percent of the 283,063 Bangladeshis and nine percent of the 1,053,411 Indians living in Britain (Peach 2006).

7. It should also be made clear that as it focuses on the *professional* game in England this chapter focuses exclusively on male players. It goes without saying that, due to the rapid increase in girls and women playing football, anti-racist strategies must acknowledge the experiences of both male and female players, and to understand the complex interplay between race and gender.

8. Commensurable to other racialized groups, British Asians are also heavily under-represented as "live" supporters at professional matches.

9. From 2007, the CRE became part of a new, broader agency known as the Equality and Human Rights Commission.

10. The initial aims of Kick It Out (1998, 5) were: to ensure that its anti-racism campaign was implemented at professional clubs; to develop educational resources for young people; to eradicate racism from amateur football; to increase British Asian participation in the game; to increase participation by minority ethnic groups in their local professional clubs; and to develop European anti-racist networks.

11. Dominant perceptions of absolute inclusion/exclusion can have significant implications for all minority ethnic groups. For example, King (2004) claims that a corollary of the increasing focus on British Asians is that the issues facing African-Caribbeans in the game may become marginalized. He argues that because British Asians are under-represented in all aspects of the game they have become the main priority for the anti-racist football movement. In contrast, due to the fact that African-Caribbeans have achieved some degree of representation—as players—their absence as coaches and managers is regarded as a less significant priority. Whilst King arguably overstates the extent to which meaningful measures are being implemented to overcome the exclusion of British Asians, he is correct in identifying the fluctuating priorities of anti-racist agendas.

12. It must also be noted that biological racism in sport is equally damaging to African-Caribbeans as it reinforces wider historical, racist stereotypes of the black body as possessing visceral and physical qualities rather than cerebral and intellectual ones.

13. It is important to stress that this state of affairs is arguably occurring in all communities, and issues regarding community representation and inter-generational conflict are certainly not exclusive to Muslim or other British Asian communities, as is often purported in dominant discourses.

References

Abbas, Tahir, ed. 2005. *Muslim Britain: communities under pressure.* London: Zed Books.

Alexander, Claire. 2002. Beyond black: re-thinking the colour/culture divide. *Ethnic and Racial Studies* 25, 4: 552-71.
———. 2006. Introduction: mapping the issues. *Ethnic and Racial Studies* 29, 3: 397-410.
Alexander, Claire, and Brian Alleyne. 2002. Introduction: framing difference—racial and ethnic studies in twenty-first century Britain. *Ethnic and Racial Studies* 25, 4: 541-51.
Alleyne, Brian. 2002. An idea of community and its discontents: towards a more reflective sense of belonging in multicultural Britain. *Ethnic and Racial Studies* 25, 4: 607-27.
Anthias, Floya, and Cathie Lloyd. 2002. Introduction: fighting racisms, defining the territory. In *Rethinking anti-racisms: from theory to practice,* ed. Floya Anthias and Cathie Lloyd, 1-21. London: Routledge.
Back, Les, Tim Crabbe and John Solomos. 2001. *The changing face of football: racism, identity and multiculture in the English game.* Oxford: Berg.
Bains, Jas and Sanjiev Johal. 1998. *Corner flags and corner shops: the Asian football experience.* London: Gollancz.
Baringhorst, Sigrid. 2000. Symbolic politics of multiculturalism: how German cities campaign against racism. In *Minorities in European cities: the dynamics of social integration at the neighbourhood level,* ed. Sophie Body-Gendrot and Marco Martiniello, 162-178. Basingstoke: Palgrave.
Bell, Vikki. 2002. Reflections on 'The end of antiracism'. In *Race Critical Theories,* ed. Philomena Essed and David Theo Goldberg, 509-12. Oxford: Blackwell.
Bonilla-Silva, E. 2006. *Racism without racists: colour-blind racism and the persistence of racial equality in the United States.* Oxford: Rowman and Littlefield.
Bunting, Madeleine, ed. 2005. *Islam, race and being British.* London: Guardian / Barrow Cadbury Trust.
Burdsey, Daniel. 2004a. Obstacle Race? 'Race,' racism and the recruitment of British Asian professional footballers. *Patterns of Prejudice* 38, 3: 279-99.
———. 2004b. 'One of the Lads?' Dual ethnicity and assimilated ethnicities in the careers of British Asian professional footballers. *Ethnic and Racial Studies* 27, 5: 757-79.
———. 2006. No ball games allowed? A socio-historical examination of the development and social roles of British Asian football clubs. *Journal of Ethnic and Migration Studies,* 32, 3: 477-96.
———. 2007. *British Asians and football: culture, identity, exclusion.* London: Routledge.
Carrington, Ben and Ian McDonald. 2003. The politics of 'race' and sports policy. In *Sport and society: a student introduction,* ed. Barrie Houlihan, 125-42. London: Sage.
Cohen, Phil 1992 'It's racism what dunnit': hidden narratives in theories of racism. In *'Race', culture and difference,* ed. James Donald and Ali Rattansi, 62-103. London: Sage.
Collins, Patricia Hill. 1998. *Fighting words: black women and the search for justice.* Minneapolis: University of Minnesota Press.
Conn, David. 2006. The clubs lost the trust of ethnic minority people. *Guardian,* October 18.
Eisenstein, Hester. 1984. *Contemporary feminist thought.* London: Allen and Unwin.
Gallagher, Charles. 2004. Racial redistricting: expanding the bodies of whiteness. In *The politics of multiracialism: challenging racial thinking,* ed. Heather Dalmage, 59-76. Albany: SUNY Press.
Gilroy, Paul. 1992. The end of anti-racism. In *'Race', culture and difference,* ed. James Donald and Ali Rattansi, 49-61. London: Sage.
Gordon, Avery and Christopher Newfield. 1996. Multiculturalism's unfinished business. In *Mapping multiculturalism,* ed. Avery Gordon and Christopher Newfield, 76-115. Minneapolis: University of Minnesota Press.

Hall, Stuart.1996. New ethnicities. In *Stuart Hall: critical dialogues in cultural studies,* ed. David Morley and Kuan-Hsing Chen, 442-51. London: Routledge.

Harvey, Lee. 1990. *Critical social research.* London: Allen and Unwin.

Houlihan, Barrie. 2000. Sporting excellence, schools and sports development: the politics of crowded policy spaces. *European Physical Education Review* 6, 2: 171-193.

Hutnyk, John. 2000. *Critique of exotica.* London: Pluto Press.

Hylton, Kevin. 2009. *'Race' and sport: critical race theory.* Abingdon: Routledge.

Ignatiev, Noel. 1995. *How the Irish became white.* London: Routledge.

Kick It Out. 1998. Annual report: 1997-98. London: Kick It Out.

Kibria, Nazli. 1998. The contested meanings of 'Asian American': racial dilemmas in the contemporary US. *Ethnic and Racial Studies* 21, 5: 939-58.

Kim, Claire Jean. 1999. The racial triangulation of Asian Americans. *Politics and Society* 27, 1: 103-36.

———. 2000-2001. Playing the racial trump card. *Amerasia Journal* 26, 3: 35-65.

———. (2004a) Imagining race and nation in multiculturalist America. *Ethnic and Racial Studies* 27, 6: 987-1005.

———. (2004b) Unyielding positions: a critique of the 'race' debate. *Ethnicities* 4, 3: 337-55.

King, Colin. 2004. *Offside racism: playing the white man.* Oxford: Berg.

Kundnani, Arun. 2002. The death of multiculturalism. *Race and Class* 43, 4: 67-72.

Lentin, Alana. 2004. *Racism and anti-racism in Europe.* London: Pluto Press.

Lloyd, Cathie. 2002. Anti-racism, social movements and civil society. In *Rethinking anti-racisms: from theory to practice,* ed. Floya Anthias and Cathie Lloyd, 60-77. London: Routledge.

Long, Jonathan, and Kevin Hylton. 2002. Shades of white: an examination of whiteness in sport. *Leisure Studies* 21: 87-103.

Long, Jonathan, Paul Robinson and Karl Spracklen. 2005. Promoting racial equality within sports organizations. *Journal of Sport and Social Issues* 29, 1: 41-59.

McDonald, Ian. 2002. Critical social research and political intervention: moralistic versus radical approaches. In *Power games: a critical sociology of sport,* ed. John Sugden and Alan Tomlinson, 100-16. London: Routledge.

Mac an Ghaill, Mairtin. 1999. *Contemporary racism and ethnicities: social and cultural transformations.* Buckingham: Open University Press.

MacInnes, Paul. 2004. Villa hit on reality TV to lift the Asian profile. *Guardian,* October 18.

Macpherson, William (Sir, of Cluny). 1999. *The Stephen Lawrence inquiry: report of an inquiry made by Sir William Macpherson of Cluny.* London: Home Office, Cm 4262-I.

Malik, Kenan. 2005. Making a difference: culture, race and social policy. *Patterns of Prejudice* 39, 4: 361-78.

Mercer, Kobena. 1994. *Welcome to the jungle: new positions in black cultural studies.* London: Routledge.

Miles, Robert. 1989. *Racism.* London: Routledge.

Modood, Tariq. 1997. Qualifications and English language. In *Ethnic minorities in Britain: diversity and disadvantage*, ed. Tariq Modood, Richard Berthoud, Jane Lakey, James Nazroo, Patten Smith, Satnam Virdee and Sharon Beishon, 60-82. London: Policy Studies Institute.

———. 2005. *Multicultural politics: racism, ethnicity and Muslims in Britain.* Edinburgh: Edinburgh University Press.

Müller, Floris, Liesbet van Zoonen and Laurens de Roode. 2008. We can't 'just do it' alone! An analysis of Nike's (potential) contributions to anti-racism in soccer. *Media, Culture and Society* 30, 1: 23-39.

Murji, Karim. 2006. Using racial stereotypes in anti-racist campaigns. *Ethnic and Racial Studies* 29, 2: 260-80.

Nayak, Anoop. 2006. After race: ethnography, race and post-race theory. *Ethnic and Racial Studies* 29, 3: 411-30.

Omi, Michael and Howard Winant. 1994. *Racial formation in the United States: 1960-1990 (second edition)*. New York: Routledge.

Peach, Ceri. 2006. Demographics of BrAsian settlement, 1951-2001. In *A postcolonial People: South Asians in Britain*, ed. Nasreen Ali, Virinder Kalra and S. Sayyid, 168-81. London: Hurst.

Rattansi, Ali. 1992. Changing the subject? Racism, culture and education. In *'Race', culture and difference*, ed. James Donald and Ali Rattansi, 11-48. London: Sage.

Razack, Sherene. 1998 *Looking white people in the eye: gender, race and culture in courtrooms and classrooms*. Toronto: University of Toronto Press.

Rhodes, Rod. 1997. *Understanding governance: policy networks, governance, reflexivity and accountability*. Maidenhead: Open University Press.

Shohat, Ella and Robert Stam. 1994. *Unthinking eurocentrism: multiculturalism and the media*. London: Routledge.

Sivanandan, Ambalavaner. 2006. Britain's shame: from multiculturalism to nativism. http:// www.irr.org.uk/2006/may/ha000024.html.

Solomos, John and Les Back. 1996. *Racism and society*. Basingstoke: Macmillan.

Song, Miri. 2004. Racial hierarchies in the USA and Britain: investigating a politically sensitive issue. In *Researching race and racism,* ed. Martin Bulmer and John Solomos, 172-86. London: Routledge.

Spracklen, Karl. 2003. Setting a standard? Measuring progress in tackling racism and promoting social inclusion in English sport. In *Leisure, Sport and Social Inclusion: Potential, Participation and Possibilities*, ed. Adrian Ibbetson, Beccy Watson and Maggie Ferguson, 41-57. Eastbourne: Leisure Studies Association.

Spracklen, Karl, Kevin Hylton and Jonathan Long. 2006. Managing and monitoring equality and diversity in UK sport: an evaluation of the Sporting Equals racial equality standard and its impact on organizational change. *Journal of Sport and Social Issues* 30, 3: 289-305.

St. Louis, Brett. 2003. Sport, genetics and the 'natural athlete': the resurgence of racial science. *Body and Society* 9, 2: 75-95.

Thomas, Paul. 1995. Kicking racism out of football: a supporter's view. *Race and Class* 36, 4: 95-101.

Werbner, Pnina. 2002. *Imagined diasporas among Manchester Muslims: the public performance of Pakistani transnational identity politics*. Oxford: James Currey.

Williams, Kim. 2004. Linking the civil rights and multiracial movements. In *The politics of multiracialism: challenging racial thinking*, ed. Heather Dalmage, 77-98. Albany: SUNY Press.

Zhou, Min and Yang Sao Xiong. 2005. The multifaceted American experiences of Asian immigrants: lessons for segmented assimilation. *Ethnic and Racial Studies* 28, 6: 1119-52.

Anti-Racism as Identity Politics:
A Constructivist Approach to the FARE
and Ad Council Campaigns

Mark D. Alleyne

Introduction

Constructivism is one way in which international relations takes a "cultural turn." By carefully interrogating the "givens" of international politics and declaring all of them to be social constructions, constructivism opens up the opportunity to question the basic credibility of all centers of power in the global order as somehow being primordial, essentialist, and natural. These include the state, the modern state system, racial identity, nationalism, and the very principles of the post-World War II international order, especially the doctrine of universality. Additionally, instead of trying to produce grand theories that purport to explain how international politics works, this paradigm is more content to give "compelling interpretations and explanations of discrete aspects of world politics, going no further than to offer heavily qualified 'contingent generalizations'" (Burchill, Devetak, Linklater, Paterson, Reus-Smit and True 2001, 222). Communicative practices are very important to this way of viewing the international scene because they are critical to how human beings discursively *construct* their social worlds (Campbell 1998). It is for this reason that the communicative practice of anti-racist campaigning, which has become popular at the turn of the new century is fair game for constructivist interrogation.

This chapter tackles this issue through a comparative analysis of two anti-racist campaigns: Football Against Racism in Europe (FARE) and the Ad Council. It begins by first locating the campaigns as events within a much wider transnational anti-racist discourse of the post-World War II order. It will then put them into the more discrete context of the period after the terrorist attacks on the United States of September 11, 2001. This will be followed by a descriptive analysis of the two phenomena utilizing textual and discourse interpretive methods.

Historical Context

Anti-racism is the area where the United Nations (UN) has one of its longest records in developing international human rights law, and racist propaganda has been outlawed under international law almost for as long as the UN has been in existence. The 1965 International Convention on the Elimination of All Forms of Racial Discrimination is the oldest and most widely ratified UN human rights convention. Under it states obligate themselves to not practice racial discrimination, to not defend the practice, to eliminate it from their legal systems, to end its use by individuals and organizations, and to encourage civic life that is multiracial and integrationist. The Convention also established the Committee on the Elimination of Racial Discrimination (CERD) to monitor compliance by states.

In addition to legalistic and bureaucratic measures such as these, the UN has had a long record of "public information" initiatives meant to massage global public opinion in favor of the principle of anti-racism. It declared 1971 the International Year for Action to Combat Racism and Racial Discrimination. It also named three Decades for Action to Combat Racism and Racial Discrimination (1973-83, 1983-93, and 1993-2003), and sponsored three "world conferences" to Combat Racism and Racial Discrimination in 1978, 1983 and 2001.

More recently the rapid growth in number of hate websites has rendered the existing international law ineffective and a number of initiatives have been launched to tackle the problem of "cyberhate," The Council of Europe produced the first international treaty dedicated to combating crimes committed over the Internet and other computer networks—the Convention on Cybercrime. The Convention set out a common criminal policy on a number of offenses committed with the use of computers, including copyright violations, pornography, "hacking," and fraud. It was supplemented by the Additional Protocol Concerning the Criminalization of Acts of a Racist and Xenophobic Nature Committed through Computer Systems. This second document criminalized the use of computer networks to transmit racially motivated threats and insults. It also criminalized the use of computer networks to deny genocide and crimes against humanity and/or to promote the perpetration of such acts. These laws came into force in July 2004.

In considering this context, it is clear that the contemporary international political order has established at least a rhetorical and legalistic condemnation of racial discrimination. However, the letter of international law was never followed. For example, the United States maintained a system of *de jure* segregation at the time the International Convention came into force, Australia had a "white Australia" policy that restricted immigration from non-white countries, and it was not until the end of the twentieth century that apartheid was dismantled in South Africa. Therefore, in exploring this new propensity for anti-racist campaigning the question becomes "Why now?" and "What for?"

Post-9/11

Following the terror attacks of September 11, 2001, mass media campaigns to promote tolerance and an anti-racist ethic received increased resources and attention in the United States. There was the assumption that the attacks and the responses to them were symptoms of the persistence of intolerance and ethnocentrism in the world and that this problem required mass communication and education programs to be eliminated.

Leading the effort was the Ad Council, which teamed with the advertising agency GSD&M to produce video public service announcements (PSAs) that stressed the cultural diversity of the United States (Raine 2001; Thacker 2001; Hassell 2001; Ad Council Extends Television Ad Campaign 2001). The Ad Council also collaborated with the Brokaw Agency to produce a PSA that decried anti-Arab/anti-Muslim attacks and admonished that "Hate has taken enough from us already ... Don't let it take you" (Billbrokaw.com 2003).

The Leadership Conference on Civil Rights/Education Fund and the singer Dave Matthews released a series of PSAs with the message that hatred was un-American (Civilrights.org 2003). The Starz Encore Group movie channels underwrote another PSA that decried anti-Arab discrimination that resulted from the terror attacks (Temman 2001). Within two weeks of the attacks another mass entertainment company, International Channel Networks, announced the production of another series of PSAs to promote tolerance and respect (International Channel Networks 2001).

In September of 2002, the Hollywood-based Entertainment Industry Foundation funded what it said was the first ever international PSA, a 90-second video that featured Moroccan Olympic gold medalist Nawal el Moutawakel-Bennis denouncing hatred and promoting forgiveness

(Entertainment Industry Foundation 2002). Another mass media and education initiative was that started by the New York-based National Video Resources, a curated collection of audio-visual materials to fight hate called *After 9.11: Videos That Promote Knowledge, Understanding and Tolerance* (After911.org 2003).

The projects in the United States came several years after the start in Europe of similar mass campaigns to promote tolerance. The most ambitious of these in terms of its geographic reach was the Football Against Racism in Europe Campaign (FARE) that was launched in February 1999 and included a network of 13 European organizations (Football Against Racism in Europe 2003; Let's Kick Racism Out of Football 2003). Increasingly, European soccer authorities have turned to strategic communication and education campaigns as tools for stemming racist taunts, neo-Nazi propaganda, and racist violence at their football events. These measures have been used in conjunction with other strategies, such as fines of offending players and clubs, and the outright banning of offending fans from particular games (Houston 2003; UEFA to Present 276,000 Dollar Charity Cheque 2002).

Interestingly, there has been some skepticism in the European trade press about the utility of such schemes as anti-racist tools (Thomas 2003). This has occurred within the context of increased immigration into a larger number of states, which has made issues of race, identity, and tolerance more central themes in political, social, and mass media discourses. The most widely-publicized examples have been in the "white" countries of Europe and Australia, where some political movements gained currency by making immigration reform a central dimension of their agendas for change. In countries such as Spain, France, and the Netherlands, new immigrants have been victimized because of their different skin color, ethnicity, culture, or religion from the majority populations (Kraft 1995; Jewkes 2001; Europe: Who Gains? 2002). This social tension and violence in turn have inspired mass media and education schemes to improve inter-ethnic and inter-religious relations and ameliorate the social and psychological conditions under which new immigrants live (C. Europa-Racismo/España 2003; Inmigration-Escuela 2003).

What makes this number of strategic mass communication campaigns very interesting is their theme of anti-racism and tolerance. So-called "public information" or "public service" campaigns were by no means a new feature of international politics, but they were rarely used so extensively before with the professed objective of fostering inter-racial, inter-ethnic and inter-religious harmony. In the 1960s and 1970s, media campaigns were employed in Africa, Asia, and Latin America as part of "development-support" strategies, especially in the health field, promoting the health benefits of such practices as breast-feeding, mosquito eradication and clean drinking water, to name a few examples. In North America and Europe, they have been popular methods to change personal behavior patterns related to such hazards as drunk driving, the spread of AIDS, and forest fires. Scores of scholarly articles and books have now been published about these various "cause marketing" cases, especially assessing the problem of how to effectively design them and how to gauge their effectiveness (Earle 2000; Rice and Atkin 2001; Stephenson 2002; Teise and Weigold 2001; Bator and Cialdini 2000; Gunther and Thorson 1992; McKinney 1988).

However, because public information campaigns on the themes of racism and intolerance have been rare, there has been scant scholarly investigation of this phenomenon. In light of the fact that racial intolerance has been long-standing problem in all corners of the globe, the question of why cause marketing strategies have been rarely used to promote inter-racial harmony and tolerance is itself worthy of study on its own. Is it because it is assumed that it would be much easier to change personal habits, such as alcohol consumption and seatbelt use, than change racial prejudice? Have the themes of racism and intolerance been considered too complex for the medium of the PSA?

Whatever the answers, all the evidence from recent developments in international politics suggests that these seemingly taboo themes are increasingly the focus of strategic national and international communication and education campaigns. They have been components of "public diplomacy" campaigns launched by the administration of President George W. Bush to win allies in the two wars—in Afghanistan and Iraq—in the wake of the 2001 attacks. These campaigns have framed the American policies as not being hostile to Islam and Arabs (White House Office of Global Communications 2003; Dunphy 2003; Benson 2001).

They also factor in the increased number of "multi-function" peacekeeping missions run by the United Nations. The particular cases of Rwanda and Bosnia—where mass media was used to mobilize genocidal acts—taught the UN the lesson that a key part of its peacekeeping role had to be strategic public information campaigns to counteract hate propaganda (Holguin 1998; Lehmann 1999; Metzl 1997; Lessons Learned in Peacekeeping 2002; United Nations 2002, 2000a). They have been considered as part of "truth and reconciliation processes" in a number of countries.

Race and ethnicity have been particularly prominent themes of the processes in South Africa and Guatemala (UN In Action Television Series 2003; Guatemala-Indigenas 2002; D. Humanos-Guatemala 2003; Misión de la ONU 2001). The new scholarly work spawned by this phenomenon has focused on the cultural politics of truth and reconciliation, especially related to mass communication, national narratives and identity construction (Lykes, Terre Blanche a Hamber 2003; Andrews 2003; Wilson 2000; Grunebaum-Ralph 2001).

Similarly, the social tension and violence that have resulted from increased global migrations have in turn inspired mass media and education schemes to improve inter-ethnic and inter-religious relations and ameliorate the social and psychological conditions under which new immigrants live (C. Europa-Racismo/España 2003; Inmigration-Escuela 2003). Popular transnational media narratives, especially in advertising, have increasingly engaged themes of racism and tolerance. In the early 1990s the Italian apparel company Benetton gained notoriety for its "United Colors of Benetton" campaign that depicted racial harmony (Kraidy and Goeddertz 2003; Foltz 1990).

The FARE Campaign

The FARE campaign includes a website devoted to ending racial abuse in European football, an annual "action week" of events at clubs across Europe to demonstrate solidarity against football racism, a budget for compensating groups for producing anti-racist media (e.g., banners, fanzines, and flyers), and support for consistent lobbying actions, such as regional conferences and dialogue with clubs and associations about the need to wipe out racism in the sport. When this European campaign was started in 1999, a similar program had been going for six years in the United Kingdom, particularly England (Home 1996).

Although Arthur Wharton had been the first black professional football player in England when he played for Darlington in 1884, black professionals were a rarity in the United Kingdom until the late 1970s (Let's Kick Racism Out of Football 2003). And as the numbers of blacks in the sport at the professional level increased, so did the practice of British crowds verbally abusing them during matches, especially the habit of calling them monkeys by throwing bananas onto the pitch at black players and doing the "monkey chant" whenever they touched the ball.

Although popular discourse in Britain tended to dismiss this behavior as that of a tiny minority who were only trying to throw the player of an opposing team "off his game," there was plenty of evidence that it was more insidious. Even when an English under-21 team defeated Denmark 4-1 in Copenhagen in 1982, the four black members of the team—Barnes, Davis, Whyte, and Regis—were harassed during play by the *English* fans (Home 1996). Also, the racist National Front used football games to recruit and organize members. "Black players did not bother to complain about racism because we were told that we had to cope with it, it was seen as a test of character," a player of the time, Garth Crooks, recalled at a FARE-sponsored conference in early 2003. "Clubs also said that racists were paying customers and were entitled to say what they want" (Syed 2003).

It was only due to a convergence of factors that the step was taken to have proactive action against racial abuse in British soccer via an anti-racist campaign: "Let's Kick Racism Out of Football" [later called "Kick It Out"]. The Commission for Racial Equality (CRE) and the Professional Footballers Association (PFA) joined together to start the British campaign because by 1993 black people rose to prominence in both organizations. By 1993 it was estimated that 20 percent of England's professional players were black. And the mainstream media were paying more attention to race and soccer by covering the theme more through video documentaries and news reports in the print and broadcast media (Home 1996).

In the mid-1990s the European Union (EU) sponsored a research project on racism in football and its implications for European integration (Merkel and Tokarski 1996), a sign that there was some recognition by then that racist abuse had ceased to be merely a British problem. Ironically, in the years since FARE was started many of the most blatant incidents of racial abuse by European fans have been in countries other than England. This has seemed to inspire the Union of European Football Associations (UEFA), the governing body of regional play in Europe, to give more money to FARE and make prominent moves to show support for FARE (European Teams Ordered to Play Behind Closed Doors 2002). One of the most poignant of these measures was UEFA's announcement in October 2002 that it would put its full support behind FARE's 10-point plan of action to fight racism in football (UEFA Backs Anti-Racism Plan 2002).

The 10 points of the FARE plan requires football clubs to:

1. Issue a statement saying the club will not tolerate racism, spelling out the action it will take against those engaged in racist chanting. The statement should be printed in all match programs and displayed permanently and prominently around the ground.

2. Make public address announcements condemning racist chanting at matches.
3. Make it a condition for season-ticket holders that they do not take part in racist abuse.
4. Take action to prevent the sale of racist literature inside and around the ground.
5. Take disciplinary action against players who engage in racial abuse.
6. Contact other clubs to make sure they understand the club's policy on racism.
7. Encourage a common strategy between stewards and police for dealing with racist abuse.
8. Remove all racist graffiti from the ground as a matter of urgency.
9. Adopt an equal opportunities' policy in relation to employment and service provision.
10. Work with all other groups and agencies, such as the players union, supporters, schools, voluntary organizations, youth clubs, sponsors, local authorities, local businesses, and police, to develop pro-active programs and make progress to raise awareness of campaigning to eliminate racial abuse and discrimination (Football against Racism in Europe 2003).

Another irony of the FARE campaign is that, though it is based on the British anti-racist campaign of Kick It Out, in recent years British teams (because they usually have the most blacks) have been the victims of some of the most egregious cases that UEFA has used to make an example of the perpetrators. In 2002 PSV Eindhoven was fined $20,000 by UEFA for abuse its fans unleashed against Arsenal's black French striker, Thierry Henry. That same year UEFA also fined Belgium's Brugge $15,000 for its supporters' racial taunting of a player from Lokomotiv Moscow (European Teams Ordered to Play behind Closed Doors 2002).

Race-based animosity has by no means gone away from the English game, as the case of English fans booing the Turkish national anthem and an outbreak of violence in a 2003 match against Turkey showed. There was the threat from UEFA that England would be thrown out of the 2004 European Championships in Portugal if such behavior was allowed to continue. That prompted the English captain, David Beckham, to make a special plea for fans to quit their racist antics because it was "going to get us into a lot of trouble" (Taylor and Kelso 2003). More recently, just a few months after England's black players were subject to racist taunts by Spanish fans in Madrid, England and Holland played a friendly at Villa Park in which both sides wore symbolic anti-racist colors instead of their national kit. About the same time another anti-racist campaign—*Stand Up, Speak Up*—was started by two prominent players of color, Rio Ferdinand and Thierry Henry (Neville Queries

Sponsors' Anti-Racism Motives 2005). Henry himself was reported to be the victim of racist abuse by none other than the Spanish manager (England Shirts to Carry Anti-Racist Message 2005).

It is very revealing that, out of the scores of articles about Kick It Out and FARE researched for this comparison, only one devoted any attention to whether there was evidence that an anti-racist campaign in football would work. It was a report published in *Marketing Week* on the news that the English Football Association (The FA) was "planning a hard-line TV campaign to root out racism among fans, citing the success of the drink-driving and seatbelt ads as good grounds for its strategy" (The Bigoted Game 2003). Although in the 30 years since the drink-driving campaign was launched the number of people killed due to drunk driving had dropped from 1,700 to 500, *Marketing Week* was skeptical of whether the same techniques could be transferred to the field of anti-racism. The chief executive of the Marketing Society, Hugh Burkitt, was quoted as explaining that "Anti-racism campaigns are normally dismissed by the majority who, rightly or wrongly, think they are not racist, and are ignored by those who know they are." Even an "FA source" doubted. "For all its strengths, the trouble with the Kick It Out campaign is that the majority of people don't see themselves as racist, so it has no effect," the source claimed. "People really don't see booing a national anthem as racist. We want to make sure people know it is wrong." *Marketing Week* also cast doubt on the effectiveness of a number of broadcast anti-racist campaigns put out over the years by the CRE (joint sponsor of Kick It Out).

The Ad Council Campaigns

The Ad Council conducts extensive qualitative research, before each campaign is produced and launched, both to understand the public's mindset with regard to each social issue, and to ensure that our public service advertisements (PSAs) are clear and will be well-received by their intended audience. The impact of Ad Council PSAs on target audiences are assessed using multiple metrics, including pre and post-launch tracking studies, fulfillment results (800# calls and unique website visitors), and other measures of success (e.g., seat belt usage rates).

The results conclusively show that public service announcements are an effective means of communication and education, as they increase awareness, reinforce positive beliefs, intensify personal concern, and move people to action (From the "Research Center" section of The Advertising Council's website http://www.adcouncil.orglresearch/impact of psas/).

Although The Advertising Council (the charity arm of the United States advertising industry) says it tests the possibility of effectiveness before launching its campaigns, that was not the case with its "I am American" campaign, which began a matter of days after the 2001 attacks on the World Trade Center and the Pentagon. The PSAs featured Americans of various ethnicities repeatedly saying the phrase "I am an American." They were among the most poignant broadcast artifacts of the period after September 11, 2001.

Media reports framed the initiative as an attempt by the Texan advertising agency GSD&M to stem any racial animosity that might have been sparked by the attacks. The *San Francisco Chronicle* reported that the agency's workers "were struck by the fact that in the chaos that followed [September 11], many Muslims and Arab Americans were cursed or attacked, and they wanted to address the injustice" (Raine 2001). GSD&M's president, Roy Spence, said at the time that the PSAs were meant to promote "diversity." "People think diversity is a new issue," he was quoted as saying in *The Houston Chronicle.* "It's not. It's at our core. Diversity is what unites us." Later in the report Spence explained that "media has the power to change behavior for good" and that his agency was "trying in our own little way to do something" (Hassell 2001).

After GSD&M produced it, the PSA was handed over to the Ad Council, which then distributed it to 3,000 media outlets in the United States, many of which aired it for free. Interestingly the Ad Council was born the last time there had been a foreign attack on American soil. The advertising industry set it up after the Japanese attack on Pearl Harbor that pushed the United States into World War II (Leff 2001). It produced mass advertising campaigns to support the war effort, one of its most famous campaigns of that time being "Loose Lips Sink Ships." Then in subsequent years it was behind a number of campaigns that had very catchy slogans, such as "Only You Can Prevent Forest Fires" and "Take A Bite *Out* Of Crime." According to the Council: "Our mission is to identify a select number of significant public issues and stimulate action on those issues through communications programs that make a measurable difference in our society. To that end, the Ad Council marshals volunteer talent from the advertising and communications industries, the facilities of the media, and the resources of the business and non-profit communities to create awareness, foster understanding and motivate action" (Adcouncil.org, 2003).

It is curious that the Ad Council's list of "significant public issues" did not include racism. The closest it ever did come to the issue was its campaign to support the United Negro College Fund (an organization that funds predominantly African-American universities). The slogan for that initiative— "A Mind Is a Terrible Thing to Waste"—became one of the Ad Council's most famous, but it was by no means an explicit message against the evils of racism, instead it merely urged people to give money to the Fund. But the very fact that there are such a large number of predominantly black universities and colleges in the United States is a direct result of the country's persistent problem of racism and racial inequality, particularly against blacks. Yet through all the years of its existence the Ad Council never found it prudent to focus resources to battling racial prejudice.

From the start it appears that anti-racism and the promotion of internationalism were not the primary objectives of the "I am an American" campaign. Interestingly the initiative could be read as much as a nationalistic strategy as an anti-racist one. "We decided the best way would be to use our advertising skills to market America's strengths," GSD&M's director of communications explained in late September, 2001 (International Eye 2001). Indeed, by the second anniversary of 9/11, the Ad Council was still producing PSAs inspired by the attacks but the implicit anti-racist message of the "I am an American" campaign had all but disappeared. By mid-September, 2003 the Ad Council had compiled a videotape of 26 PSAs based on what happened on 9/11. The majority were PSAs to assist in the recovery effort, especially those about how to deal with the psychological trauma, PSAs to support the American Red Cross, the Salvation Army, and the United Way. What was clear was that the Ad Council was making a more explicit nationalistic narrative and a not-too-subtle pitch for the government's preferred reading of the ongoing wars in Afghanistan and Iraq—i.e., there were struggles by the United States to promote "freedom."

In July 2002 the Ad Council launched its "Campaign for Freedom" that was "designed to inspire Americans by reminding them about what makes our country so extraordinary—our freedom." Unlike with the "I am an American" campaign, there was more planning. The Ad Council's research found that Americans had taken their freedom for granted. The media donated $150 million to the new campaign that would try to make Americans appreciate their freedom more. The 2003 phase features refugees from the Ukraine, Armenia, and Cambodia, in separate PSAs testifying to the fact that they gained great freedom in escaping the regimes in their homelands and coming to the United States. All the PSAs feature flickering images of American iconic symbols: such as the

Statue of Liberty, Mount Rushmore, and the American flag. The tagline is "Freedom: Appreciate it. Cherish it. Protect it" (Freedom Ads Launch for the Second Anniversary of September 11th 2003).

The campaign raises a number of interesting questions. Why were the refugees featured all from totalitarian regimes that have now fallen? Why did they not select refugees who had fled oppressive regimes that were installed and supported by the United States, such as in Chile, the former Zaire, and El Salvador? Why were there no black refugees or African-Americans testifying to what a free place was the United States for them?

In what might seem a contradictory move, in September 2003 the Ad Council helped in the distribution of two PSAs in favor of world peace that were produced by the New York agency DCODE, the History Channel, and the United Nations. They featured UN Messengers of Peace Muhammad Ali and Luciano Pavarotti and a multiracial group of children urging world peace. (Press Conference on International Day of Peace 2003).

Comparisons and Contrasts

(1) Anti-Racism as Internationalism. It is tempting to provide a shallow interpretation of the two cases described above as yet more evidence of the coming of a new internationalist age, where, under conditions of globalization (especially the globalization of mass media) there is the expansion of transnational civil society. Iriye defines *internationalism* as "an idea, a movement, or an institution that seeks to reformulate the nature of relations among nations through cross-national cooperation and interchange" (Iriye 1997, 3). The specific form of internationalism called *cultural internationalism* is defined by Iriye as "a variety of activities undertaken to link countries and peoples through the exchange of ideas and persons, through scholarly cooperation, or through efforts at facilitating cross-national understanding." Cultural internationalists believe that such activities maintain international peace. Iriye says the phenomenon originated in the late 1800s in North America and Europe to counteract "the seemingly endless preoccupation of the great powers with military strengthening and colonial domination." However, the history of cultural internationalism is contradictory because in its early days, in the late 1800s and early 1900s, its proponents only embraced the so-called "civilized" races of the world.

The League of Nations was a prime example of internationalism. The League's Committee on Intellectual Cooperation ran a campaign to get countries to revise textbooks to be less narrow and nationalistic in perspective. Other highlights of internationalism during the years after the 1919 Paris Peace Conference and the start of World War II were the effort to create a world language, Esperanto; growing popularity of international student exchange; international collaborative efforts at art preservation; and the 1928 Kellogg-Briand Pact that outlawed war as a means of settling disputes. In the post-World War II era the Atlantic Charter and the United Nations that it presaged were also examples.

Therefore, one way of seeing these anti-racist campaigns are as communicative practices put to the service of discursively constructing internationalism. The better we understand them, the better we understand internationalism and its place within wider discourses, such as terrorism, civil war and inter-state war. Within this wider framework we can ask questions about why there is a need to discursively construct internationalism. The haste in launching these campaigns does provide grounds for suspicion. This skepticism provokes a particular set of questions. We can ask whether the motivation for such projects is *mass persuasion*—conversion of a mass of people to the logic of internationalism—or *mass symbolism*—demonstrating to the mass public that the sponsoring entity is itself not racist.

My conceptual position is that mass symbolism is a rhetorical defensive strategy that has two dimensions. The first is a *naming* component. This is the use of specific language, labels, and other signs to deflect accusations of culpability for racist behavior. An example of this is the practice common among many businesses in the United States of placing the label "Equal Opportunity Employer," "Equal Housing Opportunity," or some similar statement at the end of job advertisements or solicitations for business. In light of the fact that US law forbids all businesses from discriminating in jobs or housing, the motivation for the use of these labels is worthy of investigation. Furthermore, what does this practice say about social discourse on race and racism?

The second is an *action* component. This refers to moves taken by entities when confronted with charges of racism or when put under pressure to "do something" about intolerance or racism. They sponsor "diversity workshops," community "outreach," or (as was the case with European football authorities) they launch anti-racist campaigns. The action component goes further than merely self-naming as not racist by attempting to show that the entity is willing to devote money, manpower, time and other scarce resources to combat the problem.

Mass symbolism can be more in the interest of the sponsoring body than the actual victim population. It can deflect attention from the acts, situations or structures that produced the outcry in the first place and lead to a sense that the problem has been solved, or, at least, the organization is "doing the best it can." In February 2005, English professional footballer Gary Neville raised such questions when he queried Nike's motivations for sponsoring the recent soccer anti-racist campaigns in England. Was it a sincere interest in stamping out racism from the game, or was it a ploy to get free publicity? (Neville Queries Sponsors' Anti-Racism Motives 2005).

One key to finding out whether there is a genuine interest in solving the problems campaigns are meant to combat is the scrutiny of what is done to ensure the effectiveness of the campaigns. Is previous research and experience tapped to help design the campaign? After the campaign has been launched are surveys done to monitor its effectiveness? Is there a willingness to change the strategy if the problem persists?

There is already evidence that these campaigns have performed more of a symbolic function and have not necessarily changed the culture at organizations that have sponsored them. For example, a number of organizations that have run anti-racist or "diversity" campaigns have later been found to still engage in institutionalized racism, such as Coca-Cola and London's Metropolitan Police.

The approach of viewing anti-racist campaigns as sub-discourses of a master internationalist discourse must also account for seemingly chaotic, as opposed to planned activity. There has been the tendency to see internationalism emerging not as a planned project but as a somewhat natural consequence of technological change, especially changes in communication technology that facilitated much easier contact among peoples over great distances (Angell 1913; Wallas 1915). But campaigns are deliberate acts. The term "campaign" implies a number of features:

a) They are run by an identifiable institution.
b) They have identifiable beginnings (and ends).
c) They are deliberate sequences of action that are geared to specific objectives.
d) They are run by individuals in a hierarchy.
e) They are distinct entities that can be singled out for praise or criticism. Some campaigns are awarded prizes by advertising industry bodies as part of competitions for work done during a specific time period (usually a year).

Therefore, campaigns seem to have a premeditated, rather than chaotic, relationship to internationalism. However, the utility of the constructivist paradigm is its ability to provide tools for showing how the seemingly chaotic might not be so. It is for this reason that we must now turn to a more profound reading of the two campaigns.

(2) Anti-Racism as Cultural Politics. Virginia Q. Tilley, in a constructivist critique of the role of "the state" in ethnic conflict, argues that ethnic politics is at the very foundation of the modern state system and so it is misleading to assume that states can be evenhanded players in mediating and ameliorating ethnic conflict (Tilley 2002). She argues that the state system itself is a product of ethnocentric bias concerning the optimum form of political organization. There is the assumption that "the nation-state is the fundamental normative framework for political order, and that the territorial state demarcates the nation" (ibid., 153).

State power is employed to define the ethnic composition of states, to define who is indigenous or not, and in the case of Latin America especially, to even deny the saliency of ethnic/racial cleavages that threaten the credibility of the state as representative of a seemingly homogenous national entity called a nation-state. Although the most glaring examples of the deployment of ethnic politics by states are well known (e.g., Nazi Germany and Rwanda), it is not frequently acknowledge how states play ethnic politics as part of their routine existence.

As Tilley points out, states form political and trade affiliations based on ethnic affiliation (e.g., "Arab" or "African"), and they take on specific ethnic identities over time based on convenience (e.g., Australia's move from being "white" to "Pacific" and "Asian"). Similarly, states pick and choose over time which ethnic/racial components of their populations to celebrate or exterminate (e.g., Jamaica's initial vilification of Rastafarian culture to the later utilization of it to promote the country). This approach provides us with another way of seeing contemporary anti-racist discourse of the type manifested in the FARE and Ad Council campaigns.

The similarities between the FARE initiative and that of the Ad Council begin with their being both campaigns. They share all the characteristics of campaigns identified earlier in this chapter. They were organized with the professed goal of achieving objectives, even though, as this review has already revealed, there was great variation in how clear these objectives were. Both were started by more than one entity in the midst of a perceived crisis. In the case of FARE, it was the spate of racial abuse directed at black players by fans. In the American example, the initial problem was the backlash of racial attacks against Arab-Americans (and anyone who looked "Arab") in the wake of the September 11 attacks.

The empirical evidence suggests that in both cases there seemed to be perceived pressure to "do something" in response to the crisis. The financial consequences to professional football seemed more obvious than those to the American advertising industry. However, both sponsoring entities had some incentive to deflect charges of racism directed against them because there had been a history of both European football and the American media industries in general being accused of racial insensitivity. For example, it was not until relatively recently (within the past 20 years) that there was much ethnic diversity in American advertising, and, as Garth Crooks pointed out, professional football clubs had for a long time not considered racial abuse by fans to be very serious and had even condoned the free-expression rights of racist fans.

Having noted all of the above by way of comparison, preliminary evidence suggests that the *mass symbolism* function took precedence over the *mass persuasion* function in both cases. Entities embarking on campaigns meant to systematically bring about change would engage in at least some "effects" research to determine media and strategies most likely to succeed. However, this kind of planning was absent at the start of both campaigns.

Although the initiators of the FARE and "I am an American" campaigns never made the bold assertion that they wanted to propagate internationalism, it is important to consider them within the broader framework of internationalist discourse because it is through such communicative practices at a micro level that broader trends of the type identified by Iriye take place. Also, any discourse on race, racism and anti-racism is important to the search for a better understanding of internationalism because racism is one of the chief problems of contemporary international society. Racism is actually an obstacle to internationalism if we adopt the basic position that the internationalist ethic assumes the absence of racial prejudice, so we need to understand better why and how these involved concepts of race, racism and anti-racism are "constructed." And it is precisely on this theme that one of the most fascinating points of comparison can be made. It is the argument that both campaigns engage in some way with contemporary discourses on the intersection of nationalism, racism, and anti-racism.

The FARE campaign contains this interplay because of European football's importance to both the political economy and symbolic uses of modern sport. Professional sport and the mass media have become more interlinked with the increased industrialization of both sport and the media. European football is a business where clubs "buy," "sell" and "trade" players in an international marketplace and where these clubs try to increase their profit margins by providing a "product" that is appealing to television networks that pay millions for the broadcast "rights." However, a main reason why racism in European soccer became a more serious problem in the late 20th and early 21st centuries was the inability of this seemingly rational, pragmatic sphere to separate itself from the conversely irrational and emotional dimensions of the social life of the geographic locations that clubs "represent."

In other words, although prominent clubs like Real Madrid (Spain), Liverpool (England) or Bordeaux (France) acquire the best players from all over the world in order to be competitive, these clubs compete in an emotional sphere that is as much driven by racial and national mythology as it is by the marketplace. Football and the clubs that play it in Europe have meaning in the dynamic of European identity politics. The fans and the club and association officials that run the sport have various types and degrees of psychological investment in what the clubs and the players should mean. Therefore, football matches are social and intellectual spaces where racial and national mythologies present in other aspects of societies are played out.

The clearest example of elite sport's investment in nationalism is the fact that the most prominent international sporting competitions (especially the Olympics and football's World Cup) require affiliation with national sporting bodies as prerequisites of participation. As one writer has noted, "the Olympic Games are international rather than transnational" (Bairner 2003). This has made elite sport fertile ground for critical theory analysis. One such approach has argued that the nation-states try to project the *myth* of a unified, primordial nation, but the very fact that these myths are necessary exposes the fact that the national unity ostensibly reflected by sport is artificial because national formations are always divided along several fault lines, especially those of gender and race (Rowe, McKay and Miller 1998).

Therefore, European football's anti-racism campaign originated as much in an engagement with the mythologies of internationalism and nationalism as with the crudity of racial verbal harassment and racist violence. While a popular sentiment has been to regard sport as a vehicle of national integration, the new international football environment caused by the industrialization of soccer and the expanded number of nation-states following the end of the USSR and the Eastern Bloc created a more volatile mix of factors. In the mid-1990s, when European authorities began organizing attention to racism in football, nationalism was one of the themes identified very early. In the foreword to a 1996 study on racism and xenophobia in European football, Klaus Hausch (then president of the European Parliament) wrote that the racist incidents in the sport were a reminder "of the need for those who favor closer integration to be constantly on our guard against nationalist reflexes that express themselves in the rejection of other cultures" (Merkel and Tokarski 1996). Similarly, in April of that same year, a news agency story on a speech by Dutch Crown Prince Willem Alexander before a conference on anti-racism in sport reported him as saying "[a]n increasing number of fans exceed the boundaries of normal rivalries, particularly when national pride changes into blind nationalism" (Boas 1996).

What the above quotes reveal is that, despite the popular view of sport as a vehicle to mobilize myths of unity across fault lines (especially those of race), nationalist ideology presented a dilemma for football anti-racism. Nationalist appeals could not be used in a pan-European anti-racist campaign because it seemed that the problem owed its very existence to nationalism! The ideology of nationalism is what sustains the social construction of national identity, and it poses a problem for anti-racism because national identity formation is a two-dimensional process—"one of inclusion that provides a boundary around 'us,' and one of exclusion that distinguishes 'us' from 'them'" (Schlesinger 1991, 300). So a key feature of the FARE anti-racist agenda is one of distancing soccer from the vulgar nationalist identity politics that are a part of everyday life in the region. One way of doing this has been confronting the mythology that the increased numbers of "foreign" players in European football is indicative of increased integration and tolerance in society.

Bart Vanreusel, in a mid-1990s study of racism and xenophobia in Belgium soccer, pointed out that although Antwerp football club had the highest percentage of "foreign" players (36 percent) Antwerp was a city where "extreme right-wing and racist and xenophobic ideologies attract the highest number of votes in Belgian politics." In contrast, Second Division Tongeren, in a province with high numbers of immigrants and minority ethnic groups, did not have "one single 'foreign' or minority ethnic player" (Merkel and Tokarski, 69-70). Therefore, it was important to understand that the presence of "foreign" players in clubs is primarily a function of the economic marketplace of soccer than a reflection of the social integration of immigrants.

Conversely—and very ironically—the Ad Council's texts conflate the internationalist theme with a nationalist one. "America" in this discourse means diversity—i.e., all nations under one flag. In comparison to the

European case, this is a very incredible articulation within an anti-racist narrative. In Europe hyper-nationalism uses racism as a trope: "we" are different from "them" because they are inferior to us; "we" must be unified because "we" share a lot in common; "we" must be willing to use violence to defend what "we" have from being taken over by "them." For this reason European football anti-racists and hyper-nationalists are often on different sides during the FARE campaign. But the Ad Council campaign turned this model of racist/anti-racist discourse on its head. This form of hyper-nationalism redefines *the nation*. The "we," instead of being defined in an essentialist, primordial manner along demarcations of *race,* is defined according to ideological attachment. The trope is "freedom." This hyper-nationalism seems to accommodate racial difference. Most important is the ideological affiliation for which the mantra is "freedom."

This use of nationalist mythology and myth might not seem so paradoxical if the Ad Council campaign is considered within the context of the peculiar cultural politics of the United States and of George W. Bush's "War on Terror" in particular.

Of course, a key distinction between the two campaigns is that the FARE campaign is regional while the Ad Council catered to a *national* audience, however, it has been noted that intellectual elites in the United States have made a considerable investment in promoting "the mythology of American individual freedom" based on values of self-government, liberty and equality (Calabrese and Burke 1992). These myths that are used in national identity construction are important to understand because "[i]f citizens make a strong psychological identification with the nation and internalize national symbols, political leaders are better able to mobilize public sentiment toward a political goal in times of crisis by using communication strategies that emphasize positive themes of national identity" (Hutcheson, Domke, Billeaudeaux, and Garland 2004, 29).

In addition to the problem of the highly contested nature of national identity politics that is always present, the George W. Bush administration was confronted with the additional problem of the peculiar nature of the crisis. Two fundamental components of war—the enemy and the enemy's war aims—were very unclear.

Al-Qaeda—the named perpetrators behind the 9/11 attacks—is not a state but an ominous network of terrorists that (according to the administration) could be anywhere. So, apart from attempting to put a face on the enemy—i.e., Osama Bin Laden, the Taliban and Saddam Hussein—the administration's propaganda had to establish what al-Qaeda was supposed to represent. By associating al-Qaeda with the Taliban government of Afghanistan and the Baath regime of Iraq, it was easier to make the case for war because these regimes were said to be anathema to the most cherished principles of American democracy. They dealt in terrorism, sexism, torture, denial of civil liberties, and *weapons of mass destruction*. It is therefore very significant that the two military operations launched by the administration against these two states carried the word *freedom* in their titles: "Operation Enduring Freedom" (Afghanistan) and "Operation Iraqi Freedom" (Iraq).

The administration prepared the population within the United States to accept the sacrifices that were necessary to conduct the war (especially curbs on civil liberties and deaths in military operations) by resorting to the trope of hyper-nationalism. A new Department of *Homeland* Security was established. The set of laws that compromised American freedoms was called the *Patriot* Act. All along the way the administration sustained the notion that the country was under terrorist threat, encouraging people within the United States to identify suspicious individuals and activities and report them to law enforcement. On September 26, 2001, White House Press Secretary Ari Fleischer (in response to a report that a comedian had suggested on TV that the suicide attackers were courageous) famously said that such incidents were "reminders to all Americans that they need to watch what they say, watch what they do" (Office of the White House Press Secretary 2001). The Department of Homeland Security established a color-coded "Homeland Security Advisory System" that featured various levels of "Threat Advisory": the higher the threat, the more alert law enforcement would be in imposing public inconveniences, especially more security checks at airports. A key feature of the "War on Terrorism" narrative became the ebbs and flows of these advisories that were said to be based on government intelligence about communication among the terrorists.

The alleged suicide bombers left no statement about why they supposedly did what they did and what specific changes they meant to see. Although al-Qaeda was said to be a non-state actor, even previous campaigns of violence by non-state entities included statements of purpose by these bodies. And such entities have always had "political wings" to complement the work of their "armed wings." So, in the absence of an entity that would participate in the international political discourse on the behalf of the enemy, the George W. Bush administration was free to set the discursive parameters. The administration read the attacks as a declaration of war on the nation-state that is the United States. In the months and years after 9/11 it reinforced that theme by emphasizing that "the terrorists" sought the elimination of the United States. There was a *de facto* call to all Americans to defend the state (the *Homeland*), and so the symbolism of the state became critical to the discursive sustenance of this discourse. Citizens were asked to reflect on what it meant to be part of the nation-state that is the United States, there were prominent displays of the flag, commemorative events featured the playing of the national anthem, and there were appeals to "support" the US military, the armed wing of the nation-state.

The Ad Council campaigns were part of a wider project that included this trope. The Defense Department started a propaganda campaign to bolster support for the troops called "Operation Tribute to Freedom" (Operation Tribute to Freedom 2004). Eager to show their patriotism, a number of personalities and organizations volunteered participation. For example, the National Football League dedicated the official start of its 2003-2004 season to the "men and women of the US armed forces" as part of the campaign. The NFL sponsored a free concert on the National Mall in Washington, D.C., at which members of the military were asked to attend in uniform (Defense Logistics Agency 2003).

Conclusion

At first sight, it might have appeared that the two campaigns analyzed above might not have been suited to, or worthy of, scholarly comparison. However, the work is a contribution to our acquiring a more sophisti-cated understanding of internationalism as a feature of contemporary international and domestic politics. While technological progress and the growth of a transnational human rights regime have made anti-racist campaigns a more common feature of the world scene, there is a need to understand why these campaigns are launched and the dynamic of their cultural politics. We gain a more sophisticated understanding of these phenomena if we interrogate their relationship with nationalism. Further, it is clear that not all anti-racist campaigns use nationalism the same way. Because of this, we must be cautious in placing all such cam-paigns within the framework of a seemingly widening internationalist ethic. Indeed, one lesson from this exercise is that great care should be taken when using the term cultural internationalism. There is no natural relationship between these campaigns and progress towards international peace. As the case of FARE shows, an imperative of those seeking to end racist violence is the confrontation of nationalist ideology that has been a motivation for the conflict in the first place. In contrast, the campaign in the US after the September 11 attacks initially used anti-racist rhetoric as part of a mobilization for war.

References

"Ad Council Extends Television Ad Campaign to the Email Accounts of over a Million Americans; helloNetwork and NetCreations Donate Resources and Technology to Support Video Mail." 2001. *Business Wire,* October 9.

Adcouncil.org [Web Page]. URL http://www.adcouncil.org [December 14, 2003].

After911.org [Web Page]. URL http://www.after911videos.org [September 16, 2003].

Alleyne, M. D. 1995. *International Power and International Communication.* London: Macmillan.

Alleyne, M. D. 1997. *News Revolution: Political and Economic Decisions about Global Information.* New York: St. Martin's Press.

Alleyne, M. D. 2003. *Global Lies? Propaganda, the UN and World Order.* London: Palgrave-Macmillan.

Andrews, D. L. and Jackson, S. J. (Eds.) 2001. *Sports Stars: Public Culture and the Politics of Representation.* London: Routledge.

Andrews, M. 2003. "Grand National Narratives and the Project of Truth Commissions: A Comparative Analysis." *Media, Culture & Society,* 25 (1).

Angell, N. 1913. *The Great Illusion.* New York: G. P. Putnam's Sons.

Baimer, A. 2003. "Globalization and Sport: The Nation Strikes Back." *Phi Kappa Phi Forum, 83* (4), 34-37.

Barber, B. R. 1995. *Jihad vs. McWorld: How Globalism and Tribalism Are Reshaping The World.* New York: Ballantine Books.

Bator, R. J. and Cialdini, R. B. 2000. "The Application of Persuasion Theory to the Development of Effective Proenvironmental Public Service Announcements." *The Journal of Social Issues, 56* (3).

Benson, M. 2001. "In War on Terrorism, Information Becomes a Prime Weapon." *Newhouse News Service,* October 2.

Billbrokaw.com [Web Page]. URL http://www.billbrokaw.com/what_ we _ do/gallery _ adcouncil.asp# September 12, 2003].

Boas, H. 1996. "Europeans Urge Civility by Fans at Sports Events." *Jewish Telegraphic Agency* (New York), April 17.

Burchill, S., Devetak, R., Linklater, A., Paterson, M., Reus-Smit, C. and True, J. 2001. *Theories of International Relations* (2nd Edition) Houndmills, Basingstoke: Palgrave.

C. Europa-Racismo/España ECRI Pide a España Tomar Medidas Contra Racismo y Xenofobia. 2003. *Efe News Services (US.) Inc.,* July 8.

Calabrese, A. and Burke, B. R. 1992. *Journal of Communication Inquiry,* 16 (2), Summer, 52-73.

Campbell, D. 1998. *Writing Security: United States Foreign Policy and the Politics of Identity* (Revised Edition). Minneapolis: University of Minnesota Press.

Civilrights.org [Web Page]. URL http://www.civilrights.org/issues/enforcement/details. cfm?id=5494 [September 12, 2003].

D. Humanos-Guatemala Relator ONU Denuncia Inseguridad y Violencia Contra Indigenas. 2003. *Efe News Services (US.) Inc.,* April 10, 2003.

Defense Logistics Agency. 2003. "Time is Running Out to Register for NFL Kickoff Live Concert." *PR Newswire,* August 26.

Dunphy, H. 2003. "White House: The Truth is the Best Way to Sell America to the World." *Associated Press,* January 24.

Earle, R. 2000. *The Art of Cause Marketing: How to Use Advertising to Change Personal Behavior and Public Policy.* Chicago: McGraw-Hill.

Ellul, J. 1973. *Propaganda: The Formation of Men 's Attitudes.* New York: Random House. Entertainment Industry Foundation. 2002. Morocco's Olympic Champion Teams With Hollywood 9-11 International Group to Send Worldwide Message of Peace, Tolerance, Understanding and Hope. *PR Newswire,* September 5.

"Europe: Who Gains? France, Race and Immigration." 2002. *The Economist,* March 2.

"European Teams Ordered To Play Behind Closed Doors." 2002. *The Associated Press,* October 11.

Finch, L. 2000. "Psychological Propaganda: The War of Ideas on Ideas during the First Half of the Twentieth Century." *Armed Forces and Society,* 26 (3), 367-386.

Foltz, K. 1990. "Peace on Earth—Race Relations Are the Key to Benetton's Controversial Ads." *Chicago Tribune,* April 4.

Football Against Racism in Europe [Web Page]. URL http://www.farenet.org [September 16, 2003].

Freedom Ads Launch for the Second Anniversary of September 11th 2003. *Public Service Advertising* (a publication of the Ad Council), September/October.

Goldstone, K. 2001. "Football Kicks Off Campaign Against Racism." *The Irish Times,* March 20.

Goulding, M. 2002. *Peacemonger.* London: John Murrary.

Grunebaum-Ralph, H. 2001. "Re-placing Pasts, Forgetting Presents: Narrative, Place, and Memory in the Time of the Truth and Reconciliation Commission." *Research in African Literatures,* 32 (3).

"Guatemala-Indígenas Relator Especial ONU Asegura La Discriminación Racial Es Latente." 2002. *Efe News Services (U.S.) Inc.,* September 7.

Gunther, A. C. and Thorson, E. 1992. "Perceived Persuasive Effects of Product Commercials and Public Service Announcements." *Communication Research,* 19 (5).

Hassell, G. 2001. "Altruistic Ads Try to Unite Americans." *The Houston Chronicle,* September 26.

Holguin, L. M. 1998. "The Media in Modern Peacekeeping." *Peace Review,* 10 (4).

Home, J. 1996. "Kicking Racism Out of Soccer in England and Scotland." *Journal of Sport and Social Issues,* 20 (1).

Houston, S. 2003. "Racism Gets The Red Card; New Tsar To Tackle Football Hatred." *Daily Record* (Scotland), August 25.

Huntington, S. P. 1997. *The Clash of Civilizations and the Remaking of World Order.* New York: Simon & Schuster.

Hutcheson, J., Domke, D., Billeaudeaux, A. and Garland, P. 2004. "U.S. National Identity, Political Elites, and a Patriotic Press Following September 11." *Political Communication,* 21, 27-50.

"Inmigración-Escuela Calvo Buezas: La Educación Intercultural Es Cara, Pero Necesaria." 2003. *Efe News Services (U.S.) Inc.,* May 29.

International Channel Networks. 2001. "International Channel Networks Produces Public Service Announcement Urging Cultural and Religious Tolerance in the United States; Cable Television Network Responds to Terrorists Attacks On World Trade Center and Pentagon With Message of Understanding." *PR Newswire,* September 24.

"International Eye—US Ad Industry Puts Skills to Good Use in AID of Peace." 2001. *Media Week,* September 28.

"Interpublic Plans Campaign to Boost Morale in U.S.: Sept. 11 Aftermath." 2001. *Reuters,* October 5.

Iriye, A. 1997. *Cultural Internationalism and World Order.* Baltimore: Johns Hopkins University Press.

Jewkes, S. 2001. "Italy's Immigration Quandry." *Europe,* November.

Kardam, N. 2004. "The Emerging Global Gender Equality Regime from Neoliberal and Constructivist Perspectives in International Relations." *International Feminist Journal of Politics,* 6 (1), March, 85-109.

Katzenstein, P. J. 2002. "Same War, Different Views: Germany, Japan, and the War on Terrorism." *Current History,* 101 (659), 427-435.

Kraft, S. 1995. "Regional Outlook: Is Racist Rhetoric Turning into Europe's Reality? A Spate of Violence Against Immigrants Across the Continent Has Many Worried That Animosity Is Out of Control." *Los Angeles Times,* April 18.

Kraidy, M. M. and Goeddertz, T. 2003. "Transnational Advertising and International Relations: US Press Discourses on the Benetton 'We On Death Row' Campaign." *Media, Culture & Society,* 25 (2).

"Larsson's Anti-Racism Bid." 2002. *Evening Times* (Scotland), July 22.

Lehmann, I. A. 1999. *Peacekeeping and Public Information: Caught in the Crossfire.* London: Frank Cass.

Lessons Learned in Peacekeeping [Web Page]. URL http://www.un.orgiDepts/dpko/lessons/ Multidisciplinary Peacekeeping: Lessons Learned From Recent Past [July 5, 2002].

Let's Kick Racism Out of Football [Web Page]. URL http://www.kic9-11 kitout.org [September 16, 2003].

Lindsay, James M. and Smith, C. 2003. "Rally 'Round the Flag." *The Brookings Review,* 21 (3), Summer, 20-23.

Lykes, M. B., Terre Blanche, M. and Hamber, B. 2003. "Narrating Survival and Change in Guatemala and South Africa: The Politics of Representation and a Liberatory Community Psychology." *American Journal of Community Psychology,* 31 *(112).*

"Martinez Debuts New Television and Print Advertising Campaign to Fight Housing Discrimination." .2003. *PR Newswire,* April 29.

Mayeda, D. T. 1999. "From Model Minority to Economic Threat." *Journal of Sport and Social Issues,* 23 (2).

McKinney, R. M. 1988. "Public Service Announcements: Their Effect on Smoking." *Health Marketing Quarterly,* 5 (3, 4).

Merkel, U. and Tokarski, M. 1996. *Racism and Xenophobia in European Football.* Aachen: Meyer & Meyer.

Metzl, J. F. 1997. "Information Intervention: When Switching Channels Isn't Enough." *Foreign Affairs,* 76 (6).

"Mision de la ONU: En Guatemala Hay 'Apartheid de Hecho' Contra Los Indigenas." 2001. *Agence France Presse,* September 20.

"Morocco's Olympic Champion Teams With Hollywood 9-11 International Group to Send Worldwide Message of Peace, Tolerance, Understanding and Hope." 2002. *PR Newswire,* September 5.

Office of the White House Press Secretary. 2001. White House Daily Press Briefing. September 26.

Operation Tribute To Freedom [Web Page]. URL http://www.defenselink.mil/specials/ tribute [January 5, 2004].

Polulmbaum, J. and Wieting, S. G. 1999. "Stories of Sport and Moral Order: Unraveling the Cultural Construction of Tiger Woods." *Journalism and Communication Monographs,* 1 (2).

"Press Conference on International Day of Peace." 2003. *Press Briefing* [The United Nations], September 15.

Raine, G. 2001. "Ad Industry Promotes Unity / Campaign Asks Americans to Come Together." *San Francisco Chronicle,* September 21.

Rice, R. E., and Atkin, C. K. (Eds.) 2001. *Public Communication Campaigns* 3rd Edition. Thousand Oaks, CA: Sage.

Rowe, D., McKay J., and Miller, T. 1998. in Wenner, L. A., ed. *MediaSport.* London: Routledge, 119-133.

Tilley, V. Q. 2002. in Green, D. M., (Ed.) *Constructivism and Comparative Politics.* Armonk, New York: M. E. Sharpe, 151-174.

Schlesinger, P. 1991. "Media, the Political Order and National Identity." *Media, Culture and Society,* 13, 297-308.

Sen, R. 2002. "Reflections on Durban and the War: Rinku Sen Compares U.S. Behavior at the World Conference Against Racism and After 9/11." *Colorlines Magazine,* 5 (1).

Silk, M. and Andrews, D. L. 2001. "Beyond A Boundary? Sport, Transnational Advertising, and the Reimaging of National Culture." *Journal of Sport and Social Issues,* 25 (2).

Leff, Mark H. "The Politics of Sacrifice on the American Home Front in World War II." *The Journal of American History,* 77 (4), 1991, 1296-1318.

Stabile, C. A. 2000. "Nike, Social Responsibility, and the Hidden Abode of Production." *Critical Studies in Media Communication,* 17 (2).

Stephenson, M. T. 2002. "Anti-drug Public Service Announcements Targeting Parents: An Analysis and Evaluation." *The Southern Communication Journal,* 67 (4).

Syed, M. 2003. "Conference Spells Out Cold Facts in Black and White." *The Times* (London), March 6.

Taylor, D. and Kelso, P. 2003. "England Risk Boot, Beckham Tells Fans." *The Guardian* (London), June 3.

Temman, F. 2001. "Entertainment Industry to Promote Tolerance of Arab-Americans." *Agence France Presse,* December 22.

Thacker, K. 2001. "Austin, Texas, Firm's New Ad Campaign Celebrates Nation's Diversity, Unity." *The Dallas Morning News,* September 21.

Thomas, D. 2003. "The Bigoted Game." *Marketing Week,* June 5, 2003.

Treise, D. and Weigold, M. F. 2001. "AIDS Public Service Announcements: Effects of Fear and Repetition on Predictors of Condon Use." *Health Marketing Quarterly,* 18 (3/4).

"UEFA Backs Anti-Racism Plan." 2002. *Xinhua News Agency,* October 10.

"UEFA To Present 276,000 Dollar Charity Cheque to FARE."2002. *Deutsche Presse-Agentur,* November 12.

"UN in Action Television Series." 2003. Lynching: A Continuing Scourge (videotape). New York: United Nations.

United Nations. 2000. Document A/54/2000, We The Peoples: The Role of the United Nations in the Twenty-First Century—Report of the Secretary-General.

United Nations. 2000a. Document A/55/305-S/2000/809, Report of the Panel on United Nations Peace Operations.

United Nations. 2002. Document A/AC.198/2002/5, Substantive Questions: Role of the Department of Public Information in United Nations Peacekeeping—Report of the Secretary-General.

Vande Berg, L. R. 1999. The Critical Sense: Three Decades of Critical Media Studies in the Wake of Samuel L. Becker's "Rhetorical Studies for the Contemporary World." *Communication Studies,* 50 (1), Spring, 72-81.

Viewingrace.org [Web Page]. URL http://www.viewingrace.org [September 16, 2003]. Wallas, G. 1915. *The Great Society: A Psychological Analysis.* New York: Macmillan. Wenner, L. A., (Ed.). 1998. *MediaSport.* London: Routledge.

White House Office of Global Communications [Web Page]. URL http://www.whitehouse.gov/ogc/ [September 14, 2003].

Wilson, R. A. 2000. "Reconciliation and Revenge in Post-Apartheid South Africa: Rethinking Legal Pluralism and Human Rights." *Current Anthropology,* 41 (1).

Conclusion: Anti-Racism as International Communication

Mark D. Alleyne

We see the articulation (in the sense of cultural studies) of themes of race, racism, and nationalism more clearly when a person appears wearing a "White Pride" t-shirt at the 2007 Henry County *Georgia Independence Day* (July 4th) *Festival,* just outside the city of Atlanta. The t-shirt was a souvenir from an annual "White Pride Ride" and carried the slogan "If it ain't white, it ain't right." The event to celebrate American Independence Day, where one attendee saw fit to wear this t-shirt, featured actors playing characters from the Revolutionary War against the British, food, and other forms of entertainment. But, ironically, the festival took place on Nash Farm, a battleground during the American Civil War. This fact was also commemorated at the festival, with informational displays and a tractor ride out to the center of the farm where the fighting troops encamped. In effect, the festival was as much a discourse about remembering the war that established the nation as it was about not forgetting the war fought 100 years later to keep that nation in tact.

Georgia fought on the Confederate side that lost its struggle to maintain slavery, but that racist history included the Jim Crow segregation and terrorist lynchings that were to follow, and it also includes the psychological terrorism of the present day of which the t-shirt is a part. The informational displays about the 1860-1865 war used the name "War Between the States"—a title still preferred by many in the American South instead of "Civil War."

The literature on anti-racist discourse tells us that favorable national imaginings are the axes used by multiculturalists in the United States and elsewhere to anchor the logic of their anti-racisms. However, this tendency is unsettled by the reality that the histories involved are never as glamorous as they are represented. They are as much about racial terrorism as the rise of liberal public culture. This is why racists are as much prone to deploy nationalist mythologies as anti-racists are. We cannot achieve a refined understanding of the contours of difference that fashion international politics without a careful scrutiny of both sides of this coin.

The various studies that comprise this chapter were done in this spirit of inquiry. But the variety of cases, research methodologies and theoretical frames make it a daunting task to weave the findings into a coherent fabric that shows how they are relevant to common themes. A way to solve this problem is to organize this conclusion around five key questions: (1) *How does the literature on anti-racism improve our understanding of conflict resolution?*; (2) *How does the analysis of the media's role in racist and anti-racist discourses improve the process of theorizing, writing and arbitrating international law on hate and war propaganda?*; (3) *How can research on anti-racist discourse improve UN peacekeeping?*; (4) *What implications does the literature on anti-racist discourse have for theory-building and activism for "cultural diversity" in international communication?*; and (5) *How and why should the literature on anti-racism expand research in international relations?*

1. How Does the Literature on Anti-Racism Improve Our Understanding of Conflict Resolution?

As Burdsey notes in setting out his praxis for social theory, if the analysis of a problem is wrong, then the proposed solution will also be wrong. Therefore, our attention to anti-racist discourses helps us to understand much better the nature of conflict and to devise answers more appropriate for their resolution. This was most clearly demonstrated in the chapter by Müller, van Zoonen, and de Roode where they confront directly anti-racism's problem of tending to misdefine the sources of conflict. Their specific case study was Dutch football, with its tendency to view racist conflict in the sport as limited to a minority of hooligans and hard-core racists. But, as that chapter showed, racial conflict is better conceptualized as springing from an entire system of social relations that are not limited to individual acts of violence or discrimination. Therefore, anti-racist campaigns, or entire swaths of social policy meant to deal with racism, often tend to be "barking up the wrong tree."

The definition of conflict is a problem that has haunted the literature on conflict resolution (Sambanis, Mack). The politics of memory is a powerful force in instigating and maintaining conflicts and, as the case from the American South mentioned above showed, even how we define historical events has consequences for contemporary social life. This theme of definition—naming—which is the organizing principle of the book's first part, appears repeatedly in the chapters. Falcón shows how a dispute over the definition of state-sponsored racism can stonewall international negotiations at the United Nations and ultimately thwart progress towards international anti-racist custom and law. Similarly, in Nesmith's study of Brazil we see the myth of racial democracy as a discursive strategy to deny the existence of racial conflict and propagate a positive self-definition in the country's public political culture. What activists such as *Amulherada* do is assert the argument that there is actually conflict as a first step in anti-racist praxis and social change.

2. How Does the Analysis of the Media's Role in Racist and Anti-Racist Discourses Improve the Process of Theorizing, Writing and Arbitrating International Law on Hate and War Propaganda?

Restrictions on hate propaganda are one of the most established areas of international law over mass media (Alleyne, 94-99). The main reason for this was the example the Nazis provided in showing how media agitation could be put at the service of genocide, by priming populations to first hate the intended victims, and then helping them to justify their violence and murder. This tradition in international law notwithstanding, hate propaganda has continued to be a serious problem in international politics due to advances in media technology (especially satellites, the Internet, and digital mobile communication). This is evidenced in the well-known cases at the end of the 20th century where the media were used to inflame hatreds and support mass murder (Alleyne, 118-20). It has been common to mention the Balkans and Rwanda in the 1990s as prime examples of this, but the propaganda of the United States and its allies that launched wars in Afghanistan and Iraq in 2001 and 2003 should not escape scrutiny. Apart from propaganda at the service of civil and international wars, there has also been the propaganda of non-state hate groups and networks that have used the Internet increasingly to organize and disseminate information about racial difference and hierarchy. Of course, propaganda suffers from the same problems of definition as conflict. But the central argument in favor of legal prohibitions of hate propaganda is the syllogistic logic that hate propaganda leads to violence and war (Murphey; Metzl; Drumbl; Davis). This logic is why, in 1946, Julius Streicher, who had published the anti-Semitic weekly *Der Sturmer*, was found guilty by the Nuremberg Tribunal and executed for crimes against humanity. The next time there were similar prosecutions under international law was in 2003 when three Rwandan journalists were found guilty by the UN International Criminal Tribunal for Rwanda for inciting genocide in 1994. Two were given life sentences and another 35 years (Wax).

Media complicity in racially motivated violence, and even genocide, has been difficult to prove, and that is part of the reason why these types of prosecutions under international law have been rare. But Lugo-Ocando makes a powerful argument for expanding the definition of hate campaigns and propaganda when he documents the character of reporting on asylum-seekers by some sectors of the British press. Similarly, Falcón identifies the potentialities and limits of international anti-racist bureaucracies and legislation that are supposed to be the backbone for this kind of jurisprudence.

When we set up several of the chapters against this second concluding question, an interesting contradiction in the "War on Terror" is exposed. While the US in particular has sought limits on the press, especially foreign media such as the TV network Al-Jazeera, which has broadcast the recordings of terrorist groups, it has not been as accommodating to wider definitions in the case of racism.

Another peculiarity of the topic of hate propaganda has been the restricted nature of legal discourse on the theme. Cases under international have only been against individuals in the specific circumstances of war tribunals. Lugo-Ocando's analysis opens up the argument for at least considering media institutions liable. And there is the related argument for scrutiny of state entities, such as public diplomacy organs, whose primary function in international relations is to broadcast propaganda.

3. How Can Research on Anti-Racist Discourse Improve UN Peacekeeping?

Even before the UN's role as international peacekeeper blossomed after the Cold War, its public information policies were marked by tepidity and lack of focus at best (Alleyne; Lehmann). This characteristic was not necessarily due to professional incompetence of UN staff, but more on the peculiar place of organized campaigning of this type in international politics. I have noted elsewhere how the UN and international law never really outlawed all propaganda, but rather made a demarcation between "bad propaganda"—campaigning it did not like, such as hate crusades—and "good propaganda"—campaigning in favor of values the UN promoted, such as anti-racism (Alleyne 1997). But even supposedly "good" propaganda does not achieve universal acceptance. For example, the South African apartheid regime did not consider UN anti-racism acceptable, and the UN's promotion of indigenous rights in the United States (discussed by Falcón in this volume) is just one of several cases where governments have clashed with the UN over whether these states' treatment of racialized groups within their borders has complied with international law. However, the UN's critique of governments' racial policies from afar seems a luxury when compared to the pressure the organization comes under to actually come up with social policies of its own to end racial oppression in countries where it runs peacekeeping and peace-building missions.

What scholarly research on anti-racism reveals is that UN policies in a variety of areas conveniently draw philosophical sustenance from the culturalism of the UNESCO tradition. The intellectual shortcomings of this approach, which were discussed in this book's introduction, are translated into its peacekeeping policies. Some of these weaknesses include a tendency to confuse discrimination with racism, to rely too much on public information campaigns as an anti-racist strategy, and to follow the culturalist line of celebrating diversity without tackling racial hierarchy.

Lehmann's optimism about the success of the UN's public information program in Namibia must be tempered with the suggestion that it is actually too early to determine the success of UN anti-racist peacekeeping and peace-building projects in Namibia and other countries where entrenched racism has been a source of civil conflict. The defeat of racism requires a complete social transformation. Ironically, the theoretical frame of critical race theory that is attractive to Burdsey is not very optimistic that racism can be overcome (see Bell).

4. What Implications Does the Literature on Anti-Racist Discourse Have for Theory-Building and Activism for "Cultural Diversity" in International Communication?

After these journeys into anti-racist discourses it is now possible to see that the "cultural diversity" movement, which has had a privileged spot on UNESCO's agenda at the turn of the 21st century, is actually rooted in anti-racism. The anxiety to preserve world cultural diversity was heightened in the wake of the growth of neo-liberal economic philosophy and the creation of the World Trade Organization. Neo-liberalism itself emerged after the 1980s' global debt crisis and the "structural adjustment" policies the World Bank and IMF imposed on all countries that needed help out of debt. This economic philosophy is seen as a threat to cultural diversity because of what it does to culture on the scale of social policy in countries that decide to run their economies this way and on the agenda of international negotiations. In essence, neo-liberalism widens the range of issues that should be subject to the logics of free markets with their assumed in-built efficiencies of comparative and competitive advantage. Those advocating on the behalf of cultural industries in small countries and artists from minority cultures fear that neo-liberalism will be the death knell for these kinds of cultural expression if these kinds of economic policies are not stemmed. For example, production subsidies might be stopped, world audio-visual production would be concentrated in large firms in a few rich countries, and decisions about artistic value would be made by those in the field of economics rather than culture.

As we have seen in our discussions of the archeology of the multiculturalism that succeeded the debunking of pseudo-scientific theories of race, UNESCO has been the obvious forum for international debates about culture. It has actually been the guardian of this particular multicultural form of anti-racism which views the world as comprised of hermetic cultures, each having its own value. UNESCO anti-racism defines racism as the product of ignorance or misunderstandings of cultures and it holds out hope that racism would be overcome via more educational and media programs about different cultures. It is believed that neo-liberalism threatens this potential of enrichment because the economists who would make decisions about educational and media programs would not be guided by the ethic of multiculturalism. In March 1998, UNESCO's Conference on Culture for Development concluded that globalization was undermining local and traditional cultures and that cultural groups should form global networks to counteract this trend. This was followed two years later by the establishment of the International Network for Cultural Diversity (INCD) at a meeting in Santorini, Greece, that was attended by representatives from the field of culture from 21 countries. The INCD—with headquarters in Canada—was funded by the Canadian and Swedish governments and by the Ford Foundation. In November 2001 the UNESCO General Conference adopted the Universal Declaration on Cultural Diversity, and in October 2005 that same body adopted the Convention on the Protection of the Diversity of Cultural Contents and Artistic Expressions based on the principles of the Declaration.

Among the key principles of the Convention are equal dignity of and respect for all cultures, and the complementarity of the economic and cultural aspects of development. These doctrines and the language of cultural diversity were also in the "Outcome Documents" of the World Summit on the Information Society (WSIS), a process concurrent to the negotiations for the Convention. In point 32 of the 2005 "Tunis Commitment" the WSIS participants committed themselves to

> promote the inclusion of all peoples in the Information Society through the development and use of local and/or indigenous languages in ICTs [information and communication technologies]. We will continue our efforts to protect and promote cultural diversity, as well as cultural identities, within the Information Society (International Telecommunication Union, 63).

The obvious weaknesses in the discourses on cultural diversity in the WSIS documents and the Convention show why it is so important to engage with the literature on anti-racism. For example, the Convention grants supreme privilege to the rights of states (sovereignty), but the literature on racism and anti-racism shows that states are the chief perpetrators of race-based victimization and genocide. Also, although the INCD hailed the Convention for being the first piece of international law to recognize that cultural products have both cultural and economic value (Neil), the notion of cultural rights that undergirds this particular discourse assumes that the concept of culture describes a naturally occurring phenomenon and that these cultures are hermetically sealed entities (Morris-Suzuki; Sullivan). Therefore shrewd jurisprudence in this area is heavily dependent on social theory and research. Horsti argues in this volume that the cultural diversity ethic in media programming must be understood as an outgrowth of the identity politics of the sponsoring entities, and this ethic can easily lead to tokenism.

5. How and Why Should the Literature on Anti-Racism Expand Research in International Relations?

This point about how this form of social research must inform domestic and international jurisprudence is just one way this literature enhances the understanding of international relations. However, when thinking about anti-racism in relation to international relations it is tempting to try and fit it solely into the constructivist trend. Constructivism can become a convenient nomenclature for a variety of approaches to the study of international phenomena that do not fall within the group of themes that have traditionally been considered international theory.

The persistence and growth of ethnic conflict and identity based terrorist movements are merely two examples that expose a basic intellectual dilemma: international society faces a set of serious problems with really no organized discipline and scholarly tradition to provide the tools for their solution.

This crisis has happened because the field of international relations has traditionally marginalized all research in "low politics," such as communication, anthropology, sociology, and fields outside the realm of "high politics"—strategic studies, grand political theory (such as studies of communism, authoritarianism, capitalism, etc.), and international organization.

For its part, international communication—which I consider a subfield of international relations—has not had a history of intellectual sophistication. What eventually became known as international communication originated in scholarship heavily invested in the polemics of international politics, especially World War II and the Cold War. Government money to enhance war propaganda and facilitate post-war development launched and maintained academic careers, as Shah discusses at the beginning of this book (see also Smith). Later, UNESCO underwrote research favorable to its multicultural worldview and not by any means critical of the communication and cultural implications of the entire UN project (Alleyne). This was especially evident during the period of UNESCO's sponsorship of the New World Information and Communication Order (NWICO) when much of what passed for international communication scholarship were really polemics in favor of the cultural imperialism hypothesis (see Kraidy; Stevenson).

Anti-racism scholarship has been less voluminous but suffers from similar problems. Critiques of the "race relations industry" in Britain or of "political correctness" in relation to race in the United States have often been nothing more than polemics. And some insightful writing on racism has attracted the label of polemic because of its declared anti-racist praxis. For example, van Dijk's discourse analysis of has been done on the premise that a key dimension of the reproduction of ethnic prejudice has been via "the White in-group" (van Dijk, 15).

The history of these fields notwithstanding, we have shown in this work how the literatures can learn a lot from each other. For example, Shah has shown that the modernization/development and anti-racist discourses are mutually constitutive. Attention to artistic groups, such as Nesmith's work in Brazil, point to the importance of how some actors do politics outside what has been understood traditionally as the political arena.

Regardless of whether this research falls into the category of constructivism or not, the most important point is its utility in informing the search for world peace by beginning with a set of questions and using theory and research methodology to find answers. Unlike polemicists—who start with the answers and use research to support pre-set conclusions—it is best to characterize the conversation between anti-racist research and international relations as the start of a journey for unknown answers that is not confined to the terrain of just one academic discipline.

References

Alleyne, Mark D. 2003. "Global Lies?: Propaganda, the UN, and World Order." Palgrave Macmillan.

———. 1997. *News Revolution: Political and Economic Decisions about Global Information.* 1st ed. New York: St. Martin's Press.

Bell, Derrick A. 1992. *Faces at the Bottom of the Well: The Permanence of Racism.* New York, NY: Basic Books.

Davis, Spencer W. 2006. "Incitement to Terrorism in Media Coverage: Solutions to Al-Jazeera after the Rwanda Media Trial." *The George Washington International Law Review* 38.4: 749.

Drumbl, Mark A. 2005. "Pluralizing International Criminal Justice." *Michigan Law Review* 103.6: 1295.

International Telecommunication Union. 2005. "World Summit on the Information Society Outcome Documents: Geneva 2003—Tunis 2005." Geneva: ITU.

Kraidy, Marwan M. 2002. "Ferment in Global Media Studies." *Journal of Broadcasting & Electronic Media* 46.4: 630.

Lehmann, Ingrid A. 1999. *Peacekeeping and Public Information: Caught in the Crossfire.* Cass Series on Peacekeeping, 5;. London: Portland, OR.

Mack, Raymond W. & Richard C. Snyder. 1957. "The Analysis of Social Conflict: Toward an Overview and Synthesis." *The Journal of Conflict Resolution (pre-1986)* 1.2: 212.

Metzl, Jamie Frederic. 1997. "Rwandan Genocide and the International Law of Radio Jamming." *The American Journal of International Law* 91.4: 628.

Morris-Suzuki, Tessa. 1995. "The Invention and Reinvention of 'Japanese Culture.'" *The Journal of Asian Studies* 54.3: 759.

Murphey, Dwight D. 2003. "Conceptual Issues in Prohibiting 'Hate Speech.'" *Mankind Quarterly* 43.3: 335.

Neil, Garry. 2006. "Assessing the Effectiveness of UNESCO's New Convention on Cultural Diversity." *Global Media & Communication* 2.2: 257-62.

Sambanis, Nicholas. 2004. "What Is Civil War? Conceptual and Empirical Complexities of an Operational Definition." *The Journal of Conflict Resolution* 48.6: 814.

Smith, Bruce Lannes. 1956. "Trends in Research on International Communication and Opinion, 1945-55." *The Public Opinion Quarterly* 20.1: 182-95.

Stevenson, Robert L. 2000. "Separating Polemic from Scholarship: An Exploration of International Communication as a Research Field." *International Journal of Public Opinion Research* 12.4: 420.

Sullivan, Patrick. 2005. "Searching for the Intercultural, Searching for the Culture." *Oceania* 75.3: 183.

van Dijk, Teun Adrianus. 1987. *Communicating Racism: Ethnic Prejudice in Thought and Talk.* Newbury Park, Calif.: Sage Publications.

Wax, Emily. 2003. "Journalists Sentenced in Rwanda Genocide; Prosecutor Said 'Hate Media' Urged Killings." *The Washington Post* December 4: A.20.

Contributors

Mark D. Alleyne was professor of communication at the University of Georgia before his untimely death in 2009. His main research areas were international communication policy, United Nations public information policy, and indigenous and Afro-Hispanic transnational activism. He authored numerous scholarly articles as well as the books *Global Lies?, News Revolution, and International Power* and *International Communication.*

Daniel Burdsey is a senior lecturer in sociology at the University of Brighton. His research interests focus on issues of race, ethnicity, and multiculturalism in the context of sport, leisure, and popular culture. He has published his work in a number of international journals, including *Ethnic and Racial Studies, Journal of Ethnic and Migration Studies, Patterns of Prejudice, Sociological Review,* and *Sociology.* He is the author of *British Asians and Football: Culture, Identity, Exclusion* and the editor of *Race, Ethnicity and Football: Persisting Debates and Emergent Issues* (forthcoming).

Laurens de Roode is a graduate of the Department of Communication at the University of Amsterdam.

Sylvanna M. Falcón is an assistant professor in the Department of Latin American and Latino Studies at the University of California, Santa Cruz and is a former University of California President's Postdoctoral Fellow in the Department of Women's Studies at the University of California, Riverside. She is completing her first book manuscript entitled *From Apartheid to Intersections at the United Nations: Anti-Racisms, Feminisms, Human Rights.* Her work has been published in *Gender & Society, Societies Without Borders,* and *Social Justice.* She serves on the editorial collective of *Societies Without Borders: Human Rights and the Social Science.*

Karina Horsti is an Academy of Finland post-doctoral researcher at Center for Research on Ethnic Relations and Nationalism (CEREN), University of Helsinki, director of the Nordic Research Network for Media, Migration and Society. In 2009 she was a visiting scholar in the Department of Media, Culture and Communication, New York University. Horsti's research interests focus on racist and antiracist discourses, mediatization of migration and difference, and European multicultural media policies. Her work has appeared recently in *Communication, Culture & Critique* (2009) and *Javnost-the Public* (2008).

Ingrid A. Lehmann is a lecturer in communication studies at the University of Salzburg in Austria. She previously spent 25 years with the United Nations as a political affairs officer and an information officer and headed the United Nations Information Centers in Washington, D.C., Athens, Greece and Vienna, Austria. She holds a diploma in political science and a doctorate from the University of Berlin, Germany and an M.A. in history from the University of Minnesota. She has published two books, *Peacekeeping and Public Information—Caught in the Crossfire* (1999) and *Managing Public Information in a Mediation Process* (2009).

Jairo Lugo-Ocando, Ph.D., is director of the journalism programs of the Department of Film, Media & Journalism at the University of Stirling in Scotland. He is an associated researcher at the Stirling Media Research Institute and author of several books and articles. He sits on the advisory board of the Asylum Positive Image Project run by OXFAM-GB.

Floris Müller is a research associate at the sociology department of the Erasmus University in Rotterdam.

Nakisha T. Nesmith (Niva Ayodele Flor) is an artist and vocalist in the San Francisco Bay Area. She holds a BA in music from Spelman College, an MA in ethnomusicology from the University of California–Los Angeles, and is currently a Ph.D. candidate in ethnomusicology at UCLA. Her dissertation focuses on the use of music in the promulgation of black identity, community building, and cultural tourism in Salvador, Bahia, Brazil.

Hemant Shah is professor in the School of Journalism and Mass Communication at the University of Wisconsin. He is the author of *Newspaper Coverage of Interethnic Conflict: Competing Visions of America* (2004) and co-editor of *Reorienting Global Communication: Indian and Chinese Media beyond Borders* (2010). Shah is writing *The Production of Modernization: Daniel Lerner, Mass Media, and the Passing of Traditional Society*, a book-length treatment of the intellectual history of development communication in the Cold War era.

Liesbet van Zoonen is professor of media and popular culture in Loughborough University.

Index

Ad Council, 4, 213, 215, 221-224, 227, 230-231, 233
Advertising Council, 11, 222
African Americans,
  citizenship rights, 1
  equality, 41-42, 66, 224
  incarcerated, 59
  music, 176, 179
  torture, 68
Almond Gabriel, 29, 32, 38
anti-racism,
  analysis, 154
  as cultural politics, 227
  as discourse, 4-9
  as phenomena, 97
  campaigns, 3, 10-12, 73-74, 76-86, 116-117, 122, 153, 160, 187, 206-207, 213-214, 223, 225-227, 229-230, 233
  changing visions, 86-88
  depoliticization, 162-166
  examples of defeat of racism, 1-2
  in English football, 192-194, 196, 198-201, 231
  historical context, 214-215
  in soccer, 75-76, 88-90
  internationalism, 224
  legislation, 108
  literature, 239-241, 243-247
  media, 218-221, 241-242
  militant, 59
  movements, 158, 160-161, 171-172, 189-192
  United Nation's projects, 129-130, 242-243
apartheid, 129-135, 138, 143-146, 156, 215, 243
Army's Psychological Warfare Division (PWD), 38-39
asylum seekers, 95-124, 157-158, 242

behavioralism, 32-34
Berry, Halle, 2
biological racism, 22-23, 25-26, 49, 99, 197-198
black-specific programming, 161
blacks,
  activism, 170-172, 174
  cultural movements, 176-177
  English football players, 194-196, 218-220, 227
  in Namibia, 132-145
  intellectuals, 41
  racial identity, 2, 173, 178-179, 206
  soccer players, 75-76, 88
  students, 174, 223
  view of the criminal justice system, 59-60
  women, 179-182
Blaut, James, 22-23
Boas, Franz, 7, 12, 23-24, 41
Bonnett, Alastair, 2-3, 9, 11-12
Brazil, 14-15, 169-179, 183, 241, 246
British Asians, 15, 187-192, 194-207
Bureau of Applied Social Research (BASR), 36, 39

Cabral, Amilcar, 45, 49
Center for International Studies (CENIS), 33, 41-43
citizenship rights, 1, 65
Civil Rights Act of 1964, 1, 61
Committee on Comparative Politics (CCP), 32-33, 36
Committee to Eliminate Racial Discrimination (CERD), 12, 55-69, 214
constructivism, 213, 245-247
cultural racism, 22-26, 30-31, 33-35, 41, 49
culturalism, 7, 12, 14, 203, 243

deportations, 101, 103, 124
dog whistle journalism, 105

Eggers, Rowland, 44
Ellison, Ralph, 41
English football, 187, 189-192, 194,
    199-200, 204-207

First Amendment, 61-64
Football Against Racism in Europe
    (FARE), 213, 216, 218-221, 227-228,
    230-231, 233

Gilroy, Paul, 11, 99, 104, 188, 191
Gitlow v. New York, 63-64

hate speech, 61-64, 66

If Racism Wins, Sports Loses, 73-74,
    76-77, 79-90
incarcerations, 56, 59-61, 101
Inter-American Developmental Bank
    (IADB), 3, 15
International Convention on the Elimina-
    tion of All Forms of Racial Discrimi-
    nation
(ICERD), 55-58, 63-64, 66-69
Islamophobia, 120, 205-206

land abrogation, 64-65
Lasswell, Harold, 29, 32-34, 38, 46
Lazarsfeld, Paul, 33-34, 36, 38-39
Lentin, Alana, 7-9, 12, 14, 159, 190
Lerner, Daniel, 11, 26-27, 29-31, 33-34,
    36-41, 45, 47, 50
Levy, Marion, 35-37

mass communication, 10, 21-22, 26-27,
    29-32, 38, 46-49, 187, 215-218
Mazrui, Ali, 45, 49
Mead, Margaret, 24, 34, 38
Merton, Robert, 36, 38
Middle East, 21-22, 25-27, 29-31, 39,
    41, 47-48, 144
Milliken, Max, 33, 43
miscegenation, 1, 173
modernization theory, 12, 15, 21-50
Myrdal, Gunnar, 23, 40-43

Namibia, 13-14, 129-146, 243
Nandy, Ashis, 46, 49
Native Americans, 64-65

negros, 41, 102, 172-173
Nike, 11, 73, 77, 226
non-governmental organizations
    (NGOs), 67-68, 96, 100, 116-118, 122-
    123, 129, 145, 159, 161, 179

Obama, Barack, 1-4
one drop rule, 2
Oxfam, 98-99, 111, 117-119

Parsons, Talcott, 27-29, 34-35, 38
Potter, Dalton, 47-48
Pye, Lucian, 11, 29, 31-33, 50

race,
    and Black consciousness, 170-175
    and culture, 49
    and ethnicity, 218-219
    and gender struggles, 180
    and racism, 5-6, 108, 191-193
    animosity, 220
    discourses, 12, 98, 109, 169-170, 225-
        228
    discrimination, 57, 104-106
    relations, 1-3, 22-23, 26, 32-33, 40-43,
        95, 201-202, 246
    theory, 15, 24, 190, 243-245
racialization, 13, 75, 82, 87, 194, 206
religious racism, 22-23
Request for Proposals (RFP), 10
Reservations, Understandings, and
    Declarations (RUDS), 65-66
Revolution and Development of Interna-
    tional Relations (RADIR), 33-34, 38
Rostow, Walt, 11, 29-29, 33-34, 41-43,
    45, 50

Scotland, 13, 95-124
Shah, Hemant, 5, 11-12, 246
Shils, Edward, 11, 25, 27-29, 33-39, 41,
    50
September 11 attacks, 4-5, 102, 214-215,
    222-224, 227, 233-234
soccer racism, 13, 73-77, 79, 81, 85-86,
    90, 226
Social Science Research Council
    (SSRC), 32-33
South West African People's Organiza-
    tion (SWAPO), 131-134, 138-143
Stand Up, Speak Up, 11, 73-90, 206, 220
Statement by Experts on Problems of
    Race, 6

structural functionalism, 32, 34-36, 40

tabloids, 95, 97, 99, 101-102, 104, 106-110, 112, 114, 116, 119, 122-124
Tehranian, Majid, 21
Thomas, W.I., 33, 40
Thornberry, Cedric, 136, 139, 141
Tilley, Virginia Q., 227
Tintin, 108
tokenism, 14, 187, 245
Truman, Harry, 24

United Nations,
  anti-racism campaign, 5, 8, 13-14, 214-215
  conflict with U.S. government, 12
  Namibia, 131-132, 134-136, 145-146

peacekeeping, 129, 144-145, 240, 242-243
South Africa, 130, 138-139
United Nations Economic Commission for Europe (UNECE), 41-42
United Nations Economics and Security Council (UNESCO), 6-8, 12, 14, 161, 163, 243-244, 246
United Nations Transition Assistance Group (UNTAG), 129, 132-146

Weiss, Thomas, 146
World War II, 8, 21-25, 31-33, 37-42, 106, 156, 213, 222, 225, 246

Znaniecki, Florian, 33, 40